D0717726

MOZART'S
Letters

MOZART'S
Letters

AN ILLUSTRATED SELECTION

Translated by
EMILY ANDERSON

BARRIE & JENKINS
LONDON

First published in Great Britain in 1990 by
Barrie & Jenkins Ltd
20 Vauxhall Bridge Road, SW1V 2SA

British Library Cataloguing in Publication Data
Mozart, Wolfgang Amadeus, *1756-1791*
  Mozart's letters.-Ill. ed.
  1. Austrian music. Mozart, Wolfgang Amadeus, 1756-1791
  I. Title II. Anderson, Emily
  780.92

ISBN 0-7126-2092-3

FRONTISPIECE *Mozart as a child; a posthumous portrait by Ludwig Bode, 1859*

Typeset by SX Composing Ltd
Colour separation by Chroma Graphics (Overseas) PTE Ltd.
Printed and bound in Italy by Mondadori Editore.

CONTENTS

The boy Mozart, by Pietro Antonio Lorenzoni, early 1763.

PREFACE
to the original edition

THE CELEBRATION OF A GREAT COMPOSER'S ANNIVERSARY BY A VAST INCREASE
in performances of his works is of doubtful value. If he is as great as Mozart, his
music is always with us, and it does not suddenly become more lovable or
interesting on his two-hundredth birthday. A good deal more is to be said for the
publication of personal documents less frequently before the public, especially if
they allow us to come into closer contact with an artist's personality, as Mozart's
letters certainly do. They show in many ways an ordinary boy, youth and man,
alert and attractive, but with various defects and blind spots surprising in a
genius; and then, now and again, personal superiority shows in pages suddenly
revealing quick-wittedness, decent behaviour, insight into character, or keen
judgement of other people's music and his own. He is a variable person, difficult
to size up all round, more difficult in some ways than his music is to understand
and value; yet once the man is known more intimately than he can be before a
reading of his own words, one cannot fail to penetrate several layers deeper into
his work, though the ultimate mystery of the very greatest of it remains
unfathomable. Even a mere selection from his correspondence, such as is here
presented as a birthday gift, will do much to help the reader to better
acquaintance, and he will rejoice in the odd circumstance that the gift is an
unusual one, coming from the celebrant instead of being presented to him. Still,
some profit will be his: he as well as his work will be loved the more by those
who have come to know him more intimately through these pages.

An English translation of the Mozart letters need never be attempted again.
Emily Anderson's is a classic. It is true that her version has no sort of feeling of
the eighteenth-century manner which gives the originals a peculiarly engaging
flavour; but although it is possible, for the purpose of quotation, to rewrite him in
the English of Sheridan or thereabouts – I have tried it myself – to do anything of
the kind on the large scale of a complete edition would be to weary the reader
with an intolerably sustained effort of affection. Miss Anderson turns Mozart's
epistolary usage – it can hardly be called a style – into plain, lucid, impeccable
English, which can be taken in large doses without becoming in the least
oppressive. What is more, she always succeeds in giving the precise equivalent of
the original.

The text of the letters, so far as it appears in this selection, is reproduced
exactly as it stands in the Anderson edition published by Messrs Macmillan and
Co. in 1938. There are, however, some typographical changes, made to conform
either with certain editorial notions or with the 'house style' used by the

Mozart with his father and sister; a lithograph by A. Schieferdecker after the painting by L.C. de Carmontelle.

publishers. They do not affect the translator's work or interfere in any way with its accuracy: they are concerned merely with such things as the use of capital and lower-case initials, and more particularly with that of italic type. In the present edition this is reserved entirely for foreign words and, on a larger scale, for the translation of phrases, passages, or whole letters written by Mozart in a language other than German – in fact in a language foreign to him. All the text in Roman type may be taken as being translated from the German; Latin or French words and short phrases are left in the original and printed in italics, as are also such Italian words as Miss Anderson chose to leave untranslated. An exception to these rules is made in the case of the expression 'a propos', which, not being used in its proper French sense, is left in Roman type. As used by Austrians, it does not refer to a subject just mentioned, in the sense of 'which reminds me', or 'as to that', but on the contrary introduces a new one. It could have been quite accurately translated as 'by the way' and is still so used in Austria today.

Words or sentences in angular brackets are transcribed from the cipher used by the Mozart family for secret messages. A specimen will be found on page 62; otherwise such passages are given in English only, but they are easily identifiable by those special brackets.

Where amendments occur in the text, they were supplied by Miss Anderson herself. All numbered footnotes are hers also, unless followed by the initials 'E.B.', in which case they are editorial. They are occasionally abbreviated, but never altered. . . .

In conclusion I wish to acknowledge most gratefully the ready courtesy with which Messrs Macmillan consented to the use of their edition of the letters, as well as the help and advice most generously given by Miss Emily Anderson in order that this selection from her work should be as good as possible. Apart from one or two suggestions on which I was glad to act, she is not responsible for the actual choice of the letters here given in full or in part. On the other hand she has not only agreed most willingly to this decimation of a work in three volumes, which includes letters of Mozart's family as well as his own, but has also most carefully gone through the proofs, very kindly making a considerable number of corrections, and offered valuable advice of various kinds. Without her help this edition would undoubtedly have been less acceptable than I hope it is now going to prove to a large number of readers among whom, I feel, Mozart will find many new friends.

ERIC BLOM

ITALIAN JOURNEYS WITH HIS FATHER
1769-73

Dearest Mamma!

My heart is completely enchanted with all these pleasures, because it is so jolly on this journey, because it is so warm in the carriage and because our coachman is a fine fellow who, when the road gives him the slightest chance, drives so fast. Papa will have already described the journey to Mamma. The reason why I am writing to Mamma is to show her that I know my duty and that I am with the deepest respect her devoted son.

WOLFGANG MOZART

Dearest Sister!

I have had an aching feeling, because I have been so long waiting in vain for an answer. I have had good reason, too, because I have not yet received your letter. Here ends the German booby and the Italian one begins. *You are more fluent in Italian than I had imagined. Please tell me the reason why you did not go to the play which the courtiers acted? At present we are always hearing operas. One of them is 'Ruggiero'. Oronte, father of Bradamante, is a prince. Signor Afferi takes this part. He is a fine singer, a baritone, but* forced when he sings falsetto, but not as much as Tibaldi in Vienna. *Bradamante, daughter of Oronte, is in love with Ruggiero* (she is to marry Leone, but she does not want him). *Her part is sung by a poor Baroness, who has had great misfortune, but I don't know what it was. She is singing* under an assumed name, but I do not know it. *Her voice is tolerably good and she has not a bad presence, but she sings devilishly out of tune. The part of Ruggiero, a rich prince, who is in love with Bradamante, is sung by a castrato, who sings rather* in the manner of Manzuoli *and has a very fine powerful voice and is already old. He is fifty-five and has a* flexible throat. Leone, who is to marry Bradamante, is very rich, but whether he is rich off the stage, I do not know. *His part is sung by a woman, Afferi's wife. She has a most beautiful voice, but there is so much whispering in the theatre that you can't hear anything. Irene's part is sung by a sister of Lolli, the great violinist, whom we heard in Vienna.* She has a muffled voice and always sings a semiquaver too late *or too soon. The part of Ganno is taken by someone whose name I do not know. He is singing for the first time.* After each act there is a ballet. There is a good dancer here called Monsieur Ruesler. He is a German and dances very well. One of the last times we were at the opera (but not the very last time) we asked M. Ruesler to come up to our *palco* (for we have a free entrance to the

Leopold Mozart, a portrait attributed to Pietro Antonio Lorenzoni, 1765.

11

palco of Marchese Carlotti, as we have the key) and there we had a talk with him. A propos, everyone is masked now and it is really very convenient when you wear your mask, as you have the advantage of not having to take your hat off when you are greeted and of not having to address the person by name. You just say, '_servitore umilissimo, Signora Maschera'. Cospetto di Bacco,_ what fun! But the funniest thing of all is that we go to bed between seven and half past seven. _If you guess this I shall certainly say that you are the mother of all guessers._ Kiss my mother's hand for me. I kiss you a thousand times and assure you that I shall always remain,

your sincere brother

WOLFGANG MOZART

Portez-vous bien et aimez-moi toujours.

Mozart in Verona aged thirteen, a portrait by Saverio dalla Rosa.

TO HIS SISTER
Milan, 26 January 1770

I rejoice with my whole heart that you had such a good time during that sleigh-drive and I wish you a thousand opportunities of amusement so that you may spend your life very merrily. But one thing distresses me, and that is, that you have made Herr von Mölk[1] sigh and suffer so frightfully and that you did not go sleigh-driving with him, so that he might have upset you. How many handkerchiefs will he not have used that day, weeping on your account. No doubt he will have previously taken an ounce of tartar, which will have purged his wretchedly dirty body. I have no news except that Herr Gellert, the poet, has died at Leipzig and since his death has written no more poetry. Just before I began this letter I composed an aria from 'Demetrio', which begins: 'Misero tu non sei' . . .

The opera at Mantua was charming. They played 'Demetrio'. The *prima donna* sings well, but very softly; and when you do not see her acting, but only singing, you would think that she is not singing at all. For she cannot open her mouth, but whines out everything. However, we are quite accustomed to that now. The *seconda donna* looks like a grenadier and has a powerful voice too, and, I must say, does not sing badly, seeing that she is acting for the first time. The *primo uomo, il musico*, sings beautifully, though his voice is uneven. His name is Caselli. *Il secondo uomo* is already old and I do not like him. His name is —. As for the tenors, one is called Otini.[2] He does not sing badly, but rather heavily like all Italian tenors, and he is a great friend of ours. I do not know the name of the other one. He is still young, but not particularly good. *Primo ballerino* – good. *Prima ballerina* – good, and it is said that she is not hideous, but I have seen her close to. The rest are quite ordinary. A *grotesco* was there who jumps well, but cannot write as I do, I mean, as sows piddle. The orchestra was not bad. In Cremona it is good. The first violin is called Spagnoletto. The *prima donna* is not bad; she is quite old, I should say, and not good-looking; she acts better than she sings, and she is the wife of a violinist called Masi, who plays in the orchestra. The opera was: 'La Clemenza di Tito'. *Seconda donna*, young, not at all bad on the stage, but nothing out of the ordinary. *Primo uomo, musico*, Cicognani – a delightful voice and a beautiful *cantabile*. The other two *castrati*, young and passable. The tenor's name is – *I don't know it*. He has a pleasant way with him, and resembles as though he were his natural son, Leroy in Vienna, who came to Geneva.

---

1. Anton Joseph, son of Court Chancellor Felix von Mölk, was a friend of Mozart and in love with Nannerl.

2. Appears in [Leopold's] *Reiseaufzeichnungen, p. 50, as 'Uttini'.*

LEFT Mozart's sister Maria Anna, known as Nannerl, at the age of twelve; a portrait by Pietro Antonio Lorenzoni, 1763.

RIGHT Anna Maria Mozart, Wolfgang's mother; a portait attributed to Pietro Antonio Lorenzoni, c. 1775.

Ballerino primo, good. *Ballerina prima*, good but very plain. There was a woman dancer there, who did not dance badly and, what is very remarkable, was not bad-looking on the stage and off it. The others were quite ordinary. A *grotesco* was there too, who whenever he jumped let off a fart. As for Milan I really cannot tell you very much. We have not yet been to the opera, but we have heard that it has not been a success. Aprile, *primo uomo*, sings well and has a beautiful even voice. We heard him in a church, when there happened to be a great festival. Madame Piccinelli from Paris, who sang at our concert, is acting in the opera. Monsieur Pick[1], who danced in Vienna, is dancing here too. The opera is called: 'Didone abbandonata'. This opera will soon come to an end and Signor Piccinni, who is writing the next opera, is here. I have learned that he is called: 'Cesare in Egitto'. Here there are also *feste di ballo* which begin as soon as the opera is over. The wife of Count von Firmian's steward is a Viennese. Last Friday we dined there and we are going there again next Sunday. Farewell. Kiss my mother's hands a thousand times *on my behalf*. I remain, true till death, your brother

WOLFGANG DE MOZART
The Honourable Highdale,
Friend of the Counting-house

1. His real name was Le Picq.

TO HIS MOTHER AND SISTER
Milan, 10 February 1770

Talk of the devil and he will appear. Thanks and praise be to God, I am quite well and I can scarcely await the hour when I shall receive an answer from you. I kiss Mamma's hand and to my sister I send a pock-mark of a kiss and I remain the same old . . . old what? . . . the same old buffoon,

WOLFGANG IN GERMANY, AMADEO IN ITALY,

DE MOZARTINI

TO HIS SISTER
Bologna, 24 March 1770

Oh you busy thing!

As I have been idle for so long, I have been thinking that it would not be a bad idea if I did some work again for a short while. Every post-day, when letters arrive from Germany, I enjoy eating and drinking far more than usual. Please write and tell me who is singing in the oratorios and let me know their titles as well. Tell me also how you like Haydn's[1] minuets and whether they are better than his earlier ones. . . .

I shall soon send you a minuet which Mr Pick danced in the theatre and which everyone danced to afterwards at the *feste di ballo* in Milan, solely in order that you may see how slowly people dance here. The minuet itself is very beautiful. It comes, of course, from Vienna and was most certainly composed by Deller or Starzer.[2] It has plenty of notes. Why? Because it is a stage minuet which is danced slowly. The minuets in Milan, in fact the Italian minuets generally, have plenty of notes, are played slowly, and have several bars, e.g., the first part has sixteen, the second twenty or twenty four. . . .

1. Michael Haydn.
2. Florian Deller (1729–73) and Joseph Starzer (1726–87) were well-known composers of ballet music in Vienna.

St Peter's, Rome, from a coloured engraving by Giovanni Battista Piranesi.

TO HIS SISTER
Rome, 25 April 1770

My dear Sister,
  I assure you that every post-day I look forward with an incredible eagerness to receiving some letters from Salzburg. Yesterday we were at San Lorenzo and heard vespers, and this morning the mass which was sung, and in the evening the second vespers, because it is the festival of the Madonna del Buon Consiglio. During the last few days we have been to the Campidoglio and have seen several fine things. If I were to write down all that I have seen, this small sheet would not suffice. I have played at two concerts and to-morrow I am playing at another. This evening we saw a contralto singer, a castrato, who was very like Signor Meisner, whom by the way we shall have the honour of meeting at Naples. Immediately after lunch we play boccia. That is a game which I have learnt in Rome. When I come home, I shall teach it to you. . . . When I have finished this letter I shall finish a symphony which I have begun. The aria is finished. A symphony is being copied (my father is the copyist, for we do not wish to give it out to be copied, as it would be stolen). My greetings to all my friends and please kiss Mamma's hands for me, for I am (Tra la liera)
  WOLFGANG IN GERMANIA,
  AMADEO MOZART IN ITALIA

ROMA caput mundi,
  25 April 1770,
  and next year 1771.
    Behind as in front
    And double in the middle.   *I kiss you both.*

16

TO HIS MOTHER AND SISTER
Rome, 28 April 1770

I kiss my sister's face and Mamma's hands. I have not yet seen any scorpions or spiders nor do people talk or hear anything about them. Mamma will surely recognize my handwriting? She ought to let me know this quickly, or I shall sign my name underneath.

TO HIS SISTER
Naples, 19 May 1770

... The opera, which Jommelli is composing, will begin on the 30th. We saw the King and Queen at mass in the court chapel at Portici and we have seen Vesuvius too. Naples is beautiful, but it is as crowded as Vienna and Paris. And of the two, London and Naples, I do not know whether Naples does not surpass London for the insolence of the people; for here the *lazzaroni* have their own general or chief, who receives twenty-five *ducati d'argento* from the King every month, solely for the purpose of keeping them in order.

De Amicis is singing in the opera. We have been to see her.[1] Cafaro is composing the second opera and Ciccio di Majo the third. It is not yet known who is composing the fourth. Go regularly to Mirabell[2] to hear the Litanies and to listen to the Regina Coeli or the Salve Regina and sleep soundly and do not have any bad dreams. Give Herr von Schiedenhofen my fiercest greetings, 'Tralaliera, Tralaliera', and tell him to learn to play on the clavier the repeating minuet, so that he does not forget it. He must do so soon, so that he may do me the pleasure of accompanying him one day. Do remember me to all my good friends, and do keep well and do not die, so that you may do another letter for me and that I may do another for you and that we may keep on doing until we are done. For I am the man to go on doing until there is nothing more to do.

Meanwhile I do remain

WOLFGANG MOZART

1. The autograph has 'and she recognized us at once', which Mozart struck out.
2. Schloss Mirabell, built in 1606 by Archbishop Wolf Dietrich, was remodelled in a baroque style during the years 1721–27. It is now divided up into private dwellings. The gardens are still kept in the style of the eighteenth century.

The bay of Naples, by Pietro Fabris.

The San Carlo theatre in Naples, from a drawing by G. Medrano. It was here that the Mozarts heard Jommelli's new opera Armida abbandonata.

TO HIS SISTER
Naples, 5 June 1770

. . . The opera here is one of Jommelli's; it is beautiful, but too serious and old-fashioned for the theatre. De Amicis sings amazingly well and so does Aprile, who sang in Milan. The dances are wretchedly pompous. The theatre is beautiful. The King has had a rough Neapolitan upbringing and in the opera he always stands on a stool so as to look a little taller than the Queen. She is beautiful and gracious, and on the Molo (that is a drive) she bowed to me in a most friendly manner at least six times. Every evening the nobles send us their carriages to drive out with them to the Molo. We were invited on Sunday to the ball given by the French Ambassador. I can't write anything more. My compliments to all our kind friends. Farewell.

WOLFGANG MOZART

P.S. I kiss Mamma's hand.

TO HIS SISTER
Bologna, 21 July 1770

I hope that God will always grant you good health and will let you live another hundred years and will let you die when you have reached a thousand. I hope that you will get to know me better in the future and that then you will decide how much you like me. I have no time to write much. My pen is not worth a fig nor is he who is holding it. We do not yet know the title of the opera which I have to compose in Milan. Our hostess in Rome gave me as a present the 'Arabian Nights' in Italian. It is very amusing to read.

TO HIS SISTER
Bologna, 4 August 1770

. . . My fiddle has now been restrung and I play every day. But I add this simply because Mamma wanted to know whether I still play the fiddle. More than six times at least I have had the honour of going alone to a church and to some magnificent function. In the meantime I have composed four Italian symphonies, to say nothing of arias, of which I must have composed at least five or six, and also a motet. . . .

LEFT Mozart in 1770, an engraving by I. Sichling after the drawing by Cignaroli.

RIGHT An anonymous portrait of Giovanni Battista Martini.

21

TO HIS MOTHER AND SISTER
Bologna, 21 August 1770

I too am still alive and, what is more, as merry as can be. I had a great desire to-day to ride on a donkey, for it is the custom in Italy, and so I thought that I too should try it. We have the honour to go about with a certain Dominican, who is regarded as a holy man. For my part I do not believe it, for at breakfast he often takes a cup of chocolate and immediately afterwards a good glass of strong Spanish wine; and I myself have had the honour of lunching with this saint who at table drank a whole decanter and finished up with a full glass of strong wine, two large slices of melon, some peaches, pears, five cups of coffee, a whole plate of cloves, and two full saucers of milk and lemon. He may, of course, be following some sort of diet, but I do not think so, for it would be too much; moreover he takes several little snacks during the afternoon. *Addio.* Farewell. Kiss Mamma's hands for me. My greetings to all who know me.

WOLFGANG MOZART

TO HIS SISTER
Bologna, 8 September 1770

In order not to fail in my duty, I will add a few words myself. Please write and tell me to what Brotherhoods I belong and let me know what prayers I must offer for them. I am at this moment reading 'Télémaque' and have already got to the second part. Meanwhile, farewell.

WOLFGANG MOZART

I kiss Mamma's hand.

TO THOMAS LINLEY AT FLORENCE
Bologna, 10 September 1770

My dear Friend,

Here is a letter at last! Indeed I am very late in replying to your charming letter addressed to me at Naples, which, however, I only received two months after you had written it. My father's plan was to travel to Loreto via Bologna, and thence to Milan via Florence, Leghorn and Genoa. We should then have given you a surprise by turning up unexpectedly in Florence. But, as he had the misfortune to gash his leg rather badly when the shaft-horse of our sedia fell on the road, and as this wound not only kept him in bed for three weeks, but held us up in Bologna for another seven, this nasty accident has forced us to change our plans

Elizabeth and Thomas Linley, by Thomas Gainsborough, 1768. The English violinist (1756-78) became friendly with Mozart in Florence, where they played duets together. His sister married the playwright Sheridan.

and to proceed to Milan via Parma.

Firstly, we have missed the suitable time for such a journey and, secondly, the season is over, as everyone is in the country and therefore we could not earn our expenses. I assure you that this accident has annoyed us very much. I would do everything in my power to have the pleasure of embracing my dear friend. Moreover my father and I would very much like to meet again Signor Gavard and his very dear and charming family, and also Signora Corilla and Signor Nardini, and then to return to Bologna. This we would do indeed, if we had the slightest hope of making even the expenses for our journey.

As for the engravings you lost, my father remembered you; and his order arrived in time for two other copies to be kept for you. So please let me know some means of sending them to you. Keep me in your friendship and believe that my affection for you will endure for ever and that I am your most devoted servant and loving friend.

AMADEO WOLFGANG MOZART

TO HIS MOTHER
Milan, 20 October 1770

My dear Mamma,

I cannot write much, for my fingers are aching from composing so many recitatives. Mamma, I beg you to pray for me, that my opera may go well and that we may be happy together again. I kiss Mamma's hand a thousand times and I have many things to say to my sister, but what? God and I alone know. If it is God's will, I shall soon, I hope, be able to tell them to her myself. Meanwhile I kiss her 1,000 times. . . .

TO HIS SISTER
Milan, 12 January 1771

Dearest Sister,

I have not written for a long time, for I was busy with my opera, but as I now have time, I will be more attentive to my duty. The opera, God be praised, is a success, for every evening the theatre is full, much to the astonishment of everyone, for several people say that since they have been to Milan they have never seen such crowds at a first opera. Papa and I, thank God, are well, and I hope that at Easter I shall be able to tell you and Mamma everything with my own lips. *Addio.* I kiss Mamma's hand. A propos! Yesterday the copyist called on us and said that he had orders to transcribe my opera for the court at Lisbon. Meanwhile farewell, my dear *Mademoiselle* sister. I have the honour to be and to remain from now to all eternity

   your faithful brother[1]

TO JOHANNES HAGENAUER AT SALZBURG
Venice, 13 February 1771

The particularly splendid pearl and all the other pearls too admire you very greatly. I assure you that they are all in love with you and that they hope that like a Turk you will marry them all, and make the whole six of them happy. I am writing this in Herr Wider's house. He is a fine fellow, as you told me in your letter. Yesterday we wound up the carnival at his house, dined with him and then danced and went with the pearls to the new Ridotto, which I liked immensely. When I am at Herr Wider's and look out of the window, I can see

---

1. The signature has been cut off this autograph.

the house where you lived when you were in Venice. I have no news for you. I am charmed with Venice. My greetings to your father, mother, sisters, brothers and to all my friends. Addio.

WOLFGANG AMADEO MOZART

TO HIS SISTER
Venice, 20 February 1771

God be praised, I too am still alive and well. De Amicis sang here at San Benedetto. Tell Johannes that Wider's pearls, especially Mademoiselle Catarina, are always talking about him, and that he must soon come back to Venice and submit to the *attacco*, that is, have his bottom spanked when he is lying on the ground, so that he may become a true Venetian. They tried to do it to me – the seven women all together – and yet they could not pull me down. *Addio.* I kiss Mamma's hand and we both send greetings to all our good friends. Farewell. Amen.

TO HIS SISTER
Milan, 24 August 1771

Dearest Sister,

We suffered greatly from the heat on our journey and the dust worried us most impertinently the whole time, so that we should certainly have been choked to death, if we had not been too clever for that. Here it has not rained for a whole month (or so the Milanese say). . . . The Princess had an attack of diarrhoea the other day. Apart from that I have no news. Do send me some. My greetings to all our good friends, and I kiss Mamma's hand. I am simply panting from the heat! So I am tearing open my waistcoat. *Addio.* Farewell.

WOLFGANG

Upstairs we have a violinist, downstairs another one, in the next room a singing-master who gives lessons, and in the other room opposite ours an oboist. That is good fun when you are composing! It gives you plenty of ideas.

An engraving by Marc Antonio dal Re of the interior of the theatre at Milan, La Scala.

TO HIS SISTER

Milan, 26 October 1771

Praise and thanks be to God, I too am well. As my work is now finished, I have more time to write letters. But I have nothing to say, for Papa has told you everything already. I have no news except that numbers 35, 59, 60, 61, 62 were drawn in the lottery; and so, if we had taken these numbers, we should have won. But as we did not take any tickets, we have neither won nor lost, but we have had our laugh at other people who did. The two arias which were encored in the serenata were sung by Manzuoli and by the prima donna, Girelli, respectively. . . .

TO HIS SISTER

Milan, 24 November 1771

. . . Manzuoli, who up to the present has been generally looked upon as the most sensible of the *castrati*, has in his old age[1] given the world a sample of his stupidity and conceit. He was engaged for the opera at a salary of five hundred *cigliati*, but,

1. He was forty-six.

as the contract did not mention the *serenata*, he demanded another five hundred for that, that is, one thousand *cigliati* in all. The court only gave him seven hundred and a fine gold snuff-box (quite enough, I think). But he like a true *castrato* returned both the seven hundred *cigliati* and the gold snuff-box and went off without anything. I do not know how it will all end – badly, I expect. . . .

TO HIS MOTHER AND SISTER
Milan, 30 November 1771

Lest you should think that I am unwell I am sending you these few lines. I kiss Mamma's hand. My greetings to all our good friends. I have seen four rascals hanged here in the Piazza del Duomo. They hang them just as they do in Lyons.

WOLFGANG

TO HIS SISTER
Milan, 5 December 1772

I still have fourteen pieces to compose and then I shall have finished. But indeed the trio and the duet might well count as four. It is impossible for me to write much, as I have no news and, moreover, I do not know what I am writing, for I can think of nothing but my opera and I am in danger of writing down not words but a whole aria. . . .

TO HIS SISTER
Milan, 18 December 1772

I hope that you are well, my dear sister. When you receive this letter, my dear sister, that very evening my opera will have been performed, my dear sister. Think of me, my dear sister, and try as hard as you can to imagine that you, my dear sister, are hearing and seeing it too, my dear sister. That is hard, I admit, as it is already eleven o'clock. Otherwise I believe and do not doubt at all that during the day it is brighter than at Easter. We are lunching tomorrow, my dear sister, with Herr von Mayr, and why, do you think? Guess! Why, because he has asked

LUCIO SILLA

DRAMMA PER MUSICA

DA RAPPRESENTARSI

**NEL REGIO-DUCAL TEATRO
DI MILANO**

Nel Carnovale dell' anno 1773

DEDICATO

ALLE LL. AA. RR.

IL SERENISSIMO ARCIDUCA

FERDINANDO

Principe Reale d' Ungheria , e Boemia , Arciduca d'Auftria
Duca di Borgogna , e di Lorena ec. , Cefareo Reale
Luogo-Tenente , Governatore , e Capitano
Generale nella Lombardia Auftriaca ,

E LA

SERENISSIMA ARCIDUCHESSA

MARIA RICCIARDA
BEATRICE D' ESTE

PRINCIPESSA DI MODENA.

IN MILANO,

Preffo Gio. Batifta Bianchi Regio Stampatore
Con licenza de' Superiori .

The title page of Mozart's Lucio Silla, *written when he was seventeen. The first
performance took place in the Teatro Regio Ducal on 26 December 1772.*

us. The rehearsal tomorrow is at the theatre, but Signor Castiglione, the impresario, has begged me not to tell anyone about it; otherwise a whole crowd of people will come running in and we do not want this. So, my child, I beg you not to mention it to anyone, my child, otherwise too many people will come running in, my child. That reminds me. Have you heard what happened here? I shall tell you. We left Count Firmian's to-day to go home and when we reached our street, we opened the hall door and what do you think we did? Why, we went in. Farewell, my little lung. I kiss you, my liver, and remain as always, my stomach, your unworthy

{ frater
{ brother

WOLFGANG

Please, please, my dear sister, something is biting me. Do come and scratch me.

TO HIS SISTER
Milan, 23 January 1773

. . . The first orchestral rehearsal of the second opera took place yesterday evening, but I only heard the first act, since, as it was late, I left at the beginning of the second. In this opera there are to be twenty-four horses and a great crowd of people on the stage, so that it will be a miracle if some accident does not happen. I like the music, but I do not know whether the public will like it, for only people connected with the theatre have been allowed to attend the first rehearsal. . . .

WITH HIS FATHER IN VIENNA AND MUNICH
1773-75

TO HIS SISTER
Vienna, 14 August 1773

I hope, my queen, that you are enjoying the highest degree of health and that now and then or rather, sometimes, or, better still, occasionally, or, even better still, *qualche volta*, as the Italians say, you will sacrifice for my benefit some of your important and intimate thoughts, which ever proceed from that very fine and clear reasoning power, which in addition to your beauty, and although from a woman, and particularly from one of such tender years, almost nothing of the kind is ever expected, you possess, O queen, so abundantly as to put men and even greybeards to shame. There now, you have a well-turned sentence. Farewell.

WOLFGANG MOZART

TO HIS MOTHER
Vienna, 8 September 1773

Little Wolfgang has no time to write, for he has nothing to do. He is walking up and down the room like a dog with fleas.

TO HERR VON HEFNER AT SALZBURG
Vienna, 15 September 1773

To Herr von Hefner
I hope that we shall still find you in Salzburg,
   my friendly slug.
I hope that you are well and are not an empty spider, for if so I'll be an enemy fly
Or even a friendly bug.
So I strongly advise you to write better rhymes, for
If not, our Salzburg Cathedral will see me no more.
For I'm quite *capax* to go off to Constantinople, that city whose praises all chant.
And then you won't see me again nor I you; yet
When horses are hungry, some oats they get.
Farewell, my lad, I'm ever to infinity
Or else I'll go mad. From now to all eternity.

TO HIS SISTER
Munich, 28 December 1774

My dearest Sister,
   I beg you not to forget to keep your promise before you leave, I mean, to pay
the call we both know of . . . for I have my reasons. I beg you to convey my
greetings there – but in the most definite way – in the most tender fashion – and –
oh, I need not be so anxious, for of course I know my sister and how extremely
tender she is. I am quite certain that she will do her utmost to do me a kindness –
and for her own advantage too – but that is rather nasty. But we shall quarrel
about this in Munich. Farewell.

TO HIS SISTER
Munich, 30 December 1774

   I present my compliments to Roxelana, and invite her to take tea this evening
with the Sultan. Please give all sorts of messages to Jungfrau Mitzerl[1], and tell her

1. Fräulein Maria Raab, the owner of the Mozarts' house in Hannibalplatz [later called Makartplatz and Dollfussplatz].

OPPOSITE The interior of Salzburg Cathedral, by Melchior Kussell, c. 1680.

that she must never doubt my love. I see her constantly before me in her ravishing _négligée._[2] I have seen many pretty girls here, but have not yet found such a beauty. . . . My greetings to all my good friends. I hope that you will – farewell – I see you soon in Munich to hope. I have compliments to deliver to you from Frau von Durst. . . . My mother's hand I kiss, the rest she'll have to miss. I beg you to keep very warm on the journey, or else for a fortnight at home you'll sit and beside the stove perspire a bit and not a soul will protect you one whit. But I simply refuse to have a fit; and now the lightning's beginning to spit.

YOUR MUNICH
brother, the 1774th day of _Anno_ 30, _Dicembre._

TO HIS MOTHER
Munich, 11 January, 1775

Thank God, all three of us are quite well. It is impossible for me to write a long letter, as I am off this very . . . moment to a rehearsal of my opera. To-morrow we are having the dress rehearsal and the performance takes place on Friday, the 13th. Mamma must not worry; it will go off quite well. . . .

TO HIS MOTHER
Munich, 14 January 1775

Thank God! My opera was performed yesterday, the 13th, for the first time and was such a success that it is impossible for me to describe the applause to Mamma. In the first place, the whole theatre was so packed that a great many people were turned away. Then after each aria there was a terrific noise, clapping of hands and cries of '_Viva Maestro_'. Her Highness the Electress and the Dowager Electress (who were sitting opposite me) also called out '_Bravo_' to me. After the opera was over and during the pause when there is usually silence until the ballet begins, people kept on clapping all the time and shouting '_Bravo_'; now stopping,

2. Mozart means 'with her hair undressed'.

An engraving by Valerian Funck, after François Cuvilliés and Ignaz Gunther, of the Residenztheater in Munich where Idomeneo *was first performed in 1781.*

now beginning again and so on. Afterwards I went off with Papa to a certain room through which the Elector and the whole court had to pass and I kissed the hands of the Elector and Electress and Their Highnesses, who were all very gracious. . . . I fear that we cannot return to Salzburg very soon and Mamma must not wish it, for she knows how much good it is doing me to be able to breathe freely. We shall come home soon enough. One very urgent and necessary reason for our absence is that next Friday my opera is being performed again and it is most essential that I should be present. Otherwise my work would be quite unrecognizable – for very strange things happen here. I kiss Mamma's hands 1,000 times. My greetings to all my friends. . . . Adieu. 1,000 smacks to Bimberl.[1]

1. Bimberl, Bimperl, Bimpes, or Bimbes was the family's fox-terrier bitch, who is often sent messages in the letters.

WITH THE FAMILY AT SALZBURG

TO PADRE MARTINI AT BOLOGNA
Salzburg, 4 September 1776

Most reverend Padre Maestro, my esteemed Patron,

The regard, the esteem and the respect which I cherish for your illustrious person have prompted me to trouble you with this letter and to send you a humble specimen of my music, which I submit to your masterly judgement. I composed for last year's carnival at Munich an opera buffa, 'La finta giardiniera'. A few days before my departure the Elector expressed a desire to hear some of my contrapuntal compositions. I was therefore obliged to write this motet[1] in a great hurry, in order to have time to have the score copied for His Highness and to have the parts written out and thus enable it to be performed during the Offertory at High Mass on the following Sunday. Most beloved and esteemed Signor Padre Maestro! I beg you most earnestly to tell me, frankly and without reserve, what you think of it. We live in this world in order to learn zealously and, by interchanging our ideas, to enlighten one another and thus endeavour to promote science and art. Oh, how often have I longed to be near you, most Reverend Father, so that I might be able to talk to and reason with you. For I live in a country where music leads a struggling existence, though indeed apart from those who have left us, we still have excellent teachers and particularly composers of great wisdom, learning and taste. As for the theatre, we are in a bad way for lack of singers. We have no castrati, and we shall never have them, as they insist on being handsomely paid; and generosity is not one of our faults. Meanwhile I am amusing myself by writing chamber music and music for the church, in which branches of composition we have two other excellent masters of counterpoint, Signori Haydn and Adlgasser. My father is in the service of the Cathedral and this gives me an opportunity of writing as much church music as I like. He has already served this court for thirty-six years and as he knows that the present Archbishop cannot and will not have anything to do with people who are getting on in years, he no longer puts his whole heart into his work, but has taken up literature, which was always a favourite study of his. Our church music is very different from that of Italy, since a mass with the whole Kyrie, the Gloria, the Credo, the Epistle sonata, the Offertory or Motet, the Sanctus and the Agnus Dei must not last longer than three-quarters of an hour. This applies even to the most solemn mass said by the Archbishop himself. So you see that a special study is required for this kind of composition . . . I long to win your favour and I never cease to grieve that I am far away from that one person in the world whom I love, revere and esteem most of all and whose most humble and devoted servant, most

Reverend Father, I shall always be.

WOLFGANGO AMADEO MOZART

1. K.222, 'Misericordias Domini', performed in Munich on 5 March 1775.

34

The Paris Lodron Palace, Salzburg, by Johann Michael Sattler, seen from the now demolished Mitterbach archway. In Mozart's time the hereditary marshal Count Lodron lived here, for whose wife and daughters Mozart wrote several divertimenti and the concerto for three pianos.

TO ARCHBISHOP HIERONYMUS COLLOREDO
Salzburg, 1 August 1777

Your Grace, Most Worthy Prince of the Holy Roman Empire!

I will not presume to trouble Your Grace with a full description of our unhappy circumstances, which my father has set forth most accurately in his very humble petition which was handed to you on March 14th, 1777. As, however, your most gracious decision was never conveyed to him, my father intended last June once more most respectfully to beg Your Grace to allow us to travel for a few months in order to enable us to make some money; and he would have done so, if you had not given orders that in view of the imminent visit of His Majesty the Emperor your orchestra should practise various works with a view to their performance. Later my father applied again for leave of absence, which Your Grace refused to grant, though you permitted me, who am in any case only a half-time servant, to travel alone. Our situation is pressing and my father has therefore decided to let me go alone. But to this course also Your Grace has been pleased to raise certain objections. Most Gracious Prince and Lord! Parents endeavour to place their children in a position to earn their own bread; and in this

Hieronymous, Count Colloredo, Prince-Archbishop of Salzburg (König) 1772.

36

A drawing of Salzburg by August Franz Heinrich Naumann, 1790.

they follow alike their own interest and that of the State. The greater the talents which children have received from God, the more are they bound to use them for the improvement of their own and their parents' circumstances, so that they may at the same time assist them and take thought for their own future progress. The Gospel teaches us to use our talents in this way. My conscience tells me that I owe it to God to be grateful to my father, who has spent his time unwearyingly upon my education, so that I may lighten his burden, look after myself and later on be able to support my sister. For I should be sorry to think that she should have spent so many hours at the harpsichord and not be able to make good use of her training.

Your Grace will therefore be so good as to allow me to ask you most humbly for my discharge, of which I should like to take advantage before the autumn, so that I may not be obliged to face the bad weather of the ensuing months of winter. Your Grace will not misunderstand this petition, seeing that when I asked you for permission to travel to Vienna three years ago, you graciously declared that I had nothing to hope for in Salzburg and would do better to seek my fortune elsewhere. I thank Your Grace for all the favours I have received from you and, in the hope of being able to serve you later on with greater success, I am

your most humble and obedient servant

WOLFGANG AMADÉ MOZART

37

A TOUR WITH HIS MOTHER TO MANNHEIM
—•☉••☉•— 1777-78 —•☉••☉•—

... This is what happened. I walked into the house and Madame Niesser, the actress, who was just coming out, asked me: 'I suppose you want to see the Count?' 'Yes', I replied. 'Well, he is still in his garden and goodness knows when he will return.' I asked her where the garden was. 'Well,' she said, 'I too want to see him, so let us go together.' We had hardly passed the lodge gates before the Count came towards us; and when he was about twelve paces from us, he recognized me, addressed me by name, and was extremely polite. He was already acquainted with my story. As we mounted the steps together very slowly, I disclosed to him very briefly the object of my visit. He said that I should ask immediately for an audience with His Highness the Elector and that if for any reason I was unable to see him, I should put my case before him in writing. I begged him to keep the whole thing secret and he promised me to do so. When I remarked that a first-rate composer was badly needed here, he said: 'I am well aware of it.' After this I called on the Bishop of Chiemsee and was with him for half an hour. I told him everything and he promised to do his best in the matter. He was going to Nymphenburg at one o'clock and promised to speak to Her Highness the Electress without fail. The court returns to Munich on Sunday evening. ...

At nine o'clock to-day, the 30th, I went as arranged with M. Woschitka to court. Everyone was in hunting dress. Baron Kern was acting chamberlain. I might have gone there yesterday evening, but did not want to tread on the toes of M. Woschitka, who of his own accord had offered to procure me an audience with the Elector. At ten o'clock he showed me into a little narrow room through which His Highness was to pass on his way to hear mass before going to hunt. Count Seeau went by and greeted me in the most friendly fashion, saying: 'How do you do, my very dear Mozart!' When the Elector came up to me, I said: 'Your Highness will allow me to throw myself most humbly at your feet and offer you my services.' 'So you have left Salzburg for good?' 'Yes, your Highness, for good.' 'How is that? Have you had a row with him?' 'Not at all, your Highness. I

Maximilian Joseph III and Joseph Anton, Count Seeau, 1755.

only asked him for permission to travel, which he refused. So I was compelled to take this step, though indeed I had long been intending to clear out. For Salzburg is no place for me, I can assure you.' 'Good Heavens! There's a young man for you! But your father is still in Salzburg?' 'Yes, your Highness. He too throws himself most humbly at your feet, and so forth. I have been three times to Italy already, I have written three operas, I am a member of the Bologna Academy, where I had to pass a test, at which many *maestri* have laboured and sweated for four or five hours, but which I finished in an hour. Let that be a proof that I am competent to serve at any court. My sole wish, however, is to serve your Highness, who himself is such a great – ' 'Yes, my dear boy, but I have no vacancy. I am sorry. If only there were a vacancy – ' 'I assure your Highness that I should not fail to do credit to Munich.' 'I know. But it is no good, for there is no vacancy here.' This he said as he walked away. Whereupon I commended myself to his good graces. Herr Woschitka has advised me to put in an appearance at court as often as I can. This afternoon I went to see Count Salern. The Countess, his daughter, is now a maid of honour. She had gone out hunting with the rest. Ravani and I were in the street when the whole company passed by. The Elector and the Electress greeted me in a most friendly manner. Countess Salern recognized me at once and waved her hand to me repeatedly. Baron Rumling, whom I saw beforehand in the antechamber, has never been so civil to me as he was on this occasion. How I got on with Salern I shall tell you in my next letter. It was quite satisfactory. He was very polite – and frank.

P.S. *Ma très chère soeur.* I shall send you a letter all for yourself very soon. My greetings to A.B.C.M.R. and more letters of the alphabet of that kind. *Addio.* I do beg you to take great care of your health. I kiss Papa's hands 100,000 times and always remain your most obedient son

WOLFGANG AMADÉ MOZART

Someone built a house here and wrote on it:
  To build a house is good fun, 'tis true.
  That 'twould cost so much I never knew.
During the night someone scrawled underneath:
  That to build a house would cost so much brass
  You ought to have known, you silly ass.

TO HIS FATHER

Munich, 2–3 October 1777

Yesterday, October 1st, I called on Count Salern again and to-day, the 2nd, I actually lunched there. During the last three days I have had quite enough playing, I think, but I have thoroughly enjoyed it. Papa must not suppose that I like to go to Count Salern's on account of —. Not at all, for unfortunately, she is in service at court and therefore is never at home. But about ten o'clock to-morrow morning I shall go to court with Madame Hepp, née Tosson, and shall then see her. For the court leaves on Saturday and will not return until the 20th. I

40

am lunching to-morrow with Frau and Fräulein De Branca, who is now half my pupil, as Siegl seldom turns up and Becke, who usually accompanies her on the flute, is not here. At Count Salern's during those three days I played several things out of my head, and then the two Cassations I wrote for the Countess and finally the *Finalmusik* with the Rondo, all from memory. You cannot imagine how delighted Count Salern was. But he really understands music, for all the time he kept shouting '*Bravo*', where other noblemen would take a pinch of snuff, blow their noses, clear their throats – or start a conversation. I said to him that I only wished that the Elector could be there, for then he might hear something. As it is, he knows nothing whatever about me. He has no idea what I can do. Why do these gentlemen believe what anyone tells them and never try to find out for themselves? Yes, it is always the same. I am willing to submit to a test. Let him get together all the composers in Munich, let him even summon a few from Italy, France, Germany, England, and Spain. I undertake to compete with any of them in composition. I told Salern what I had done in Italy and I begged him, whenever the conversation should turn on me, to trot out these facts. He said: 'I have very little influence, but what I can do, I will do with my whole heart.' He too is strongly of the opinion that if I could stay on here for a time, the problem would solve itself. If I were here alone, it would not be impossible for me to manage somehow, for I should ask for at least 300 gulden from Count Seeau. As for food, I should not have to worry, for I should always be invited out, and whenever I had no invitation, Albert would only be too delighted to have me at table. I eat very little, drink water, just at dessert I take a small glass of wine. I should draw up a contract with Count Seeau (all on the advice of my good friends) on the following lines: to compose every year four German operas, some *buffe*, some *serie*; and to be allowed a *sera* or benefit performance of each for myself, as is the custom here. That alone would bring me in at least 500 gulden, which with my salary would make up 800 gulden. But I should certainly make more, for Reiner, the actor and singer, took in 200 gulden on the occasion of his benefit; and I am very popular here. And how much more popular I should be if I could help forward the German national theatre! And with my help it would certainly succeed. For when I heard the German *singspiel*, I was simply itching to compose. The leading soprano is called Mlle Kaiser. She is the daughter of a cook by a count here and is a very attractive girl; pretty on the stage, that is; but I have not yet seen her near. She is a native of the town. When I heard her, it was only her third appearance. She has a beautiful voice, not powerful but by no means weak,

Nicolo Piccinni; an engraving by Louis Jacques Cathelin after Julien Robineau. Mozart first met Piccinni on 2 February 1770 at a dress rehearsal of Cesare in Egitto.

very pure and her intonation is good. Valesi has taught her; and from her singing you can tell he knows how to sing as well as how to teach. When she sustains her voice for a few bars, I have been astonished at the beauty of her *crescendo* and *decrescendo*. She still takes her trills slowly and I am very glad. They will be all the truer and clearer when later on she wants to trill more rapidly, as it is always easier to do them quickly in any case. People here are delighted with her – and I am delighted with them. Mamma was in the pit. She went in as early as half-past four in order to secure a seat; but I did not turn up until half-past six, as I have the *entrée* to all the boxes, for I am so well known. I was in the Brancas' box and I kept my opera-glasses on Mlle Kaiser and she often drew a tear from me. I kept on calling out '*Brava, Bravissima*', for I could not forget that it was only her third appearance on the stage. The play was 'The Fishermaiden', a very good translation of Piccinni's opera. As yet they have no original plays. They would like to produce a German *opera seria* soon, and they are very anxious that I should compose it. Professor Huber, whom I have already mentioned, is one of the people who want this. Now I must go to bed, for I have come to an end of my tether. It is ten o'clock sharp.

Baron Rumling paid me a compliment the other day by saying: 'I love the theatre, good actors and actresses, good singers, and, last but not least, a first-rate composer like yourself.' Only words, it is true, and it is very easy to talk. But he has never spoken to me before in such a flattering manner. I wish you good night

– to-morrow, God willing, I shall have the honour of talking to you again, my dearest Papa, in writing.

October 2nd. Number four on the second floor. . . .

I am writing this on October 3rd. The court is leaving tomorrow and will not return until the 20th. If it had stayed, I should have kept on hammering, and I should have stayed on myself for some time. As it is, I hope next Tuesday to continue my journey with Mamma, but the position is this: in the meantime the company, about which I wrote to you the other day, will be formed; so that, when we are tired of travelling, we shall have a safe place to return to. Herr von Krimmel was with the Bishop of Chiemsee to-day; he had a good many things to settle with him, including that matter of the salt. Von Krimmel is a curious fellow. Here they call him 'Your Grace', I mean, the flunkeys do. He would like nothing better than that I should remain here, and spoke about me very warmly to the Prince. He said to me: 'Just leave it to me. I shall talk to the Prince. I know how to deal with him, as I have often been of service to him.' The Prince promised him that I should certainly be taken into the court service, but added that things could not be done quite so quickly. As soon as the court returns, he will speak most seriously and earnestly to the Elector. At eight o'clock this morning I saw Count Seeau. I was very brief and merely said: 'I have come, your Excellency, solely in order to explain myself and produce my credentials. It has been cast up at me that I ought to travel to Italy. Why, I have spent sixteen months in Italy and, as everyone knows, I have written three operas. My other achievements your Excellency will learn about from these papers.' I then showed him my diplomas and added: 'I am showing these to your Excellency and I am telling you all this so that, if ever my name is mentioned and any injustice should be done to me, you may be justified in taking my part.' He asked me if I was now going to France. I replied that I was staying on in Germany. But he thought I meant Munich and asked with a pleasant smile: 'What? So you are staying on here?' 'No', I said, 'I should have liked to; and, to tell the truth, the only reason why I should have been glad of a subsidy from the Elector is that I might have been able to serve your Excellency with my compositions and without asking for anything in return. I should have regarded it as a pleasure.' At these words he actually raised his skull-cap. At ten o'clock I was at court with the Countess Salern, who has already received the arias. The Robinigs just say, of course, whatever comes into their heads. Afterwards I lunched with the Brancas. Privy Councillor von Branca had been invited to the French Ambassador's, and so was not at home. He is addressed as 'Your Excellency'. His wife is a Frenchwoman, who hardly knows a word of German, so I spoke French to her all the time, and I talked quite boldly. She told me that I did not speak at all badly and that I had one good habit, that is, of talking slowly, which made it quite easy to understand me. She is an excellent woman with the most charming manners. Her daughter plays quite nicely, but her time is still poor. I thought at first that it was due to her own carelessness or that her ear was at fault, but I can now blame no one but her teacher, who is far too indulgent and is satisfied with anything. I made her play to me to-day. I wager that after two months' lessons from me she would play quite well and accurately. She asked me to send her greetings to you and to the whole Robinig family. She was at the convent at the same time as Fräulein Louise. Later in the day a certain Fräulein Lindner, who is now at Count Salern's as governess to the two young countesses, also requested me to send all sorts of messages to the Robinigs and to Fräulein Louise von Schiedenhofen, with whom she was at the same convent. At four o'clock I went to Frau von Tosson, where I found Mamma and Frau von Hepp. I played there until eight o'clock and then we went home. About half-past nine in the evening a small orchestra of five players, two clarinets, two horns and one bassoon, came up to the house. Herr Albert (whose name-day is to-morrow) had ordered this music in his and my honour. They did not play at all badly together. They were the same people who play in Albert's dining-hall during the meals. But you can tell at once that Fiala has trained them. They played some of his compositions and I must say that they were very pretty and that he has some very good ideas.

To-morrow we are going to have a little scratch-concert among ourselves, but, I should add, on that wretched clavier. Oh! Oh! Oh! Well, I wish you a very restful night and I improve on this good wish by hearing to hope soon that Papa is well quite. I forgiveness your crave for my disgraceful handwriting, but ink, haste, sleep, dreams and all the rest. . . . I Papa your, my hands kiss, a thousand times dearest, and my embrace, the heart, sister I with all my brute of a, and remain, now and for ever, amen,

WOLFGANG most obedient your
AMEDÉ MOZART son

Munich, 3 October 1777

To all good friends, to all bad friends, good friends, bad friends, all sorts of messages.

TO HIS FATHER
Munich
10–11 October 1777

... Mysliveček showed me too some letters in which my name was frequently mentioned. I am told that he has expressed great surprise when people here have talked about Beecke or other clavier-players of the same kind, and has always exclaimed: 'Make no mistake. No one can play like Mozart. In Italy, where the greatest masters are to be found, they talk of no one but Mozart. When he is mentioned, everyone is silent.' I can now write the letter to Naples when I choose, but the sooner the better. First, however, I should like to have the opinion of that very wise Court *Kapellmeister*, Herr von Mozart!

I have an inexpressible longing to write another opera. It is a long way to go, it is true, but it would be a long time before I should have to write it. Many things may happen before then. But I think that I ought to accept it. If in the meantime I fail to secure an appointment, *eh bien*, then I can fall back on Italy. I shall still have my certain 100 ducats at the carnival and once I have conposed for Naples, I shall be in demand everywhere. Moreover, as Papa is well aware, there are also *opere buffe* here and there in the spring, summer and autumn, which one can write for practice and for something to do. I should not make very much, it is true, but, all the same, it would be something; and they would bring me more honour and credit than if I were to give a hundred concerts in Germany. And I am happier when I have something to compose, for that, after all, is my sole delight and passion. And if I secure an appointment or if I have hopes of settling down somewhere, then the *scrittura* will be an excellent recommendation will give me restige and greatly enhance my value. But all this is only talk – talk out of the fullness of my heart. If Papa can prove conclusively that I am wrong, well, then I shall acquiesce, although unwillingly. For I have only to hear an opera discussed, I have only to sit in a theatre, hear the orchestra tuning their instruments – oh, I am quite beside myself at once ...

Immediately after lunch yesterday I went with Mamma to a coffee party at the two Fräulein Freysingers'. Mamma, however, drank no coffee, but had two bottles of Tyrolese wine instead. She went home at three o'clock to put a few things together for our journey. I went with the two young ladies to the said Herr von Hamm, where the three ladies each played a concerto and I played one of Eichner's at sight and then went on improvising. Miss Simplicity von Hamm's teacher is a certain clergyman of the name of Schreier. He is a good organist, but no cembalist. He kept on staring at me through his spectacles the whole time. He is a dry sort of fellow, who does not say much: but he tapped me on the shoulder, sighed and said: 'Yes – you are – you know – yes – that is true – you are first-rate.' A propos. Does Papa not recall the name Freysinger? The Papa of the two beautiful young ladies whom I have mentioned says that he knows Papa quite well, and was a student with him. He still remembers particularly Wessobrunn, where Papa (this was news to me) played on the organ amazingly well. 'It was quite terrifying', he said to me, 'to see how rapid your Papa was with his feet and hands. Indeed, he was absolutely amazing. Ah, he was a great fellow. My father thought the world of him. And how he fooled the clerics to the top of their bent about becoming a priest! You are the very image of him, as he then was, absolutely the very image. But when I knew him, he was just a little shorter.' A propos. Now for something else. A certain Court Councillor, Öfele by name, who is one of the best Court Councillors here, sends his most humble greetings to Papa. He could have been Chancellor long ago, but for one thing – his love of the bottle. When I first saw him at Albert's, I thought, and so did Mamma, 'Goodness me, what a superlative idiot!' Just picture him, a very tall fellow, strongly built, rather corpulent, with a perfectly absurd face. When he crosses the room to go to another table, he places both hands on his stomach, bends over them and hoists his belly aloft, nods his head and then draws back his right foot with great rapidity. And he performs the same trick afresh for every person in turn. He says he knows Papa infinitely well. I am now off to the theatre for a while. Later on I shall write more. I simply cannot do so now, for my fingers are aching horribly.

TO HIS FATHER
Augsburg, 14 October 1777

. . . just hear how kind and generous these good Augsburg gentlemen have been! In no place have I been overwhelmed with so many marks of honour as here. My first visit was to the magistrate, Longotabarro. My uncle, a most excellent and lovable man and an honourable townsman, accompanied me and had the honour of waiting upstairs on the landing like a lackey until I should come out of the Arch-Magistrate's room. I did not forget to deliver at once my Papa's most humble respects. He was so good as to remember our whole history and asked me: 'How has he fared all this time?' Whereupon I at once replied: 'Very well, thanks and praise be to God. And I trust that you too have fared very well?' After that he began to unbend, and addressed me in the second person, while I

A view of Augsburg, engraved by P. van der Aa in 1729. Leopold Mozart was born here in 1719.

continued to address him as 'Your Highness', as I had done from the very first. He would not let me go and I had to follow him upstairs to his son-in-law (on the second floor); and meanwhile my uncle had the honour of waiting, seated on a stool in the lobby. I had to restrain myself, most manfully, otherwise I should have said something, quite politely, of course. Upstairs I had the honour of playing for about three-quarters of an hour upon a good clavichord by Stein in the presence of the dressed-up son and the long-legged young wife and the stupid old lady. I improvised and finally I played off at sight all the music he had, including some very pretty pieces by a certain Edelmann. They were all exceedingly polite and I too was very polite. For it is my custom to treat people as I find them; it pays best in the end. I told them that after lunch I was going to see Stein. The young gentleman of his own accord offered to take me there. I thanked him for his kindness and promised to call again at two o'clock, which I did. We all set off together, accompanied by his brother-in-law, who looked the perfect student. Although I had asked them to keep my identity a secret, yet Herr von Langenmantel was so thoughtless as to say to Herr Stein: 'I have the honour of introducing you to a virtuoso on the clavier', and began to snigger. I at once protested and said that I was only an unworthy pupil of Herr Siegl in Munich, who had asked me to deliver 1,000 compliments to him. He shook his head – and said finally: 'Is it possible that I have the honour of seeing Herr Mozart before me?' 'Oh no,' I replied, 'my name is Trazom and I have a letter for you.' He took the letter and wanted to break the seal at once. But I did not give him time to do so and asked: 'Surely you do not want to read that letter now? Open the door, and let us go into your room. I am most anxious to see your pianofortes.' 'All right,' he said, 'just as you wish. But I feel sure that I am not mistaken.' He opened the door and I ran straight to one of the three claviers which stood in the room. I began to play. He could scarcely open the letter in his eagerness to make sure. He only read the signature. 'Oh', he cried and embraced me. He kept crossing himself and making faces and was as pleased as Punch. I shall tell you all about his claviers. He then took me straight to a coffee-house. When I entered I thought that I should drop down, overcome by the stink and fumes of tobacco. But with God's help I had to stand it for an hour; and I pretended to enjoy it all; though to me it seemed as if we were in Turkey. He then talked a great deal about a certain composer, called Graf, who, however, has only written flute concertos. He said 'Now Graf is something quite exceptional', and all that kind of exaggerated talk. I was sweating with fright, my head, my hands, and my whole body. This Graf is the brother of the two who live at The Hague and at Zürich respectively. My host would not let me off, but took me to him at once. Graf is indeed a most noble fellow. He had a dressing-gown on, which I should not be ashamed to be seen wearing in the street. His words are all on stilts and he generally opens his mouth before he knows what he wants to say; and often it shuts again without having done anything. After many compliments he performed a concerto for two flutes. I had to play the first violin part. This is what I think of it. It is not at all pleasing to the ear, not a bit natural. He often plunges into a new key far too brusquely and it is all quite devoid of charm. When it was over, I praised him very highly, for he really deserves it. The poor fellow must have taken a great deal of trouble over it and he must have studied hard enough. At last a clavichord, one of Stein's, was brought out of the inner room, an excellent instrument, but covered with dust and dirt. Herr Graf, who is Director here, stood there transfixed, like someone who has always imagined that his wanderings from key to key are quite unusual and now finds that one can be even more unusual and yet not offend the ear. In a word, they were all astounded. . . .

TO HIS FATHER
Augsburg, 16–17 October 1777

. . . she undoubtedly must have a gift for music, as she has only been learning for three years and yet can play several pieces really well. But I find it difficult to give you an idea of the impression she makes on me when she is playing. She seems to me so curiously affected. She stalks over the clavier with her long bony fingers in such an odd way. It is true that she has not yet had a really good teacher, and if she stays in Munich she will never, never become what her father is so anxious that she should be: and that is, a first-rate performer on the clavier. If she comes to Papa at Salzburg, her gain will be twofold; both in musical knowledge and in intelligence, which is not exactly her strong point at present. She has made me laugh a great deal already at her expense and you would certainly get plenty of entertainment for your pains. She would not eat much, for she is far too simple. You say that I ought to have tested her playing. Why, I simply could not do so for laughing. For whenever, by way of example, I played a passage with my right hand she at once exclaimed *Bravissimo!* in a tiny mouse-like voice. . . .

. . . Now Papa must know that at Herr von Stein's young Herr von Langenmantel had declared that he would undertake to get up a concert . . . for the patricians alone, as a special honour for me. . . . We arranged that I should call on him the next day and hear the decision. I went. This was October 13th. He was very polite, but said that he could not tell me anything definite yet. I played to him again for about an hour and he invited me to lunch on the following day, the 14th. In the morning he sent a message asking me to come at eleven o'clock and bring some music, as he had invited some of the orchestra and they would like to play something. I sent him some music at once and arrived myself at eleven o'clock. He mumbled a whole string of excuses and remarked quite coolly: 'Look here, a concert is quite out of the question. Oh, I assure you I lost my temper yesterday on your account. The patricians told me that their funds are very low and that you were not the type of virtuoso to whom they could offer a *souverain d'or.*' I smiled and said 'I quite agree'. . . . But I did not let it worry me. We went up to lunch. The old man was also at table; he was very polite, but did not say a word about the concert. After lunch I played two concertos, improvised something and then played the violin in one of Hafeneder's trios. I would gladly have done some more fiddling, but I was accompanied so badly that it gave me the colic. He said to me in a very friendly manner: 'You must spend the day with us and we will go to the play and then you will come back to supper with us.' We were all very merry. When we got back from the theatre, I played again until we went to supper. He had already questioned me in the morning about my cross and I had

An anonymous portrait, commissioned by Padre Martini, of Mozart as a Chevalier of the Order of the Golden Spur, 1777.

explained quite clearly how I had got it and what it was. He and his brother-in-law kept on saying: 'We must get our crosses too, so that we may belong to the same body as Mozart.' But I took no notice. They also addressed me frequently: 'Hello, you fine gentleman, Knight of the Spur.' I said nothing; but during supper things really got beyond a joke. They asked me 'About how much does it cost? Three ducats? Must one have permission to wear it? Does this permission cost something too? We really must send for our crosses.' A certain Baron Bagge, an officer who was there, called out: 'Come! You ought to be ashamed of yourselves. What would you do with the cross?' That young ass, von Kurzenmantel, winked at him. I saw him and he knew it. Then we had a little peace. He offered me snuff and said: 'There, take a pinch.' I still said nothing. At last he began again in a jeering tone: 'Well, to-morrow I shall send someone to your inn and perhaps you will be so kind as to lend me the cross for a moment. I shall return it immediately. I only want to have a word with our goldsmith. He is quite a character and I am sure that if I ask him what its value is, he will say: "About a Bavarian thaler." And it is not worth more, for it is not gold at all, only copper. Ha! Ha!' 'You are wrong there', I said, 'it is tin. Ha! Ha!' I was burning with anger and rage. 'But do tell me,' he said, 'I suppose that, if necessary, I can leave out the spur?' 'Oh yes', I replied.'You do not need one, for you have one in your head already. I have one in mine too, but of a very different kind, and indeed I should not like to exchange it for yours. Here, take a pinch of snuff.' I offered him some. He turned rather pale, but began again: 'The other day – your order looked fine on that grand waistcoat of yours.' I said nothing. At length he called out to a servant: 'Hi, there, you will have to show more respect to my brother-in-law and myself when we wear the same cross as Herr Mozart. Here, take a pinch of snuff.' 'That is really very strange', I began, as though I had not heard what he said, 'but it would be easier for me to obtain all the orders which it is possible for you to win than for you to become what I am, even if you were to die twice and be born again. Take a pinch of snuff on that.' With that I stood up. They all got up too and were exceedingly embarrassed. I took my hat and sword and said: 'I shall have the pleasure of seeing you to-morrow.' 'Oh, I shall not be here to-morrow.' 'Well, then, the day after, if I am here myself.' 'Why, you surely do not mean to – ' 'I mean nothing. You are a lot of mean pigs. Good-bye for the present.' And off I went. . . .

. . . The leading nobles were very polite to me, especially a certain Baron Relling, an officer, who is also a Director or some such animal. He himself unpacked my music. I had brought a symphony too, which was performed and in which I played the fiddle. But the Augsburg orchestra is enough to give one a fit. That young puppy von Langenmantel was quite polite, though he still had a sneer on his face. 'I really thought you would slip away from us', he said; 'I even thought that perhaps you might have taken offence at our joke the other day.' 'Not at all', I said, 'you are still very young. But I advise you to be more careful in future. I am not used to such jokes. And the subject you were joking about does you no honour at all, and has served no purpose, for I still wear my cross. It would have been better to have tried some other joke.' 'I assure you', he said, 'it was only my brother-in-law who – ' 'Well, let us say no more about it', I said. 'We were nearly deprived of the pleasure of seeing you', he added. 'Yes', I said, 'if it had not been for Herr von Stein, I should certainly not have come. And, to tell you the truth, I have only come so that you, gentlemen of Augsburg, may not be laughed at in other countries, when I tell people that I spent a week in the town where my father was born without anyone taking the trouble to hear me.' I played a concerto which, save for the accompaniment, went very well. Finally I played another sonata. Baron Relling, on behalf of the whole company, thanked me most politely, asked me to take the will for the deed and gave me two ducats. They have not yet left me in peace, for they want me to give a public concert before next Sunday. Perhaps I will. But I have already had such a sickener of it that I can hardly express what I feel. I shall be honestly glad to go off again to a place where there is a court. I may say that if it were not for my good uncle and aunt and my really charming cousin, I should have as many regrets at having come to Augsburg as I have hairs on my head. I must now say a few words about my dear little cousin. But I shall save that for to-morrow, for one must be in very good spirits if one wants to praise her as she deserves.

On the morning of this day, the 17th, I write and declare that our little cousin is beautiful, intelligent, charming, clever and gay; and that is because she has mixed with people a great deal, and has also spent some time in Munich. Indeed we two get on extremely well, for, like myself, she is a bit of a scamp. We both laugh at everyone and have great fun. . . .

TO HIS FATHER
Augsburg, 17–18 October 1777

Mon très cher Père!

This time I shall begin at once with Stein's pianofortes. Before I had seen any of his make, Späth's claviers had always been my favourites. But now I much prefer Stein's, for they damp ever so much better than the Regensburg instruments. When I strike hard, I can keep my finger on the note or raise it, but the sound ceases the moment I have produced it. In whatever way I touch the keys, the tone is always even. It never jars, it is never stronger or weaker or entirely absent; in a word, it is always even. It is true that he does not sell a pianoforte of this kind for less than three hundred gulden, but the trouble and the labour which Stein puts into the making of it cannot be paid for. His instruments have this special advantage over others that they are made with escape action. Only one maker in a hundred bothers about this. But without an escapement it is impossible to avoid jangling and vibration after the note is struck. When you touch the keys, the hammers fall back again the moment after they have struck the strings, whether you hold down the keys or release them. He himself told me that when he has finished making one of these claviers, he sits down to it and tries all kinds of passages, runs and jumps, and he polishes and works away at it until it can do anything. For he labours solely in the interest of music and not for his own profit; otherwise he would soon finish his work. He often says: 'If I were not myself such a passionate lover of music and had not myself some slight skill on the clavier, I should certainly long ago have lost patience with my work. But I do like an instrument which never lets the player down and which is durable.' And his claviers certainly do last. He guarantees that the sounding-board will neither break nor split. When he has finished making one for a clavier, he places it in the open air, exposing it to rain, snow, the heat of the sun and all the devils in order that it may crack. Then he inserts wedges and glues them in to make the instrument very strong and firm. He is delighted when it cracks, for he can then be sure that nothing more can happen to it. Indeed he often cuts into it himself and then glues it together again and strengthens it in this way. He has finished making three pianofortes of this kind. To-day I played on one again.

... The device too which you work with your knee is better on his than on other instruments. I have only to touch it and it works; and when you shift your knee the slightest bit, you do not hear the least reverberation. Well, to-morrow perhaps I shall come to his organs – I mean, I shall come to write about them; and I am saving up his little daughter for the very last. When I told Herr Stein that I should very much like to play on his organ, as that instrument was my passion,

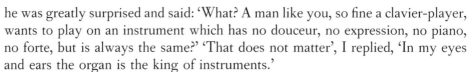
he was greatly surprised and said: 'What? A man like you, so fine a clavier-player, wants to play on an instrument which has no douceur, no expression, no piano, no forte, but is always the same?' 'That does not matter', I replied, 'In my eyes and ears the organ is the king of instruments.'

'Well,' he said, 'as you like.' So off we went together. I noticed at once from what he had said that he thought that I would not do much on his organ; that I would play, for instance, in a thoroughly pianistic style. He told me that he had taken Schubart at his own request to the same organ. 'I was rather nervous,' he said, 'for Schubart had told everyone and the church was pretty full. For I thought of course that this fellow would be all spirit, fire, and rapid execution, qualities which are not at all suited to the organ. But as soon as he began I changed my opinion.' All I said to Stein was: 'Well, Herr Stein, do you think that I am going to canter about on your organ?' 'Ah, you,' he replied, 'that is quite another matter.' We reached the choir and I began to improvise, when he started to laugh; then I played a fugue. 'I can well believe', he said, 'that you like to play the organ, when you play so well.'

TO HIS FATHER

Augsburg, 23–24 October 1777

... Everyone praised my beautiful, pure tone. Afterwards they brought in a small clavichord and I improvised and then played a sonata and the Fischer variations. Then the others whispered to the Dean that he should just hear me play something in the organ style. I asked him to give me a theme. He declined, but one of the monks gave me one. I put it through its paces and in the middle (the fugue was in G minor) I started off in the major key and played something quite lively, though in the same tempo; and after that the theme over again, but this time arseways. Finally it occurred to me, could I not use my lively tune as the theme for a fugue? I did not waste much time in asking, but did so at once, and it went as neatly as if Daser had fitted it. The Dean was absolutely staggered. 'Why, it's simply phenomenal, that's all I can say', he said. 'I should never have believed what I have heard. You are a first-rate fellow. My Abbot told me, it is true, that he had never in his life heard anyone play the organ so smoothly and so soundly.' (For he had heard me a few days before, when the Dean was away.) At last someone produced a sonata in fugal style and wanted me to play it. But I said:

'Gentlemen, this is too much. Let me tell you, I shall certainly not be able to play that sonata at sight.' 'Yes, that I can well believe', said the Dean very pressingly, for he was my strong supporter. 'It is too much to expect. No one could tackle that.' 'However,' I said, 'I should like to try it.' I heard the Dean behind me all the time: 'Oh, you little villain, oh, you rascal, oh, you – !' I played until eleven o'clock, for I was bombarded and besieged with themes for fugues. When I was in Stein's house the other day he put before me a sonata by Beecke – I think that I have told you that already. That reminds me, now for his little daughter. Anyone who sees and hears her play and can keep from laughing must, like her father, be made of stone.[1] For instead of sitting in the middle of the clavier, she sits right up opposite the treble, as it gives her more chance of flopping about and making grimaces. She rolls her eyes and smirks. When a passage is repeated, she plays it more slowly the second time. If it is to be played a third time, then she plays it even more slowly. When a passage is being played, the arm must be raised as high as possible, and according as the notes in the passage are stressed, the arm, not the fingers, must do this, and that too with great emphasis in a heavy and clumsy manner. But the best joke of all is that when she comes to a passage which ought to flow like oil and which necessitates a change of finger, she does not bother her head about it, but when the moment arrives, she just leaves out the notes, raises her hands and starts off again quite comfortably – a method by which she is much more likely to strike a wrong note, which often produces a curious effect. I am simply writing this in order to give Papa some idea of clavier-playing and clavier-teaching, so that he may derive some profit from it later on. Herr Stein is quite crazy about his daughter, who is eight and a half and who now learns everything by heart. She may succeed, for she has a great talent for music. But she will not make progress by this method – for she will never acquire great rapidity, since she definitely does all she can to make her hands heavy. Further, she will never acquire the most essential, the most difficult and the chief requisite in music, which is time, because from her earliest years she has done her utmost not to play in time. Herr Stein and I discussed this point for two hours at least and I have almost converted him, for he now asks my advice on everything. He used to be quite crazy about Beecke; but now he sees and hears that I am the better player, that I do not make grimaces, and yet play with such expression that, as he himself confesses, no one up to the present has been able to get such good results

1. Mozart puns on the word 'Stein', which means 'stone'.

out of his pianofortes. Everyone is amazed that I can always keep strict time. What the people cannot grasp is that in *tempo rubato* in an Adagio, the left hand should go on playing in strict time. With them the left hand always follows suit. Count Wolfegg, and several other passionate admirers of Beecke, publicly admitted at a concert the other day that I had wiped the floor with him. The Count kept running about in the hall, exclaiming: 'I have never heard anything like this in my life.' And he said to me: 'I really must tell you, I have never heard you play as you played to-day. I shall tell your father so too as soon as I return to Salzburg.'...

TO HIS FATHER
Mannheim, 31 October 1777

... I went with Herr Danner to-day to M. Cannabich, who was exceedingly courteous. I played to him on his pianoforte, which is a very good one, and we went together to the rehearsal. I thought I should not be able to keep myself from laughing when I was introduced to the people there. Some who knew me by repute were very polite and fearfully respectful; others, however, who had never heard of me, stared at me wide-eyed, and certainly in a rather sneering manner. They probably think that because I am little and young, nothing great or mature can come out of me; but they will soon see. Herr Cannabich himself is taking me to-morrow to Count Savioli, the Intendant of the orchestra. It is a good thing that the Elector's name-day falls very soon. The oratorio, which is being rehearsed, is by Handel[1], but I did not stay to hear it, for, before it came on, they rehearsed a Psalm – a Magnificat – by Vogler, the Vice-*Kapellmeister* here, and it lasted almost an hour. Now I must close, for I have still to write to my little cousin. I kiss Papa's hands and my sisterly beloved I embrace shortly and sweetly, as is proper.

JOHANNES[***] CHRYSOSTOMUS SIGISMUNDUS[**]

WOLFGANG[*] GOTTLIEB MOZART

[*]To-day is my name-day! [**]That is my confirmation name! [***]January 27th is my birthday!

1. Handel's 'Messiah', Part I, was performed on 1 November. Vogler conducted it. Berlin and Hamburg had already given performances of this oratorio.

TO HIS FATHER
Mannheim, 4 November 1777

... This is my second letter from Mannheim. I am with Cannabich every day. Mamma came too with me to-day to his house. He is quite a different person from what he used to be and the whole orchestra say the same thing. He has taken a great fancy to me. He has a daughter who plays the clavier quite nicely; and in order to make a real friend of him I am now working at a sonata for her, which is almost finished save for the Rondo. When I had composed the opening Allegro and the Andante I took them to their house and played them to them. Papa cannot imagine the applause which this sonata won. It so happened that some members of the orchestra were there, young Danner, a horn-player called Lang, and the oboist whose name I have forgotten, but who plays very well and has a delightfully pure tone. I have made him a present of my oboe concerto, which is being copied in a room at Cannabich's, and the fellow is quite crazy with delight. I played this concerto for him to-day on the pianoforte at Cannabich's, and, although everybody knew that I was the composer, it was very well received. Nobody said that it was not well composed, because the people here do not understand such matters – they had better consult the Archbishop, who will at once put them right.[1] I played all my six sonatas[2] to-day at Cannabich's. Herr *Kapellmeister* Holzbauer himself took me to-day to Count Savioli, the Intendant, and Cannabich happened to be there. Herr Holzbauer spoke to the Count in Italian, suggesting that the Elector ought to grant me the favour of a hearing. He added that I had been here fifteen years ago, when I was seven, but that now I was older and more developed in music as well as in body. 'Ah,' said the Count, 'that is – ' Goodness knows who he thought I was. But Cannabich stepped in at once, and I pretended not to hear and fell into conversation with some older people. I noticed, however, that he was speaking to the Count about me with an earnest expression. The latter then said to me: 'I hear that you play the clavier quite passably.' I bowed.

Now I must tell you about the music here. On Saturday, All Saints' Day, I was at High Mass in the *Kapelle*. The orchestra is excellent and very strong. On either side there are ten or eleven violins, four violas, two oboes, two flutes and two clarinets, two horns, four violoncellos, four bassoons and four double basses, also trumpets and drums. They can produce fine music, but I should not care to have one of my masses produced here. Why? On account of their shortness? No,

1. This is ironical.
2. K.279–84.

everything must be short here too. Because a different style of composition is required? Not at all. But because, as things are at present, you must write principally for the instruments, as you cannot imagine anything worse than the voices here. Six sopranos, six altos, six tenors and six basses against twenty violins and twelve basses is just like zero to one. Is that not so, Herr Bullinger? The reason for this state of affairs is that the Italians are now in very bad odour here. They have only two *castrati*, who are already old and will just be allowed to die off. The soprano would actually prefer to sing alto, as he can no longer take the high notes. The few boys they have are miserable. The tenors and basses are like our funeral singers. Vice-*Kapellmeister* Vogler, who had composed the mass which was performed the other day, is a dreary musical jester, an exceedingly conceited and rather incompetent fellow. The whole orchestra dislikes him. But to-day, I heard a mass by Holzbauer, which he wrote twenty-six years ago, but which is very fine. He is a good composer, he has a good church style, he knows how to write for voices and instruments, and he composes good fugues. They have two organists here who alone would be worth a special visit to Mannheim. I have had an opportunity of hearing them properly, for it is not the custom here to sing the Benedictus, but during that part of the service the organist has to play the whole time. On the first occasion I heard the second organist and on the second, the first organist. But in my opinion the second is even more distinguished than the first. For when I heard him, I enquired: 'Who is playing the organ?' I was told, the second organist. He played abominably. When I heard the other one, I asked: 'Who is playing now?' I was told, our first organist. He played even more wretchedly and I think that if they were thrown together, something even worse would be the result. To watch these gentlemen is enough to make one die of laughing. The second, when seated at the organ, is like a child at stool, for his face tells you what he can do. The first, at any rate, wears spectacles. I went and stood at the organ and watched him in the hope of learning something from him. At every note he lifts his hands right up in the air. His forte is to play in six parts, but chiefly in five and eight parts! He often leaves out the right hand for fun and plays with the left hand alone. In short, he can do just what he likes, for he is completely master of his instrument. . . .

Abbé George Joseph Vogler, the vice-Kapellmeister at Mannheim, whom Mozart disparages frequently in his letters.

59

TO HIS COUSIN AT AUGSBURG
Mannheim, 5 November 1777

Dearest Coz Fuzz!

I have received reprieved your dear letter, telling selling me that my uncle carbuncle, my aunt can't and you too are very well hell. Thank God, we too are in excellent health wealth. To-day the letter setter from my Papa Ha! Ha! dropped safely into my claws paws. I hope that you too have got shot the note dote which I wrote to you from Mannheim. If so, so much the better, better the much so. . . . You say lay that you will keep the compromise[1] which you made me before I left Augsburg and that you will do so soon boon. Well, that will certainly be a shock to me. You write further, you pour out, disclose, divulge, notify, declare, signify,

Mozart's caricature of Bäsle, his cousin Maria Anna Thekla Mozart.

inform, acquaint me with the fact, make it quite clear, request, demand, desire, wish, would like, order me to send lend you my portrait. *Eh bien*, I shall certainly despatch scratch it to you. *Oui, par ma foi.* . . .

No. 1. A letter or letters addressed to me will reach you, which I must ask you to – to what? Why, a fox is no hare, well . . . Now, where was I? . . . Yes, of course, at reach. Yes, they will reach you – well, what will? – Why, now I remember. Letters, why, letters will reach you . . . But what sort of letters? – Why, of course, letters addressed to me, which I must ask you to forward without fail. I shall let you know where I go on to from Mannheim.

---

1. Mozart uses instead of *Versprechen* (promise) the word *Verbrechen* (crime).

Now for No. 2. I must ask you, why not? – I must ask you, dearest dunce, why not? – if you happen to be writing to Madame Tavernier at Munich, to send my regards to the two Misses Freysinger, why not? – Strange! Why not? And say that I beg the youngest one, Fräulein Josepha, to forgive me, why not? – Why should I not beg her to forgive me? Strange! Why should I not? Say that she must forgive me for not having yet sent her the sonata I promised her and that I shall send it as soon as possible. Why not? – What? – Why not? – Why should I not send it? – Why should I not despatch it? – Why not? – Strange! I don't know why I shouldn't – Well, then – you will do me this favour. – Why not? Why should you not do it? – Why not? – Strange! I shall do the same for you when you want me to. Why not? Why should I not do it for you? Strange! Why not? – I can't think why not?

Do not forget also to send my compliments to the Papa and Mamma of the two young ladies, for it is a gross fault to forget must shall will have one's duty to father and mother. When the sonata is finished, I shall send it to you and the letter as well; and you will be good enough to send it on to Munich. Now I must close, though it makes me morose. . . . I kiss you 1,000 times and remain, as always, your little old piggy wiggy

WOLFGANG AMADÉ ROSY POSY

A thousand compliments from us two travellers to my aunt and uncle. My greetings bleatings to all my good friends sends. *Addio*, booby looby.

333 to the grave, if my life I save.

Miehnnam, Rebotco eht ʰᵗᵗ5, 7771.

TO HIS FATHER

Mannheim, 8 November 1777

I wrote out at Cannabich's this morning the Rondo to the sonata for his daughter, with the result that they refused to let me go. The Elector the Electress and the whole court are very much pleased with me. At the concert, on both occasions when I played, the Elector and the Electress came up quite close to the clavier. After the concert Cannabich arranged for me to speak to them. I kissed the Elector's hand. He remarked: 'I think it is about fifteen years since you were here last.' 'Yes, Your Highness, fifteen years since I had the honour of – ' 'You play admirably.' When I kissed the Princess's hand she said to me: '*Monsieur, je vous assure, on ne peut pas jouer mieux.*' I went yesterday with Cannabich on the visit Mamma has already referred to and there I talked to the Elector as to an old friend. He is a most gracious and courteous gentleman. He said to me: 'I hear that you have written an opera at Munich.' 'Yes, your Highness,' I replied, 'I commend myself to your Highness's good graces. My dearest wish is to write an opera here. I beg you not to forget me utterly. Thanks and praise be to God, I know German too', and I smiled. 'That can easily be managed', he answered. . . . I was in such excellent spirits to-day – words fail me to describe my feelings. I improvised and then I played three duets with violin accompaniment which I had never seen and the composer of which I had never even heard of. They were all so delighted that I had to kiss the ladies. In the daughter's case this was no hardship, for she is not at all bad-looking. Afterwards we went back to the nmthrefculn kfndlr dlo Cuhrihrotln[1] ⟨Elector's natural children⟩. There I played again with my whole heart. I played three times. The Elector himself kept on asking me for more. He sat down each time beside me and did not move an inch. I also asked a certain Professor to give me a theme for a fugue which I proceeded to develop. . . .

TO HIS FATHER
Mannheim, 13 November 1777

. . . I improvised and played my sonatas in B^b and D. In short, he was very polite and I was the same, but perfectly serious. We fell to talking of various things, amongst others of Vienna, and how the Emperor was no great lover of music. 'That is true', he said; 'he knows something about counterpoint, but that is all. I can still remember (here he rubbed his forehead) that when I had to play to him, I had not the least idea what to play. So I started to play fugues and such-like foolery, and all the time I played I was laughing up my sleeve.' When I heard this, I was scarcely able to contain myself and felt that I should love to say to him: 'Sir, I well believe that you laughed, but surely not as heartily as I should have done,

---

1. The Mozarts used a simple substitution cipher for personal remarks they did not wish to be understood by others – particularly about the Archbishop of Salzburg and other exalted persons. The words above, shown as a specimen, read 'natürlichen Kinder des Churfürsten'. Henceforth words written in cipher will be given in plain language, distinguished by angular brackets. –E.B.

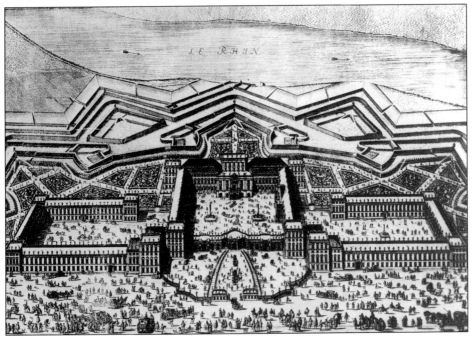

The Residenz at Mannheim, by H.K. Ostertag and Bartolomeo Anton Coentgen, 1720.

had I been listening to you.' He went on to say (which is quite true) that music is performed in the Imperial apartments which would drive a dog away. I remarked that whenever I heard that kind of music and could not get away from it, it always gave me a headache. 'Oh, it does not affect me at all', he retorted. 'Bad music never gets on my nerves; on the other hand, beautiful music does; and then I sometimes get a headache.' Once more I thought to myself: 'Yes, a shallow pate like yours no doubt begins to ache, when it hears something which it cannot understand.'

Now for some news from Mannheim. Yesterday I had to go with Cannabich to Count Savioli, the Intendant, to fetch my present. It was just as I expected. No money, but a fine gold watch. At the moment ten carolins would have suited me better than the watch, which including the chains and the mottoes has been valued at twenty. What one needs on a journey is money; and, let me tell you, I now have five watches. I am therefore seriously thinking of having an additional watch pocket on each leg of my trousers so that when I visit some great lord, I shall wear both watches (which moreover, is now the '*mode*'); so that it will not occur to him to present me with another one. . . .

Another of Mozart's drawings of Bäsle, made in 1777 or 1778.

TO HIS COUSIN AT AUGSBURG
Mannheim, 13 November 1777

... Ma très chère nièce! cousine! fille! mère, soeur et épouse!

Bless my soul, a thousand curses, Croatians, damnations, devils, witches, sorcerers, hell's battalions to all eternity, by all the elements, air, water, earth and fire, Europe, Asia, Africa and America, Jesuits, Augustinians, Benedictines, Capuchins, Minorites, Franciscans, Dominicans, Carthusians and Brothers of the Holy Cross, Canons regular and irregular, all slackers, knaves, cowards, sluggards and toadies higgledy-piggledy, asses, buffaloes, oxen, fools, nit-wits and dunces! What sort of behaviour is that, my dears – four smart soldiers and three bandoliers? ... Such a parcel to get, but no portrait as yet! I was all eagerness – in fact, I was quite sure – for you yourself had written the other day that I was to have it soon, very soon. Perhaps you doubt that I shall keep my word? Surely you do not doubt me? Well, anyhow, I implore you to send me yours – the sooner, the better. And I trust that you will have it done, as I urged you, in French costume.

... Now I must close, however that may be, for I am not yet dressed and we are lunching this very moment, so that after that we may shit again, however that may be. Do go on loving me, as I love you, then we shall never cease loving one another, though the lion hovers round the walls, though doubt's hard victory has not been weighed and the tyrant's frenzy has crept to decay; yet Codrus, the wise philosopher, often eats soot instead of porridge, and the Romans, the props of my arse, have always been and ever will be – half-castes. . . .

TO HIS FATHER
Mannheim, 20 November 1777

Mon très cher Père

I must be quite brief to-day, as I have no more paper in the house. Yesterday, Wednesday, the 19th, the gala began again. I went to the service, brand new music composed by Vogler. I had already been to the afternoon rehearsal the day before yesterday, but went off immediately after the Kyrie. I have never in my life heard such stuff. In many places the parts simply do not harmonize. He modulates in such a violent way as to make you think that he is resolved to drag you with him by the scruff of the neck, not that there is anything remarkable about it all to make it worth the trouble; no, it is all clumsy plunging. I will not say anything about the way in which the ideas are worked out. I will only say that it is impossible that a mass of Vogler's should please any composer who is worthy of the name. To put it briefly, if I hear an idea which is not at all bad – well – it will certainly not remain not at all bad for long, but will soon become – beautiful? God forbid! – bad and thoroughly bad; and that in two or three different ways. Either the idea has scarcely been introduced before another comes along and ruins it; or he does not round it off naturally enough to preserve its merit; or it is not in the right place; or, finally, it is ruined by the instrumentation. That's Vogler's music. Cannabich is now a much better composer than he was when we knew him in Paris. But what Mamma and I noticed at once about the symphonies here is that they all begin in the same manner, always with an introduction in slow time and in unison. . . .

TO HIS FATHER
Mannheim, 22 November 1777

. . . All that you write about ⟨Mannheim⟩ I know already – but I never like to write about anything prematurely. Everything will be all right. In my next letter I may perhaps be able to tell you something very good for you, but only good for me, or something very bad in your eyes, but tolerable in mine; or it may be something tolerable for you, but very good, precious and valuable for me! Rather in the style of an oracle, is it not? Well, it is obscure, yet intelligible. . . .

Well, there's nothing left for me to write except to wish you all a thoroughly good rest and that you will all sleep soundly until I wake you up with this present letter. Adieu. I kiss Papa's hands 100,000,000 times and embrace my sister, that darling blister, with all my heart, until I smart, just a little or not at all, and remain your most obedient son, hoping away you will not run,

WOLFGANG AMADÉ MOZART

Knight of the Golden Spur and, as soon as I marry, of the Double Horn, Member of the Grand Academies of Verona and Bologna. *Oui, mon ami!*

TO HIS FATHER
Mannheim, 26 November 1777

. . . The reason why we are still here is that I am thinking of staying on for the winter. I am only waiting for a reply from the Elector. Count Savioli, the Intendant, is a very honest gentleman, and I told him to be so kind ⟨as to tell the Elector that, as in any case the weather is at present bad for travelling, I should like to stay here and teach the young Count⟩. He promised me to do his best, but begged me to have patience until the gala-days were over. All this took place with the knowledge and at the instigation of Cannabich. When I told him that I had been to Savioli and what I had said to him, he remarked that he would sooner believe that it would happen than that it would not. Cannabich had himself mentioned the matter even before [the Count spoke to the Elector]. I must now wait and see. To-morrow I shall draw my 150 gulden from Herr Schmalz, as I have no doubt that our landlord would rather hear the sound of money than of music. I never imagined I should get a watch for a present here, but such is the case. I should have left long ago if they hadn't all said: 'Where will you spend the winter then? – It's a very bad time of the year for travelling. Stay where you are.' Cannabich is very anxious for me to stay on. So I have now put out a feeler, and, as an affair of this sort cannot be huried up, I must just wait patiently. I hope soon to be able to send you really good news. I already have two pupils in prospect (not counting my Arch-pupil)[1], who will most probably give me a *louis d'or* each per month. But without the Arch-one, it is true, it can't be managed. Now do let me drop all that, how it is and how it will be. What is the use of needless speculation? What will happen we know not – and yet we do know! It is God's will. Cheer up then, *Allegro, don't be so lazy*. If after all we do leave Mannheim, we shall go straight to – where do you think? – to Weilburg, or whatever the place is called, to the Princess, the sister of the Prince of Orange, whom we knew so well *à la Haie*. And there we shall remain, that is to say, as long as the officers' table is to our taste; and we shall get at least six *louis d'or*. . . . *Addio*. If I had room I would write something more, at least my compliments to my good friends. But it is impossible, for I don't know where I could work them in. I can't write anything sensible to-day, as I am rails off the quite. Papa be annoyed not must. I that just like to-day feel, I help it cannot. Warefell. I gish you nood-wight. Sound sleeply. Next time I'll sensible more writely.

TO HIS FATHER

Mannheim, 3 December 1777

. . . ⟨If I stay here, I am to go to Paris in Lent⟩ in the company of Wendling, Ramm, who plays very beautifully, and Lauchéry, the ballet-master. Wendling assures me that I shall never regret it. He has been twice to Paris; and has only just returned. He maintains that it is still the only place where one can make money and a great reputation. He said: 'Why, you are a fellow who can turn your hand to anything. I will tell you the way to set about it. You must compose all sorts, *opera seria, opéra comique*, oratorio, everything, in fact. Once a man has written a couple of operas in Paris, he is sure of a settled yearly income. Then there is the *Concert Spirituel* and the *Académie des Amateurs*, which pay five *louis d'or* for a symphony. If you take pupils, the usual fee is three *louis d'or* for twelve lessons. Further, you can get sonatas, trios and quartets engraved *par souscription*. Cannabich and Toeschi send a great deal of their music to Paris.' Wendling is an experienced traveller. Please let me have your views about this scheme, which strikes me as being useful and sensible. I shall be travelling with a man who

---

1. i.e. the young Count.

knows Paris (present-day Paris, for it has changed considerably) thoroughly. My expenses will be no greater. Indeed I don't think that I shall spend half as much, as I shall only have myself to pay for, since Mamma would stay here, probably with the Wendlings. Herr Ritter, a fine bassoon-player, is off to Paris on December 12th. Now if I had been alone, this would have been an excellent opportunity for me. He mentioned it to me himself. Ramm, the oboist, is a very good, jolly, honest fellow of about 35, who has already travelled a great deal, and consequently has plenty of experience. The chief and best musicians here are very fond of me and show me great respect. . . .

TO HIS FATHER
Mannheim, 6-7 December 1777

Mon très cher Père!

I can still tell you nothing more. I'm beginning to get sick of this joke. I am only curious now as to how it will end. ⟨Count Savioli⟩ has already spoken three times ⟨to the Elector and each time his reply has been⟩ a shrug of the shoulders and the remark that he would certainly ⟨give me an answer, but that he had not yet made up his mind.⟩ My good friends quite agree with me that all this hesitation and reserve is rather a good sign than a bad one. ⟨For if the Elector had no intention of taking me on at all, he would have said so at once; as it is⟩, I attribute this delay to – ⟨*we are a little stingy with the cash*⟩. Moreover I know for a fact that ⟨the Elector likes me⟩. *A buon conto*, we must just wait a little longer. I may say at once that I shall be glad ⟨if the affair turned out well⟩, as otherwise I should regret ⟨having sat about here for so long and wasted our money⟩. . . . His[1] daughter who is fifteen[2], his eldest child, is a very pretty and charming girl. She is very intelligent and steady for her age. She is serious, does not say much, but when she does speak, she is pleasant and amiable. Yesterday she again gave me indescribable pleasure; she played the whole of my sonata – excellently. The Andante (which must not be taken too quickly) she plays with the utmost expression. Moreover she likes playing it. I had already finished the Allegro, as you know, on the day after my arrival, and thus had only seen Mlle Cannabich once. Young Danner asked me how I thought of composing the Andante. I said

---

1. Cannabich's. – E.B.
2. He corrects this to thirteen later in the same letter. – E.B.

that I would make it fit closely the character of Mlle Rosa. When I played it, it was an extraordinary success. Young Danner told me so afterwards. It really is a fact. She is exactly like the Andante. . . .

TO HIS FATHER

Mannheim, 10–11 December 1777

Mon très cher Père!

There's nothing to be hoped for at present ⟨from the Elector⟩. The day before yesterday I went to the concert at court to get ⟨his answer. Count Savioli⟩ studiously avoided me, but I made my way up to him. When he saw me, he shrugged his shoulders. 'What', I said, 'no answer yet?' 'Please forgive me', he replied, 'unfortunately none.' '*Eh bien,*' I said, 'the Elector might have told me so before.' 'True', he said, 'but he would not have made up his mind even now, if I had not prodded him and pointed out that you have been hanging on here for such a long time and were using up all your money at the inn.' 'That's what worries me most of all', I retorted. 'It's not at all nice. However, I am very much obliged to you, Count (we don't address him as Your Excellency), for having taken such an interest in me, and I beg you to thank ⟨the Elector⟩ on my behalf for his gracious, though belated reply and to say that I can assure him that he would never have regretted it if he had taken me on.' 'Oh', he replied, 'I am surer of that than you think.' I then told Wendling about the decision. He went quite red in the face and remarked very angrily: 'We must find some way out. You must stay here, at least for the next two months until we can go to Paris together. . . .'

Let me tell you just one thing more. The other day I went to lunch at Wendling's as usual. 'Our Indian', he said, meaning a Dutchman, a gentleman of means and a lover of all the sciences, who is a great friend and ⟨admirer⟩ of mine, 'our Indian is really a first-rate fellow. He is willing to give you 200 *gulden* if you will compose for him three short, simple concertos and a couple of quartets for the flute. Through Cannabich you can get at least two pupils who will pay well. You can compose duets for clavier and violin here and have them engraved *par souscription*. Your lunch and supper you can always have with us. You can lodge at the Privy Court Councillor's.[1] All that will cost you nothing. For your mother we shall find some cheap lodging for the next two months until you have written home about all our plans. Your Mamma can then travel home and we can go on to Paris.' Mamma is quite satisfied with this arrangement and it only remains for you to give your consent. I am so certain of it that if it were now the time to travel, I should go off to Paris without waiting for an answer. For no other answer could be expected from a father who is so sensible and has shown himself up to the present so anxious for the welfare of his children. . . .

TO HIS FATHER
Mannheim, 20 December 1777

I wish you, dearest Papa, a very happy New Year, and hope that every day your health, which is so precious to me, may get better and better, to the advantage and delight of your wife and children, to the satisfaction of your true friends and the vexation and annoyance of your enemies! I beg you during the coming year to love me with the same fatherly affection as you have shown me hitherto! I for my part shall endeavour to my utmost to deserve more and more the love of so excellent a father. . . .

TO HIS FATHER
Mannheim, 27–28 December 1777

. . . Some time soon we, that is, the Cannabichs, Wendlings, Serrariuses and Mozarts, are going to the Lutheran church, where I shall have some good fun on the organ. I tried the full organ before, during that test, about which I wrote to you, but didn't play much, only a prelude and a fugue. I have now added Herr Wieland to the list of my acquaintances. But he doesn't know as much about me as I know about him, for he has never heard any of my compositions. I had imagined him to be quite different from what I found him. He strikes you as slightly affected in his speech. He has a rather childish voice; he keeps on quizzing you over his glasses; he indulges in a sort of pedantic rudeness, mingled

---

1. Serrarius.

occasionally with a stupid condescension. But I am not surprised that he permits himself such behaviour here, even though he may be quite different in Weimar and elsewhere, for people stare at him as if he had dropped from Heaven. Everyone seems embarrassed in his presence, no one says a word or moves an inch; all listen intently to every word he utters; and it's a pity they often have to wait so long, for he has a defect of speech that makes him speak very slowly and he can't say half a dozen words without stopping. Apart from that, he is what we all know him to be, a most gifted fellow. He has a frightfully ugly face, covered with pock-marks, and he has a rather long nose. . . .

TO HIS FATHER
Mannheim, 10–11 January 1778

. . . Now for some sensible talk. I know for a fact that ⟨the Emperor⟩ is proposing to ⟨establish German opera in Vienna⟩ and that he is making every effort ⟨to find a young *Kapellmeister*⟩ who understands the ⟨German language⟩, is talented and is capable of striking out a new line. ⟨Benda of Gotha⟩ is applying, but ⟨Schweitzer⟩ is determined to get it. I think it would ⟨be a good thing for me⟩ – provided, of course, that ⟨the pay⟩ is good. ⟨If the Emperor will give me a thousand *gulden*, I will write a German opera for him: if he won't have me⟩, it's all the same to me. Please write to all ⟨our friends in Vienna⟩ you can think of and tell them ⟨that it is in my power to do honour to the Emperor⟩. If he won't take me on any other terms, then let him ⟨try me with an opera⟩ – after that he can do what he likes for all I care. Adieu. But please set the ball rolling at once, or ⟨someone may forestall me⟩. . . .

TO HIS FATHER
Mannheim, 17 January 1778

Next Wednesday I am going for a few days to Kirchheim-Bolanden to visit the Princess of Orange. People here have said such nice things to me about her that I have at last decided to go. A Dutch officer, a good friend of mine, got a terrible scolding from her for not bringing me with him when he went to offer her his New Year wishes. I shall get eight *louis d'or* at least, for, as she is passionately

*The Nationaltheater in Mannheim, engraved by Johann Sebastian and Johann Baptist
Klauber after Johann Fritz von der Schlichten, 1782.*

fond of singing, I have had four arias copied for her and, as she has a nice little
orchestra and gives a concert every day, I shall also present her with a symphony.
Moreover the copying of the arias will not cost me much, for it has been done by
a certain Herr Weber, who is accompanying me there. I don't know whether I
have already written about his daughter or not – she sings indeed most admirably
and has a lovely pure voice. The only thing she lacks is dramatic action; were it
not for that, she might be the *prima donna* on any stage. She is only sixteen. She
sings most excellently my aria written for De Amicis with those horribly difficult
passages[1], and she is to sing it at Kirchheim-Bolanden. She is quite well able to
teach herself. She accompanies herself very well and she plays *galanterie* quite
respectably. What is most fortunate for her at Mannheim is that she has won the
praise of all honest people of good will. Even the Elector and the Electress are
only too glad to receive her, provided it doesn't cost them anything. She can go to
the Electress whenever she likes, even daily; and this is due to her good
behaviour. . . .

1. Giunia's aria, No. 11, 'Ah, se il crudel' in Mozart's opera 'Lucio Silla', composed in 1772.

TO HIS FATHER
Mannheim, 4 February 1778

... I propose to remain here and finish entirely at my leisure that music for De Jean, for which I am to get 200 *gulden*. I can stay here as long as I like and neither board nor lodging costs me anything. In the meantime Herr Weber will endeavour to get engagements here and there for concerts with me, and we shall then travel together. When I am with him, it is just as if I were travelling with you. The very reason why I am so fond of him is because, apart from his personal appearance, he is just like you and has exactly your character and way of thinking. If my mother were not, as you know, too comfortably lazy to write, she would tell you the very same thing! I must confess that I much enjoyed travelling with them. We were happy and merry; I was hearing a man talk like you; I had nothing to worry about; I found my torn clothes mended; in short, I was waited on like a prince.

I have become so fond of this unfortunate family that my dearest wish is to make them happy; and perhaps I may be able to do so. My advice is that they should go to Italy. So now I should like you to write to our good friend Lugiati, and the sooner the better, and enquire what are the highest terms given to a *prima donna* in Verona – the more the better, one can always climb down – perhaps too it would be possible to obtain the Ascensa in Venice.[1] As far as her singing is concerned, I would wager my life that she will bring me renown. Even in a short time she has greatly profited by my instruction, and how much greater will the improvement be by then! I am not anxious either about her acting. If our plan succeeds, we, M. Weber, his two daughters[2] and I will have the honour of visiting my dear Papa, and my dear sister for a fortnight on our way through Salzburg. My sister will find a friend and a companion in Mlle Weber, for, like my sister in Salzburg, she has a reputation for good behaviour, her father resembles my father and the whole family resemble the Mozarts. True, there are envious folk, as there are in Salzburg, but when it comes to the point, they have to speak the truth. Honesty is the best policy. I can say that I shall look forward immensely to going to Salzburg with them, if only that you may hear her sing ... I beg you to do your best to get us to Italy. You know my greatest desire is – to write operas.

I will gladly write an opera for Verona for 50 *zecchini*, if only in order that she may make her name; for if I do not compose it, I fear that she may be victimized. By that time I shall have made so much money on the other journeys we propose to undertake together, that I shall not be the loser. I think we shall go to

1. i.e. the contract to sing in the opera performed on the occasion of the Festival of the Ascension.
2. Josefa and Aloysia.

Switzerland and perhaps also to Holland. Do write to me soon about this. If we stay anywhere for long, the eldest daughter will be very useful to us; for we could have our own *ménage*, as she can cook. A propos, you must not be too much surprised when you hear that I have only 42 *gulden* left out of 77. That is merely the result of my delight at being again in the company of honest and like-minded people. I paid one half of the expenses, for I could not do otherwise, but I shall not do so on our other journeys and I have already told them so; I shall then pay only for myself.

. . . My mother is quite satisfied with my ideas. It is impossible for me to travel with people – with a man – who leads a life of which the veriest stripling could not but be ashamed; and the thought of helping a poor family, without injury to myself, delights my very soul. . . .

TO HIS FATHER
Mannheim, 7 February 1778

. . . I had already told you in my previous letter my chief reason for not going to Paris with these people. My second reason is that I have thought carefully what I should have to do there. I could not get on at all without pupils, which is a kind of work that is quite uncongenial to me – and of this I have an excellent example here. I could have had two pupils. I went three times to each, but finding one of them out, I never went back. I will gladly give lessons as a favour, particularly when I see that my pupil has talent, inclination and anxiety to learn; but to be obliged to go to a house at a certain hour – or to have to wait at home for a pupil – is what I cannot do, no matter how much money it may bring me in. I find it impossible, so must leave it to those who can do nothing else but play the clavier. I am a composer and was born to be a *Kapellmeister*, and I neither can nor ought to bury the talent for composition with which God in his goodness has so richly endowed me (I may say so without conceit, for I feel it now more than ever); and this I should be doing were I to take many pupils, for it is a most unsettling *métier* ½; and I would rather, if I may speak plainly, neglect the clavier than composition, for in my case the clavier with me is only a side-line, though, thank God, a very good one. . . .

TO HIS FATHER
Mannheim, 19 February 1778

Monsieur
   mon très cher Père!

I hope you received my last two letters safely. In the last one I discussed my mother's journey home, but I now see from your letter of the 12th that this was quite unnecessary. I always thought that you would disapprove of my undertaking a journey ⟨with the Webers⟩, but I never had any such intention – I mean, of course, in our present circumstances. I gave them my word of honour, however, to write to you about it. Herr Weber does not know how we stand – and I shall certainly never tell anyone. I wish my position were such that I had no cause to consider anyone else and that we were all comfortably off. In the intoxication of the moment I forgot how impossible it is at present to carry out my plan, and therefore also – to tell you what I have now done. The reasons why I have not gone off to Paris must be sufficiently evident to you from my last two letters. If my mother had not first raised the point, I should certainly have gone with my friends; but when I saw that she did not like the scheme, then I began to dislike it myself. For as soon as people lose confidence in me, I am apt to lose confidence in myself. . . .

What you say about Mlle Weber is all perfectly true; and at the time I wrote that letter I knew quite as well as you do that she is still too young and that she must first learn how to act and make frequent appearances on the stage. But with some people one must proceed – by degrees. These good people are as tired of being here as – you know whom and where[1]; and they think that every scheme is practicable. I promised them to write everything to my father; but when the letter was on its way to Salzburg, I kept on telling them: 'She must be patient a little longer, she is a bit too young yet, etc.' They do not mind what I say to them, for they have a high opinion of me. On my advice the father has engaged Madame Toscani (an actress) to give his daughter lessons in acting. . . .

1. Mozart and his father in Salzburg.

TO HIS FATHER
Mannheim, 22 February 1778

Monsieur

mon très cher Père,

I have been confined to the house for two days and have been taking antispasmodics, black powders and elderberry tea to make me sweat, as I have had catarrh, a cold in the head, headache, a sore throat, pains in my eyes and earache. But, thank God, I am better now and I hope to go out to-morrow, as it is Sunday. I received your letter of the 16th and the two unsealed letters of introduction for Paris. I am glad that you like my French aria. Please forgive my not writing much now, but really I cannot – I am afraid of bringing back my headache, and besides I feel no inclination to write today. It is impossible to put on paper all that we think – at least I find it so. I would rather say it than write it. My last letter will have told you just how things stand. Please believe what you like of me, but not anything bad. There are people who think that no one can love a poor girl without having evil designs; and that charming word *maîtresse*, wh—e in our tongue, is really much too charming! But I am no Brunetti! no Mysliveček! I am a Mozart; and a young and clean-minded Mozart. So you will forgive me, I hope, if in my eagerness I sometimes get excited, – if that is the expression I should use, though indeed I would much rather say, if I sometimes write naturally. I have much to say on this subject, but I cannot; for I find it impossible to do so. Among my many faults I have also this one, a persistent belief that my friends who know me, really do know me. Therefore many words are not necessary: for if they do not know me, oh, then where could I ever find words enough? It is bad enough that one needs words at all – and letters into the bargain. All this, however, is not intended for you, my dear Papa. No, indeed! You know me too well and besides you are too good-natured thoughtlessly to rob anyone of his good name. I only mean those people – and they know that I mean them – who believe such a thing. I have made up my mind to stay at home to-day, although it is Sunday, because it is snowing so hard. To-morrow I must go out, for our house nymph, Mlle Pierron, my highly esteemed pupil, is to scramble through my concerto (written for the high and mighty Countess Lützow) at the French concert which is held every Monday. I too, prostitution though it be, shall ask them to give me something to strum and shall contrive to thump it out *prima fista*. For I am a born wood-hitter and all I can do is to strum a little on the clavier. Now please let me stop, for I am not at all in the humour for writing letters to-day, but feel far more inclined to compose. . . .

TO HIS FATHER
Mannheim, 28 February 1778

. . . I was at Raaff's yesterday and brought him an aria which I composed for him the other day.[1] The words are: 'Se al labbro mio non credi, bella nemica mia', etc. I don't think that Metastasio wrote them.[2] He liked it enormously. One must treat a man like Raaff in a particular way. I chose these words on purpose, because I knew that he already had an aria on them: so of course he will sing mine with greater facility and more pleasure. I asked him to tell me candidly if he did not like it or if it did not suit his voice, adding that I would alter it if he wished or even compose another. 'God forbid', he said, 'the aria must remain just as it is, for nothing could be finer. But please shorten it a little, for I am no longer able to sustain my notes.' 'Most gladly', I replied, 'as much as you like. I made it a little long on purpose, for it is always easy to cut down, but not so easy to lengthen.' After he had sung the second part, he took off his spectacles, and looking at me with wide-open eyes, said: 'Beautiful! Beautiful! That is a charming *seconda parte*.' And he sang it three times. When I took leave of him he thanked me most cordially, while I assured him that I would arrange the aria in such a way that it would give him pleasure to sing it. For I like an aria to fit a singer as perfectly as a well-made suit of clothes.[3] For practice I have also set to music the aria 'Non so d'onde viene', etc.[4] which has been so beautifully composed by Bach.[5] Just because I know Bach's setting so well and like it so much, and because it is always ringing in my ears, I wished to try and see whether in spite of all this I could not write an aria totally unlike his. And, indeed, mine does not resemble his in the very least. At first I had intended it for Raaff; but the beginning seemed to me too high for his voice. Yet I liked it so much that I would not alter it; and from the orchestral accompaniment, too, it seemed to me better suited to a soprano. So I decided to write it for Mlle Weber. Well, I put it aside and started off on the words 'Se al labbro' for Raaff. But all in vain! I simply couldn't compose, as the first aria kept on running in my head. So I returned to it and made up my mind to compose it exactly for Mlle Weber's voice. It's an *Andante sostenuto* (preceded by a short recitative); then follows the second part, 'Nel seno a destarmi', and then the

---

1. K.295.
2. They were from Antonio Salvi's libretto for Hasse's 'Arminio'. – E.B.
3. The autograph of the aria shows corrections and cuts which Mozart made to suit Raaff.
4. K.294, recitative and aria on a text from Metastasio's 'Olimpiade', written for Aloysia Weber. In 1787 Mozart set the same words to music for the famous bass singer, Ludwig Fischer, K.512.
5. Johann Christian Bach.

sostenuto again. When it was finished, I said to Mlle Weber: 'Learn the aria yourself. Sing it as you think it ought to go; then let me hear it and afterwards I will tell you candidly what pleases me and what displeases me.' After a couple of days I went to the Webers and she sang it for me, accompanying herself. I was obliged to confess that she had sung it exactly as I wished and as I should have taught it to her myself. This is now the best aria she has; and it will ensure her success wherever she goes. Yesterday at Wendling's I sketched the aria which I had promised his wife, adding a short recitative. She had chosen the words herself – from 'Didone', 'Ah, non lasciarmi, no'.[1] She and her daughter are quite crazy about it. I have also promised the daughter some more French ariettas, and began one to-day.[2] When they are ready I shall send them to you on small paper as I did my first aria. I still have two of the six clavier sonatas to compose[3], but there's no hurry, for I can't have them engraved here. Nothing is done in this place by subscription; it is a miserly spot, and the engraver will not do them at his own expense, but he wants to go halves with me in the sale. So I prefer to have them engraved in Paris, where the engravers are delighted to get something new and pay handsomely and where it is easier to get a thing done by subscription. I would have had these sonatas copied and sent to you long ago; but I thought to myself: 'No, I prefer to send them to him when they have been engraved.' I am looking forward most particularly to the Concert Spirituel in Paris, for I shall probably be asked to compose something for it. The orchestra is said to be so excellent and is very large: and my favourite type of composition, the chorus, can be well performed there. I am indeed glad that the French value choruses highly. The only fault found with Piccinni's new opera 'Roland'[4], is that the choruses are too meagre and weak, and that the music on the whole is a little monotonous, otherwise it was universally liked. To be sure, they are accustomed to Gluck's choruses in Paris. Do rely on me. I shall do my very best to bring honour to the name of Mozart and I have not the slightest fear. My last letters will have given you full particulars as to how things are now, and as to what my intentions are. I do entreat you never to allow the thought to cross your mind that I can ever forget you, for I cannot bear it. My chief purpose was, is and ever shall be to

1. K.486a, recitative and aria on a text from Metastasio's 'Didone abbandonata', written for Dorothea Wendling.
2. Probably K.308, 'Dans un bois solitaire'.
3. K.301, 302, 303, and 305 were composed at Mannheim, K.304 and 306 in Paris.
4. 'Roland', the first opera which Piccinni wrote for Paris, was performed on 27 January 1778.

endeavour to bring about our speedy and happy reunion! But we must be patient. You yourself know even better than I do how often things go awry – but they will soon go straight – only do have patience! Let us place our trust in God, Who will never forsake us. I shall not be found wanting. How can you doubt me? Surely it is to your interest that I should work as hard as I can, so that I may have the joy and happiness (the sooner the better too) of embracing with all my heart my most beloved and dearest father? There – you see! Nothing in this world is wholly free from self-interest! If war should break out ⟨in Bavaria⟩, follow us at once, I beg you. I have full confidence in three friends, all of them powerful and invincible, God, your head and mine. Our heads, I admit, are very different, but each in its own way is good, serviceable and useful, and I hope that in time mine will by degrees equal yours in those branches in which it is now inferior. Well, good-bye! Be merry and cheerful. Remember that you have a son who has never, knowingly, forgotten his filial duty to you, who will endeavour to become more and more worthy of so good a father and who will remain unchangingly your most obedient

WOLFGANG MOZART

I embrace my sister with all my heart!

TO HIS COUSIN AT AUGSBURG
Mannheim, 28 February 1778

Mademoiselle ma très chère Cousine!

Perhaps you think or are even convinced that I am dead? That I have pegged out? Or hopped a twig? Not at all. Don't believe it, I implore you. For believing and shitting are two very different things! Now how could I be writing such a beautiful hand if I were dead? How could that be possible? I shan't apologize for my very long silence, for you would never believe me. Yet what is true is true. I have had so many things to do that I had time indeed to think of my little cousin, but not to write, you see. So I just had to let things be. But now I have the honour to inquire how you are and whether you perspire? Whether your stomach is still in good order? Whether indeed you have no disorder? Whether you still can like me at all? Whether with chalk you often scrawl? Whether now and then you have me in mind? Whether to hang yourself you sometimes feel inclined? Whether you have been wild? With this poor foolish child? Whether to make peace with me you'll be so kind? If not, I swear I'll let off one behind! Ah, you're laughing! Victoria! Our arses shall be the symbol of our peacemaking! I knew that you wouldn't be able to resist me much longer. Why, of course, I'm sure of success, even if to-day I should make a mess, though to Paris I go in a fortnight or less. So if you want to send a reply to me from that town of Augsburg yonder, you see, then write at once, the sooner the better, so that I may be sure to receive your letter, or else if I'm gone I'll have the bad luck, instead of a letter to get some muck. Muck! – Muck! – Ah, muck! Sweet word! Muck! chuck! That too is fine. Muck, chuck! – muck! – suck – *o charmante*! muck, suck! That's what I like! Muck, chuck and suck! Chuck muck and suck muck!

. . . Well, I must tell you something before I close, for I must really stop soon, as I am in a hurry, for just at the moment I have nothing whatever to do; and also because I have no more room, as you see; the paper will soon be at an end; and besides I am tired and my fingers are twitching from so much writing; and finally even if I had room, I really don't know what I could tell you, apart from this story which I am proposing to relate. Now listen, it happened not very long ago, it all took place here and it made a great sensation too, for it seemed almost unbelievable; and, between ourselves, no one knows how the affair is going to turn out. Well, to make a long story short, about four hours from here – I have forgotten the name of the place – at some village or other – and indeed it is all one, whether the village was Tribsterill, where muck runs into the sea, or Burmesquik, where the crooked arse-holes are manufactured – in short, it was a village. Now in that village there was a peasant or shepherd, who was well advanced in years, but was still hale and hearty. He was unmarried and very comfortably off and led a jolly life. But, before I finish my story, I must tell you that when he spoke he had a dreadful voice, so that whenever he said anything, people were always terrifed of him. Well, to make a long story short, you must know that he had a dog called Bellot, a very fine large dog, white with black spots. Now one day the shepherd was walking along with his sheep, of which he had eleven thousand, and was carrying in his hand a stick with a beautiful rose-coloured ribbon. For he always carried a stick. It was his habit to do this. Well, let's go on. After he had walked for a good hour or so, he got tired and sat down near a river and fell asleep, and dreamt that he had lost his sheep. He awoke in terror, but to his great joy found all his sheep beside him. So he got up and walked on, but not for very long; for he had hardly walked for half an hour before he came to a bridge, which was very long but well protected on both sides in order to prevent people from falling into the river. Well, he looked at his flock and, as he was obliged to cross the river, he began to drive his eleven thousand sheep over the bridge. Now please be so kind as to wait until the eleven thousand sheep have reached the other side and then I shall finish my story. I have already told you that no one knows how the affair is going to turn out. But I hope that before I send you my next letter the sheep will have crossed the river. If not, I really don't care very much; as far as I am concerned, they could have remained this side of the water. So you must just be content with this instalment. I have told you all I know; and it is much better to stop than to make up the rest. If I did so, you would not believe any of the story; but as it is, you will surely believe – not even half of it. Well, I must close, though it makes me morose. Whoever begins must cease, or else he gives people no peace. . . . Adieu, little cousin, I am, I was, I should be, I have been, I had been, I should have been, oh that I were, oh that I might be, would to God I were, I shall be, if I should be, oh that I should be, I shall have been, oh that I had been, would to God that I had been, what? – a duffer. *Adieu, ma chère cousine*, where have you been? I am your same old faithful cousin.

WOLFGANG AMADÉ MOZART

TO HIS FATHER
Mannheim, 7 March 1778

. . . Once I am happily settled in Paris and, as I hope, our circumstances with God's help have improved and we are all more cheerful and in better spirits, I shall tell you my thoughts more fully and ask you for a great favour. But I must tell you that I was absolutely horrified and that tears came into my eyes when I read in your last letter that ⟨you have to go about so shabbily dressed⟩. My very dearest Papa! That is certainly not my fault – you know it is not! We ⟨economize⟩ in every possible way here; food and lodging, wood and light have cost us nothing⟩, and what more can we want! As for dress, you surely know that in places where you are not known, it is out of the question ⟨to be badly dressed⟩, for appearances must be kept up. I have now set all my hopes on Paris, for the German princes are all skinflints. I mean to work with all my strength so that I may soon have the happiness ⟨of helping you out of your present distressing circumstances⟩. . . .

TO HIS FATHER
Paris, 24 March 1778

Mon très cher Père,

Yesterday, Monday the 23rd, at four o'clock in the afternoon we arrived here, thank God, both safe and sound, having been nine and a half days on our journey. We really thought that we should not be able to hold out; for never in all my life have I been so bored. You can easily imagine what it meant for us to leave Mannheim and so many dear, kind friends and then to have to spend nine and a half days, not only without these good friends, but without anyone, without a single soul with whom we could associate or converse. Well, thank Heaven! we are at our journey's end and I trust that with the help of God we will go well. To-day we are going to take a *fiacre* and look up Grimm and Wendling. To-morrow morning, however, I intend to call on the Minister of the Palatinate, Herr von Sickingen (a great connoisseur and passionate lover of music, for whom I have two letters from Herr von Gemmingen and Mr Cannabich). Before leaving Mannheim I had copies made for Herr von Gemmingen of the quartet[1] which I composed one evening at the inn at Lodi, and also of the quintet[2] and the variations on a theme by Fischer.[3] On receiving them he sent a most polite note, expressing his pleasure at the *souvenir* which I was leaving him and enclosing a letter for his intimate friend Herr von Sickingen with the words: 'I feel sure that you will be a greater recommendation for the letter than it can possibly be for you.' To cover the expenses of copying he sent me three *louis d'or*. He assured me of his friendship and asked me for mine. I must say that all the courtiers who knew me, Court Councillors, Chamberlains and other worthy people, as well as all the court musicians, were very reluctant and sorry to see me go. There is no doubt about that. We left on Saturday, the 14th, and on the previous Thursday there was an afternoon concert at Cannabich's, where my concerto for three claviers was played. Mlle Rosa Cannabich played the first, Mlle Weber the second, and Mlle Pierron Serrarius, our house nymph, the third. We had three rehearsals of the concerto and it went off very well. Mlle Weber sang two arias of mine, the 'Aer tranquillo' from 'Il Rè pastore' and my new one, 'Non so d'onde viene'. With the latter my dear Mlle Weber did herself and me indescribable honour, for everyone said that no aria had ever affected them as did this one; but then she sang it as it ought to be sung. As soon as it was over, Cannabich called

---

1. K.80 written in 1770, with a final rondo of 1773 or 1774.
2. K.174, composed in 1773.
3. K.179, composed in 1774.

The Hotel de Beauvais, in the rue St Antoine, Paris, engraved by Jean Marot. The Mozarts had lodged here with the Bavarian ambassador, Count Eyck, when they first arrived in Paris in 1763.

out loudly; '*Bravo! Bravissimo, maestro! Veramente scritta da maestro!*' It was the first time I had heard it with orchestral accompaniment and I wish you also could have heard it, exactly as it was performed and sung there with that accuracy in interpretation, *piano* and *forte*. Who knows, perhaps you may hear it yet – I hope so. The members of the orchestra never ceased praising the aria and talking about it. I have many good friends in Mannheim (people of position and means), who wished very much to keep me there. Well, if they pay me decently, they can have me. Who knows, perhaps it will come off. I wish it would. And I still have a feeling and I still cherish the hope that it will. Cannabich is an honest, worthy man and my very good friend, but he has just one failing, which is, that although no longer young, he is rather careless and absent-minded. If you are not perpetually after him, he forgets everything. But when it's a matter of helping a real friend, he roars like a bull and takes the deepest interest in him; and that means a great deal, for he has influence. But on the whole I can't say much of his courtesy and gratitude, for I must confess that, in spite of their poverty and obscurity, and although I did much less for them, the Webers have shown themselves far more grateful. For M. and Mme Cannabich did not say a word to me, not did they even offer me the smallest keepsake, not even a bagatelle, to show their kindly feeling. They gave me nothing at all, they didn't even thank me, after I had spent so much time and trouble on their daughter. She can now perform before anyone, and for a girl of fourteen and an amateur she plays quite well; and it is thanks to me, as all Mannheim knows. She now has taste and can play trills; her time is good and her fingering is much better; formerly she had nothing of this. So in three months' time they will miss me sorely; for I fear she will soon be spoiled again and will spoil herself, because, unless she has a master constantly beside her, and one who knows his job, she will be no good, as she is still too childish and careless to practise seriously and to any purpose by herself. Mlle Weber out of the goodness of her heart has knitted me two pairs of mittens in filet, which she has given me as a remembrance and a small token of her gratitude. And Herr Weber copied out gratis whatever I required, supplied me with music paper and also made me a present of Molière's comedies (as he knew that I had not yet read them) with this inscription: *Accept, my friend, the works of Molière in token of gratitude and think of me sometimes.* And once, when alone with Mamma, he said: 'Indeed our best friend, our benefactor, is about to leave us. Yes, that is certain, we owe everything to your son. He has done a great deal for my daughter and has taken an interest in her and she can never be grateful enough to him.' The day before I left they wanted me to have supper with them, but I could not do so, as I had to be at home. All the same I had to spend two hours before supper at their house. They thanked me repeatedly, saying that they only wished they were in a position to show their gratitude, and when I left, they all wept. Forgive me, but my eyes fill with tears when I recall the scene. Herr Weber came downstairs with me, and remained standing at the door until I had turned the corner and called out after me – *Adieu!* The expenses of our journey, food and drink, lodging and tips, amounted to over four *louis d'or*, for the farther we penetrated into France, the dearer things became. This very moment I have received your letter of the 16th. Please don't worry, I will certainly make good. And I have one request to make, which is, to show in your letters a cheerful spirit. If war breaks out near Salzburg, come and join us. My greetings to all our good friends. I kiss your hands a thousand times and embrace my sister with all my heart and remain your most obedient son

WOLFGANG AMADÉ MOZART

TO HIS FATHER
Paris, 5 April 1778

... When he saw my first chorus, Mr Gossec, whom you doubtless know, said to M. Le Gros (I was not present) that it was *charmant* and would certainly produce a good effect, and that the words were well arranged and on the whole excellently set to music. He is a very good friend of mine and at the same time a very dull fellow. I am not simply going to compose an act for an opera, but a whole opera *en deux actes*. The poet has already written the first act, Noverre (at whose house I lunch as often as I like) arranged the whole thing and indeed suggested the ideas.

Baron Friedrich Melchior Grimm, by Louis Carrogis de Carmontelle, 1758.

I think it is to be called 'Alexandre et Roxane'. Madame Jenomé is also in Paris. I am now going to compose a *sinfonia concertante* for flute, Wendling; oboe, Ramm; horn, Punto; and bassoon, Ritter. Punto plays *magnifique*. I have this moment returned from the Concert Spirituel. Baron Grimm and I often give vent to our musical rage at the music here, I mean, between ourselves, of course. For in public we shout: *Bravo, Bravissimo*, and clap our hands until our fingers tingle. Now farewell. I kiss your hands a hundred times and remain

WOLFGANG AMADÉ MOZART

M. Raaff is here. He is staying with M. Le Gros, so we meet almost every day. My dearest Papa, I must really beg you once more not to worry so much, not to be so anxious; for now you have no reason to be so. I am at last in a place where it is certainly possible to make money, though this requires a frightful amount of effort and work. But I am willing to do anything to please you. What annoys me most of all in this business is that our French gentlemen have only improved their *goût* to this extent that they can now listen to good stuff as well. But to expect them to realize that their own music is bad or at least to notice the difference – Heaven preserve us! And their singing! Good Lord! Let me never hear a French-woman singing Italian arias. I can forgive her if she screeches out her French trash, but not if she ruins good music! It's simply unbearable. . . .

TO HIS FATHER
Paris, 1 May 1778

Mon très cher Père!

We have received your letter of April 12th. I waited for it and that is the reason why it is so long since I wrote. Please do not take it amiss if now and then I leave you for a long time without a letter, but postal fees are very heavy here and, unless one has something absolutely necessary to say, it is not worth while spending twenty-four *sous* and sometimes more. I had intended to postpone writing until I had news and could tell you more about our circumstances. But now I feel compelled to give you an account of a few matters which are still in doubt. The little violoncellist Zygmontofsky and his worthless father are here. Perhaps I have told you this already – but I merely mention it *en passant*, as I have just remembered that I met him at a place about which I now want to tell you, I mean, at the house of Madame la Duchesse de Chabot. M. Grimm gave me a letter to her, so I drove there. The main object of this letter was to recommend me to the Duchesse de Bourbon (who was in a convent the last time I was here), to introduce me to her again and to recall me to her mind. Well, a week went by without any news. However, as she had asked me to call on her after a week had elapsed, I kept my word and went. I had to wait for half an hour in a large ice-cold, unheated room, which hadn't even a fireplace. At last the Duchesse de Chabot appeared. She was very polite and asked me to make the best of the clavier in the room, as none of her own were in good condition. Would I perhaps

The Place Louis XV (now the Place de la Concorde), by A.-J. Noel.

try it? I said that I should be delighted to play something, but that it was impossible at the moment, as my fingers were numb with cold; and I asked her to have me taken at least to a room where there was a fire. '*Oh oui, Monsieur, vous avez raison*', was all the reply I got. She then sat down and began to draw and continued to do so for a whole hour, having as company some gentlemen, who all sat in a circle round a big table, while I had the honour to wait. The windows and doors were open and not only my hands but my whole body and my feet were frozen and my head began to ache. There was *altum silentium* and I did not know what to do for cold, headache and boredom. I kept on thinking: 'If it were not for M. Grimm, I would leave this house at once.' At last, to cut my story short, I played on that miserable, wretched pianoforte. But what vexed me most of all was that Madame and all her gentlemen never interrupted their drawing for a moment, but went on intently, so that I had to play to the chairs, tables and walls. Under these detestable conditions I lost my patience. I therefore began to play the Fischer variations and after playing half of them I stood up. Whereupon I received a shower of *éloges*. Upon which I said the only thing I had to say, which was, that I could not do myself justice on that clavier; and that I should very much like to fix some other day to play, when a better instrument would be available. But, as the Duchess would not hear of my going, I had to wait for another half hour, until her husband came in. He sat down beside me and listened with the greatest attention and I – I forgot the cold and my headache and in spite of the wretched clavier, I played – as I play when I am in good spirits. Give me the best clavier in Europe with an audience who understand nothing, or don't want to undertand and who do not feel with me in what I am playing, and I shall cease to feel any pleasure. I told Grimm all about it afterwards. You say that I ought to pay a good many calls in order to make new acquaintances and revive the old ones. That, however, is out of the question. The distances are too great for walking – or the roads too muddy – for really the mud in Paris is beyond description. To take a carriage means that you have the honour of spending four to five *livres* a day and all for nothing. People pay plenty of compliments, it is true, but there it ends. They arrange for me to come on such and such a day, I play and hear them exclaim: '*Oh, c'est un prodige, c'est inconcevable, c'est étonnant!*', and then it is – *Adieu*. At first I spent a lot of money driving about – often to no purpose, as the people were not at home. Those who do not live in Paris cannot imagine how annoying this is. Besides, Paris is greatly changed; the French are not nearly as polite as they were fifteen years ago; their manners now border on rudeness and they are detestably self-conceited. Well, I must give you an account of the Concert Spirituel – which reminds me that I must tell you briefly that my work on those choruses turned out in fact to be useless, for Holzbauer's Miserere in itself was too long and did not please. Thus they only performed two of my choruses instead of four, and left out the best. But that was of no consequence, for few people knew that I had composed some of the music and many knew nothing at all about me. However, there was great applause at the rehearsal and I myself (for I attach little value to Parisian praises) am very well satisfied with my choruses. There appears, however, to be a hitch with regard to the *sinfonia concertante*, and I think that something is going on behind the scenes and that doubtless here too I have enemies. Where, indeed, have I not had them? – But that is a good sign. I had to write the *sinfonia* in a great hurry and I worked very hard at it. The four performers were and still are quite in love with it. Le Gros kept it for four days to have it copied, but I always found it lying in the same place. The day before yesterday I couldn't find it – I searched carefully among the music – and discovered it hidden away. I pretended not to notice it, but just said to Le Gros: 'A propos. Have you given the *sinfonia concertante* to be copied?' 'No', he replied. 'I forgot all about it.' As of course I could not command him to have it copied and performed, I said nothing; but when I went to the concert on the two days when it should have been performed, Ramm and Punto came up to me in the greatest rage to ask me why my *sinfonia concertante* was not being played. 'I really don't

know', I replied. 'It's the first I've head of it. I know nothing about it.' Ramm flew into a passion and in the music-room he cursed Le Gros in French, saying it was a dirty trick and so forth. What annoys me most in the whole affair is that Le Gros never said a word to me about it – I alone was to be kept in the dark. If he had even made an excuse – that the time was too short or something of the kind – but to say nothing at all! I believe, however, that Cambini, an Italian *maestro* here, is at the bottom of the business. For in all innocence I swept the floor with him at our first meeting at Le Gros's house. He has composed some quartets, one of which I heard at Mannheim. They were quite pretty. I praised them to him and played the beginning of the one I had heard. But Ritter, Ramm and Punto, who

Joseph le Gros, the director of the Concert Spirituel (Macret after Le Clerc).

were there, gave me no peace, urging me to go on and telling me that what I could not remember I myself could supply. This I did, so that Cambini was quite beside himself and could not help saying: *'He's a first-rate fellow!'* – But I am convinced that he did not enjoy it. If this were a place where people had ears to hear, hearts to feel and some measure of understanding of and taste for music, these things would only make me laugh heartily; but, as it is (so far as music is concerned), I am surrounded by mere brute beasts. How can it be otherwise? For in all their actions, emotions and passions they are just the same. There is no place in the world like Paris. You must not think that I exaggerate when I talk thus of the music here. Ask anyone you like – provided he is not a Frenchman born – and, if he knows anything at all of the matter, he will say exactly the same. Well, I am here. I must endure it for your sake. But I shall thank Almighty God if I escape with my taste unspoiled. I pray to God daily to give me grace to hold out with fortitude and to do such honour to myself and to the whole German nation as will redound to His greater honour and glory; and that He will enable me to prosper and make a great deal of money, so that I may help you out of your present difficulties; and that He will permit us to meet again soon, so that we may all live together in happiness and contentment. For the rest, may His will be done on earth as it is in heaven. But I entreat you, dearest Papa, in the meantime, to do your best so that I may soon revisit Italy, where after this experience I may revive. Do me this favour, I beg you. And now I implore you to keep up your spirits. I shall hack my way through here as best I can, and I hope to get out without any bones broken! Adieu. I kiss your hands a thousand times and embrace my sister with all my heart and remain your most obedient son

WOLFGANG AMADÉ MOZART

TO HIS FATHER
Paris, 14 May 1778

I have so much to do already, that I wonder what it will be like in winter! I think I told you in my last letter that the Duc de Guines, whose daughter is my pupil in composition, plays the flute extremely well, and that she plays the harp *magnifique*. She has a great deal of talent, even genius, and in particular a marvellous memory, so that she can play all her pieces, actually about two hundred, by heart. She is, however, extremely doubtful as to whether she has any talent for composition, especially as regards invention or ideas. But her father who, between ourselves, is somewhat too infatuated with her, declares that she certainly has ideas and that it is only that she is too bashful and has too little self-confidence. Well, we shall see. If she gets no inspirations or ideas (for at present she really has none whatever), then it is to no purpose, for – God knows – I can't give her any. Her father's intention is not to make a great composer of her. 'She is not', he said, 'to compose operas, arias, concertos, symphonies, but only grand sonatas for her instrument and mine.' I gave her her fourth lesson to-day and, so far as the rules of composition and harmony are concerned, I am fairly well satisfied with her. She filled in quite a good bass for the first minuet, the melody of which I had given her, and she has already begun to write in three parts. But she very soon gets bored, and I am unable to help her; for as yet I cannot proceed more quickly. It is too soon, even if there really were genius there, but unfortunately there is none. Everything has to be done by rule. She has no ideas whatever – nothing comes. I have tried her in every possible way. Among other things I hit on the idea of writing down a very simple minuet, in order to see whether she could not compose a variation on it. It was useless. 'Well', I thought, 'she probably does not know how she ought to begin.' So I started to write a variation on the first bar and told her to go on in the same way and to keep to the idea. In the end it went fairly well. When it was finished, I told her to begin something of her own, – only the treble part, the melody. Well, she thought and thought for a whole quarter of an hour and nothing came. So I wrote down four bars of a minuet and said to her: 'See what an ass I am! I have begun a minuet and cannot even finish the melody. Please be so kind as to finish it for me.' She was positive she couldn't, but at last with great difficulty – something came, and indeed I was only too glad to see something for once. I then told her to finish the minuet, I mean, the treble only. But for home work all I asked her to do was to alter my four bars and compose something of her own. She was to find a new beginning, use, if necessary, the same harmony, provided that the melody should be different. Well, I shall see tomorrow what she has done. I shall soon, I believe, get the libretto for my opera *en deux actes.* Then I must first present it to the Director M. de Vismes, to see if he will accept it, though there is no doubt about that, for Noverre suggested it and De Vismes owes his appointment to him. Noverre is also going to arrange a new ballet for which I am going to compose the music. Rodolphe (who plays the French horn) is in the Royal service here and is a very good friend of mine; he understands composition thoroughly and writes well. He has offered me the post of organist at Versailles, if I will accept it. The salary is 2,000 *livres* a year, but I should have to spend six months at Versailles and the other six in Paris, or wherever I like. I do not think that I shall accept it, but I have yet to hear the advice of some good friends on the subject. After all, 2,000 *livres* is not such a big sum. It would be so in German money, I admit, but here it is not. . . .

TO HIS FATHER
Paris, 12 June 1778

. . . I have lunched at least six times with Count Sickingen, Minister of the Palatinate – where people always stay from one to ten in the evening. But the time flies so quickly in his company that you simply don't notice it. He is very fond of me and I like being with him; he is such a friendly, sensible person with such excellent judgement and he has a real insight into music. I was there again to-day with Raaff. I took some of my own compositions, as the Count had asked

The Palace of Versailles, an engraving by Jan Caspar Philips, 1756.

me long ago to do so. I brought along the new symphony which I have just finished and with which the Concert Spirituel will open at Corpus Christi. They both liked it very much and I too am quite pleased with it. But I cannot say whether it will be popular – and, to tell the truth, I care very little, for who will not like it? I can answer for its pleasing the few intelligent French people who may be there – and as for the stupid ones, I shall not consider it a great misfortune if they are not pleased. I still hope, however, that even asses will find something in it to admire – and, moreover, I have been careful not to neglect *le premier coup d'archet* – and that is quite sufficient. What a fuss the oxen here make of this trick! The devil take me if I can see any difference! They all begin together, just as they do in other places. It is really too much of a joke. Raaff told me a story of Abaco's about this. He was asked by a Frenchman, at Munich or somewhere – '*Monsieur, vous avez été à Paris?*' '*Oui.*' '*Est-ce que vous étiez au Concert Spirituel?*' '*Oui.*' '*Que dites-vous du premier coup d'archet? Avez-vous entendu le premier coup d'archet?*' '*Oui, j'ai entendu le premier et le dernier.*' '*Comment, le dernier? Que veut dire cela?*' '*Mais oui, le premier et le dernier – et le dernier même m'a donné plus de plaisir.*' Now I must close. Please give my greetings to all my good friends, and particularly to Herr Bullinger. I kiss your hands a thousand times and embrace my sister with all my heart and remain your most obedient son

WOLFGANG AMADÉ MOZART

TO HIS FATHER
Paris, 3 July 1778

Monsieur
mon très cher Père!

I have very sad and distressing news to give you, which is, indeed, the reason why I have been unable to reply sooner to your letter of June 11th. My dear mother is very ill. She has been bled, as in the past, and it was very necessary too. She felt quite well afterwards, but a few days later she complained of shivering and feverishness, accompanied by diarrhoea and headache. At first we only used our home remedies – antispasmodic powders; we would gladly have tried a black powder too, but we had none, and could not get it here, where it is not known even by the name of *pulvis epilepticus*. As she got worse and worse (she could hardly speak and had lost her hearing, so that I had to shout to make myself

93

Louis Philibert Debucourt's painting of les Halles during celebrations on the birth of the Dauphin in 1782.

understood), Baron Grimm sent us his doctor. But she is still very weak and is feverish and delirious. They give me hope – but I have not much. For a long time now I have been hovering day and night between hope and fear – but I have resigned myself wholly to the will of God – and trust that you and my dear sister will do the same. How else can we manage to be calm or, I should say, calmer, for we cannot be perfectly calm! Come what may, I am resigned – for I know that God, Who orders all things for our good, however strange they seem to us, wills it thus. Moreover I believe (and no one will persuade me to the contrary) that no doctor, no man living, no misfortune and no chance can give a man his life or take it away. None can do so but God alone. These are only the instruments which He usually employs, though not always. For we see people around us swoon, fall down and die. Once our hour has come, all means are useless; they rather hasten death than delay it. This we saw in the case of our late friend Hefner. I do not mean to say that my mother will and must die, or that all hope is lost. She may recover health and strength, but only if God wills it. After praying to Him with all my might for health and life for my dear mother, I like to indulge in these consoling thoughts, because they hearten, soothe and comfort me; and you may easily imagine that I need comfort! Now let us turn to something else. Let us banish these sad thoughts; let us hope, but not too much; let us put our trust in God and console ourselves with the thought that all is well, if it is in accordance with the will of the Almighty, as He knows best what is profitable and beneficial to our temporal happiness and our eternal salvation.

I have had to compose a symphony for the opening of the Concert Spirituel. It was performed on Corpus Christi day with great applause, and I hear, too, that there was a notice about it in the 'Courier de l'Europe', – so it has given great satisfaction. I was very nervous at the rehearsal, for never in my life have I heard a worse performance. You have no idea how they twice scraped and scrambled through it. I was really in a terrible way and would gladly have had it rehearsed again, but as there was so much else to rehearse, there was no time left. So I had to go to bed with an aching heart and in a discontented and angry frame of mind. I decided next morning not to go to the concert at all; but in the evening, the weather being fine, I at last made up my mind to go, determined that if my symphony went as badly as it did at the rehearsal, I would certainly make my way into the orchestra, snatch the fiddle out of the hands of Lahoussaye, the first violin, and conduct myself! I prayed God that it might go well, for it is all to His greater honour and glory; and behold – the symphony began. Raaff was standing beside me, and just in the middle of the first Allegro there was a passage which I felt sure must please. The audience were quite carried away – and there was a tremendous burst of applause. But as I knew, when I wrote it, what effect it would surely produce, I had introduced the passage again at the close – when there were shouts of '*da capo*'. The Andante also found favour, but particularly the last Allegro, because, having observed that all last as well as first Allegros begin here with all the instruments playing together and generally *unisono*, I began mine with two violins only, *piano* for the first eight bars – followed instantly by a *forte*; the audience, as I expected, said 'hush' at the soft beginning, and when they heard the *forte*, began at once to clap their hands. I was so happy that as soon as the symphony was over, I went off to the Palais Royal, where I had a large ice, said the rosary as I had vowed to do – and went home – for I always am and always will be happiest there, or else in the company of some good, true, honest German who, if he is a bachelor, lives alone like a good Christian, or, if married, loves his wife and brings up his children properly. Now I have a piece of news for you which you may have heard already, namely, that the godless arch-rascal Voltaire[1] has pegged out like a dog, like a beast! That is his reward! You are quite right, we owe Theresa wages for five quarters. That I do not like being here, you must long ago have noticed. I have very many reasons, but, as I am here, it is useless to go into them. It is not my fault, however, that I dislike Paris, and it never shall be, for I will do my very best. Well, God will make all things right! I have a project in my mind for the success of which I daily pray to Him. If it is His divine will, it will succeed, and if not, then I am content also – at least I shall have done my part. When all this has been set going and if all turns out as I wish, you too must do your part, or the whole work would be incomplete – I trust to your kindness to do so. Only don't indulge in unnecessary conjectures now. I only wanted to beg one favour of you beforehand, which is, not to ask me to reveal my thoughts more clearly, until it is time to do so . . .

---

1. Voltaire died on 30 May 1778. No doubt Mozart had heard the infamous stories circulated at the time by Voltaire's Catholic opponents.

The gardens of the Palais Royale in about 1778.

TO THE ABBÉ BULLINGER AT SALZBURG
Paris, 4 July 1778 (dated 3 July)

Most beloved Friend!

For you alone.

Mourn with me, my friend! This has been the saddest day of my life – I am writing this at two o'clock in the morning. I have to tell you that my mother, my dear mother, is no more! God has called her to Himself. It was His will to take her, that I saw clearly – so I resigned myself to His will. He gave her to me, so He was able to take her away from me. Only think of all my anxiety, the fears and sorrows I have had to endure for the last fortnight. She was quite unconscious at the time of her death – her life flickered out like a candle. Three days before her death she made her confession, partook of the Sacrament and received extreme unction. During the last three days, however, she was constantly delirious, and to-day at twenty-one minutes past five o'clock the death agony began and she lost all sensation and consciousness. I pressed her hand and spoke to her – but she did not see me, she did not hear me and all feeling was gone. She lay thus until she expired five hours later at twenty-one minutes past ten. No one was present but myself, Herr Heina (a kind friend whom my father knows) and the nurse. It is quite impossible for me to describe to-day the whole course of her illness, but I am firmly convinced that she was bound to die and that God had so ordained it. All I ask of you at present is to act the part of a true friend, by preparing my poor father very gently for this sad news. I have written to him by this post, but only to say that she is seriously ill; and now I shall wait for his answer and be guided by it. May God give him strength and courage! O my friend! Not only am I now comforted, but I have been comforted for some time. By the mercy of God I have borne it all with fortitude and composure. When her illness became dangerous, I prayed to God for two things only – a happy death for her, and strength and courage for myself; and God in His goodness heard my prayer and gave me those two blessings in the richest measure. I beg you, therefore, most beloved friend, watch over my father for me and try to give him courage so that, when he hears the worst, he may not take it too hardly. I commend my sister to you also with all my heart. Go to them both at once, I implore you – but do not tell them yet that

The churchyard of the church of the Holy Innocents, by Jean Nicolas Le Sobre, 1787.
Mozart's mother was buried here on 4 July 1778.

99

she is dead – just prepare them for it. Do what you think best – use every means to comfort them – but so act that my mind may be relieved – and that I may not have to dread another blow. Watch over my dear father and my dear sister for me. Send me a reply at once, I entreat you. *Adieu.* I remain your most obedient and grateful servant

WOLFGANG AMADÉ MOZART

TO HIS FATHER

Paris, 9 July 1778

Monsieur mon très cher Père!

I hope that you are now prepared to hear with fortitude one of the saddest and most painful stories; indeed my last letter of the 3rd will have told you that no good news could be hoped for. On that very same day, the 3rd, at twenty-one minutes past ten at night my mother fell asleep peacefully in the Lord; indeed, when I wrote to you, she was already enjoying the blessings of Heaven – for all was then over. I wrote to you during that night and I hope that you and my dear sister will forgive me for this slight but very necessary deception; for as I judged from my own grief and sorrow what yours would be, I could not indeed bring myself suddenly to shock you with this dreadful news! But I hope that you have now summoned up courage to hear the worst, and that after you have at first given way to natural, and only too well justified tears and anguish, you will eventually resign yourself to the will of God and worship His unsearchable, unfathomable and all-wise providence. You will easily conceive what I have had to bear – what courage and fortitude I have needed to endure calmly as things grew gradually and steadily worse. And yet God in His goodness gave me grace to do so. I have, indeed, suffered and wept enough – but what did it avail? So I have tried to console myself: and please do so too my dear father, my dear sister! Weep, weep, as you cannot fail to, but take comfort at last. Remember that Almighty God willed it thus – and how can we rebel against Him? Let us rather pray to Him, and thank Him for His goodness, for she died a happy death. In those distressing moments, there were three things that consoled me – my entire and steadfast submission to the will of God, and the sight of her very easy and beautiful death which made me feel that in a moment she had become so happy; for how much happier is she now than we are! Indeed I wished at that moment to depart with her. From this wish and longing proceeded finally my third source of consolation – the thought that she is not lost to us for ever – that we shall see her again – that we shall live together far more happily and blissfully than ever in this world. We do not yet know when it will be – but that does not disturb me; when God wills it, I am ready. Well, His heavenly and most holy will has been fulfilled. Let us therefore say a devout Paternoster for her soul and turn our thoughts to other matters, for all things have their appropriate time. I am writing this in the house of Madame D'Épinay and M. Grimm, with whom I am now living. I have a pretty little room with a very pleasant view, and, so far as my condition permits, I am happy. It will be a great help to restoring my tranquillity to hear that my dear father and sister are submitting wholly and with calmness and fortitude to the will of God – are trusting Him with their whole heart in the firm belief that He orders all things for the best. My dearest father! Do not give way! Dearest sister! Be firm! You do not as yet know your brother's good heart – for he has not yet been able to prove it. My two loved ones! Take care of your health. Remember that you have a son, a brother, who is doing his utmost to make you happy – knowing well that one day you will not refuse to grant him his desire and his happiness – which certainly does him honour, and that you also will do everything in your power to make him happy. Oh, then we shall live together as peacefully, honourably and contentedly as is possible in this world – and in the end, when God wills it, we shall all meet again in Heaven – for which purpose we were destined and created.

I have received your last letter of the 29th and see with pleasure that you are both, thank God, in good health. I had to laugh heartily about Haydn's tipsy fit. If I had been there, I should certainly have whispered in his ear 'Adlgasser!' It is really disgraceful that such an able man should through his own fault render himself incapable of performing his duties – at a service instituted in honour of God – in the presence of the Archbishop too and the whole court – and with the church full of people. How disgusting! That is one of my chief reasons for detesting Salzburg – those coarse, slovenly, dissolute court musicians. Why, no honest man, of good breeding, could possibly live with them! Indeed, instead of wanting to associate with them, he would feel ashamed of them. It is probably for this very reason that musicians are neither popular nor respected among us. Ah, if only the orchestra were organized as they are at Mannheim. Indeed I would like you to see the discipline which prevails there and the authority which Cannabich wields. There everything is done seriously. Cannabich, who is the best conductor I have ever seen, is both beloved and feared by his subordinates. Moreover he is respected by the whole town and so are his soldiers. But certainly they behave quite differently from ours. They have good manners, are well dressed and do not go to public-houses and swill. This can never be the case in Salzburg, unless the Prince will trust you or me and give us full authority as far as the music is concerned – otherwise it's no good. In Salzburg everyone – or rather no one – bothers about the music. If I were to undertake it, I should have to have complete freedom of action. The Chief Steward should have nothing to say to me in musical matters, or on any point relating to music. For a courtier can't do the work of a *Kapellmeister*, but a *Kapellmeister* can well be a courtier … You acted most skilfully, indeed like Ulysses, throughout the whole affair with Count Starnbock – only continue as you have begun and do not allow yourself to be hoodwinked – and be especially on your guard, should you by any chance have to talk to that crested goose. I know her, and, believe me, she has pepper in her head and heart, even though she has sugar and honey in her mug. It is quite natural ⟨that the whole affair should still be in an unsettled state, and many points must be conceded before I could accept the offer; while, even if they were, I should still prefer to be anywhere than in Salzburg⟩. But I need not worry, for it is ⟨highly improbable that all I ask will be granted, as I am asking a great deal⟩. Yet nothing is impossible; and ⟨if everything were properly organized, I should no longer hesitate⟩ – if only to have the happiness ⟨of being with you. If the people of Salzburg want to have me, then they must fall in with all my wishes – or they will certainly never get me⟩ … I spoke to Piccinni at the Concert Spirituel. He is most polite to me and I to him when – by chance – we do meet. Otherwise I do not seek acquaintanceship, either with him or with any other composer. I understand my job – and so do they – and that is enough. I told you already that my symphony at the Concert Spirituel was a tremendous success. If I am commissioned to compose an opera, I shall have annoyance in plenty, but that I shall not mind very much, for I am pretty well inured to it; if only that confounded French tongue were not so detestable for music. It really is hopeless; even German is divine in comparison. And then the men and women singers! Indeed they hardly deserve the name, for they don't sing – they yell – howl – and that too with all their might, through their noses and throats. For next Lent I have to compose a French oratorio[1] which is to be performed at the Concert Spirituel.

1. There is no trace of this work. Probably this plan, like those for two French operas, was never carried out.

A view of Paris from the Quai de la Rapée, by Pierre Denis Martin.

Monsieur Le Gros, the Director, is amazingly taken with me. You must know that, although I used to be with him every day, I have not been near him since Easter; I felt so indignant at his not having performed my *sinfonia concertante*. I often went to the same house to visit Monsieur Raaff and each time I had to pass his rooms. His servants and maids often saw me and I always sent him my compliments. It is really a pity that he did not perform it, as it would have made a great hit – but now he no longer has an opportunity of doing so, for where could four such players be found to perform it? One day, when I went to call on Raaff, I was told that he was out but would certainly be home very soon and I therefore waited. M. Le Gros came into the room and said: 'It is really quite wonderful to have the pleasure of seeing you again.' 'Yes, I have a great deal to do.' 'I hope you will stay to lunch with us to-day?' 'I am very sorry but I am already engaged.' 'M. Mozart, we really must spend a day together again soon.' 'That will give me much pleasure.' A long pause; at length, 'A propos. Will you not write a grand symphony for me for Corpus Christi?' 'Why not?' 'Can I then rely on this?' 'Oh yes, if I may rely with certainty on its being performed, and that it will not have the same fate as my *sinfonia concertante*.' Then the dance began. He excused himself as well as he could, but did not find much to say. In short, the symphony was highly approved of – and Le Gros is so pleased with it that he says it is his

very best symphony. But the Andante has not had the good fortune to win his approval; he declares that it has too many modulations and that it is too long. He derives this opinion, however, from the fact that the audience forgot to clap their hands as loudly and to shout as much as they did at the end of the first and last movements. For indeed the Andante is a great favourite with myself and with all connoisseurs, lovers of music and the majority of those who have heard it. It is just the reverse of what Le Gros says – for it is quite simple and short. But in order to satisfy him (and, as he maintains, some others) I have composed a fresh Andante – each is good in its own way – for each has a different character. But the last pleases me even more . . .

TO FRIDOLIN WEBER AT MANNHEIM
Paris, 29 July 1778

Monsieur mon très cher et plus cher Ami!

I have this moment received your letter of July 15th, for which I had been waiting with such longing and about which I had thought so much! *Basta!* Well, your esteemed letter has restored my peace of mind – save for its chief contents which made my blood boil – so that – but I will stop – you know me, my friend – so you will understand all that I felt when I read it through. I cannot omit to do so – I must reply at once, for I think it is most necessary. Yet I must ask you whether you too received my letter of June 29th? I sent you three – one after another – one dated the 27th, addressed to you direct – one of the 29th, sent to Herr Heckmann and one of the 3rd to the same address. Now to the point. Didn't I always tell you that the Elector would make his residence in Munich? I have heard already that Count Seeau has been appointed Intendant both for Munich and Mannheim! Well, I have something really important to tell you, which, however, I cannot possibly express in German. You will soon find it out. Meanwhile I hope that, whether the court moves to Munich or remains in Mannheim, your salary will be increased and your daughter will get a good one – so that you may pay off all your debts and that you may all breathe a little more freely. Things must improve in time. If not, well then – our present circumstances are so favourable that we can afford to be patient, to wait for a suitable time, and then settle down somewhere else, in better surroundings. My friend, if I had the money which many a man, who does not earn it, squanders so disgracefully – how gladly would I then help you! But unfortunately – he who can does not want to and he who wants to cannot! Well, listen. I wanted to use my influence (and perhaps not altogether in vain) to bring you and your daughter to Paris this winter. But the position is as follows: M. Le Gros, Director of the Concert Spirituel, to whom I have already spoken about my friend, your daughter, can't have her here this winter – because he has already engaged Madame Le Brun for the season – and at the moment he is not in such a fortunate position as to be able to pay two such singers as they deserve (and I shall not agree to any other arrangement). So there is no money to be made here – but this plan will be quite practicable the following winter. I only wanted to tell you that if you really can't endure it any longer – I say, not any longer – you can come to Paris. The journey, food, lodging, wood and light will cost you nothing. However, that is not enough. For allowing that you manage to get through the winter – as there are private concerts and I might perhaps arrange something for you at the Concert des Amateurs – what would you do in the summer? Indeed I am not nervous about the following winter, when you would certainly get an engagement for the Concert Spirituel. *Basta*, send me your views about this – I shall then undertake to do all I can. Most beloved friend! I am almost ashamed to make you such a proposal – which, even if you were to accept, would be still uncertain – and not so advantageous as you deserve and as I desire! But – just remember that my intention is good – the will is there. I would gladly help but – I look in every direction to see whether something cannot be arranged and whether it cannot be managed. Wait. I shall see. If what I now have in mind succeeds – but patience – we should never hurry up a thing too much – if so, it goes wrong or does not work out at all. Meanwhile press as hard as you can to have your own salary raised and to get a good one for your daughter. Apply frequently in writing – and mind, if our heroine is to sing at court – and in the meantime you have received no reply, or at least no favourable one to your application – then just don't let her sing – make the excuse of some slight indisposition – do it often – I beg you – and when you have often done so, then all of a sudden let her sing again – and you will see how effective that dodge will be. But you must do it with great subtlety and cunning. You must seem to be extremely sorry that Louisa should be indisposed just when she has to perform. Of course, if you do this three or four times in succession, people will begin to see the joke! and that is just what I want – and when she does sing again, then, of course, you must make it quite clear that she is only doing it to oblige! She must still be slightly indisposed – she is only doing her best to please the Elector – you understand – and, at the same time, she must sing with great passion, with all her

The Comédie Française in 1780.

heart and soul; and meanwhile you must continue to make known to the world, both verbally and in writing, your complaints, which are only too well justified; and if the Intendant perhaps (or someone else who you know gossips about it) enquires about your daughter's health – tell him as a great secret that it's no wonder – the poor girl suffers from hypochondria, a disease which can hardly be cured in Mannheim – that she has devoted herself to singing with great zest and industry and has really made progress – which nobody can deny – and that unfortunately she now realizes that all her trouble and hard work have been in vain and that her eagerness and delight to be able to serve His Highness the Elector have been frustrated – and that she would have lost all her love of music too, have neglected herself and really given up singing – had you not said to her: 'My daughter, your trouble and hard work have not been in vain. If you are not rewarded here, people will reward you elsewhere – and that too is what I intend. I cannot stand it any longer – I cannot any longer let my child make to me such well-justified reproaches.' And then – suppose he asks you, 'Where are you off to?' – tell him, 'I don't know yet. Put that in your pipe and smoke it.' But only do this if you think that all hope is lost – which I cannot possibly believe: because the Elector really cannot keep her dangling any longer – for, when he sees that he can't get anything out of your daughter, without tossing a salary at her, he will just have to pay her – for he must have her – he really needs her. After all, whom has he got in Mannheim? Franziska Danzi? As sure as I'm writing this, she won't stay. And in Munich? Why, there he will certainly not find someone at once. For I know Munich in and out; I have been there five times. So he must have her – he cannot let her go – and as for you, your chief complaint must always be – your debts. But now, so that you may not be made a fool of, if it should happen that nothing can be done (which I truly hope will not be the case), you would do well to look about in secret for something permanent, of course, at some court. Rest assured that I too shall do all I can. My idea for yourself is that you should apply privately to Mainz. Why, you were there quite recently. You will at any rate know someone who can – who really can – do something. But for God's sake don't mention that Seyler company to me – I couldn't bear to think that your daughter – or even if she were not your daughter – even if she were only a foundling – I should be very sorry indeed that she with her talent should fall among players – which would mean that she is only good enough to be a stop-gap – for the main thing with the Seylers, indeed with all theatrical companies, is always the play – the *singspiel* is just put in to give occasional relief to the players now and then – indeed, very often in order to give the actors time and room to change – and generally as a diversion. You must always think of your reputation. I at least always think of mine. Well, there you have my very candid opinion – perhaps you won't like it, but with my friends it is my custom to be sincere. Besides, you can do what you like – I shall never take the liberty of prescribing anything. I shall just advise you as a true friend. You see that I am not *entêté* that you should remain in Mannheim – I should be quite pleased if you were to go to Mainz – but provided it is with honour and reputation. By Heaven, my joy at going to Mainz would be considerably lessened if I should have to look up your daughter amongst the players – which might easily happen. It is not at all impossible, of course, between ourselves, that I may go to Mainz, I need hardly add, under contract. Only to you, my friend, do I tell my affairs, just as you tell me yours. One thing more. Could you, my friend, bear to have your daughter acting with players in that very same place where Mlle Hellmuth (who cannot be compared with her) has an engagement at court? – and would consequently take precedence of her? Dearest friend – let this be my last, my most drastic argument for preventing it. Well, I am going briefly to sum up all this. You seem to me (but you must not take this remark amiss) to get very easily depressed – you lose all your courage at a go – you give up hope too quickly – you cannot deny this, for I know your circumstances – they are distressing, it is true, but not at all as distressing as you think. I know how pained and hurt is an honest man when he is forced to run up debts – I know it from experience. But let us look at things in the right way – who is running up these debts? You? No – the Elector is. – If you were to leave to-day and stay away – and never pay your debts – you could not do anything which could more easily be justified, – and no one, not even the Elector himself, would say a word – but – you need not do this – you will certainly find yourself in a position – to be able to pay these debts. I advise you, therefore, to be patient until the winter after next – and meanwhile to do your best to improve your position in Mannheim – and at the same time to try to get another appointment. If either of these alternatives comes off, so much the better; if they do not, then come to Paris the winter after next. By that time I guarantee that you will be able to earn sixty *louis d'or* at least. At the same time Louisa will have improved in her singing and especially in her acting. In the meantime I shall look about for an opera for her in Italy. When she has sung in one opera there – then she will be launched. If in the meantime Madame Le Brun should come to Mannheim – both of you should make friends with her. For she might be useful to you for London. She is coming here this winter – and when she does, I shall immediately press your case. Although, as I am sure you do not doubt, I should prefer to see you here to-day – rather than to-morrow, yet as a true friend I must dissuade you from coming here – even this winter – in the way I suggested (the only possible way at the moment). First of all, it would be a little uncertain – and then it would not be good for your reputation to come here without an engagement. Besides, it is not very pleasant to have to be supported by someone else. But indeed, if I were in the fortunate position of being able to entertain you absolutely free of charge, then you could certainly come without the slightest fear that such a procedure would be bad for your reputation – for I swear to you on my honour – that not a soul should know it. Well, I have given my views, my opinions and my advice. Do what you think best. But please do not imagine that I am trying to prevent you from setting out on your travels and to persuade you to stay in Mannheim or to get some engagement in Mainz, simply because I have hopes of getting work in one of these places – I mean, in order to have the pleasure of embracing you very soon. Not at all – it is just because I am convinced that for many reasons it would be advisable for you to wait a little longer. Indeed, most beloved friend, if I could arrange for us to live together in the same place joyfully and happily – that is what I should certainly like best of all – that is what I should prefer – but rest assured that I value your happiness more than my own well-being and pleasure – and that I would sacrifice all my pleasure just to know that you are all happy and cheerful. I have absolute confidence in God Who will surely grant me once more the joy of seeing those whom I love so dearly with all my heart and soul, and perhaps – even of being able to live with them. Be patient, therefore, dearest, most beloved friend – and meanwhile keep on looking out for an engagement. I must now tell you something about my own affairs. You have no idea what a dreadful time I am having here. Everything goes so slowly; and until one is well known – nothing can be done in the matter of composition. In my previous letters I told you how difficult it is to find a good libretto. From my description of the music here you may have gathered that I am not very happy, and that (between ourselves) I am trying to get away as quickly as possible. Unfortunately Herr Raaf will not be in Mannheim until the end of August. But he is then going to do his best for me, so that perhaps we may hope that something will turn up. If not, I shall very probably go to Mainz. Count Sickingen (at whose house I was yesterday and to whom I said a great deal about you) has a brother there – and the Count himself suggested that his brother might do something for me. So I think that things may move a bit. Now you know my prospects, which have been kept a secret from everyone except the Count and yourself. But, sad as my present position is, I am infinitely more disappointed to think that I am not able to serve you – as I should like to do, and this I swear to you on my honour. *Adieu*, most beloved friend, farewell. Write to me soon – reply to all my questions – and to my previous letters, I beg you. Give my best greetings to your wife, and to all your loved ones; and rest assured that I shall use every effort to help you to improve your position. If I hadn't a father and a sister, to whom I must sacrifice everything and whom I must try to support, I would completely renounce my own interests with the greatest pleasure – and consult your interests only. For your welfare – your pleasure – your happiness are the very foundation of mine. Farewell, your constant

MOZART

TO ALOYSIA WEBER AT MANNHEIM
Paris, 30 July 1778

Dearest Friend!

Please forgive me for not sending you this time the variations I have composed on the aria which you sent me. But I have thought it so necessary to reply as quickly as possible to your father's letter that I have not had time to copy them and therefore cannot let you have them. But you shall certainly have them in my next letter. I am hoping that my sonatas will be engraved very soon – and I shall send in the same parcel the 'Popoli di Tessaglia', which is already half finished.[1] If you are as pleased with it as I am, I shall be delighted. Meanwhile until I have the pleasure of hearing from you whether you really like this scena – for, since I have composed it for you alone I desire no other praise than yours – I can only say that of all my compositions of this kind – this scena is the best I have ever composed. I shall be delighted if you will set to work as hard as you can at my Andromeda scena 'Ah, lo previdi'[2], for I assure you that it will suit you admirably – and that you will do yourself great credit with it. I advise you to watch the expression marks – to think carefully of the meaning and the force of the words – to put yourself in all seriousness into Andromeda's situation and position! – and to imagine that you really are that very person. With your beautiful voice and your fine method of producing it you will undoubtedly soon become an excellent singer, if you continue to work in this way. The greater part of the next letter which I shall have the honour of sending you will consist of a short explanation of the manner in which I should like you to sing and act this scene. At the same time I urge you to work at it for a little by yourself – and then you will see the difference – which will be a very useful lesson for you – although indeed I am quite sure that there won't be very much to correct or alter – and that you will sing my passages in the way I desire – for you know by experience how I like my compositions to be sung. – In the aria 'Non so d'onde viene', which you learnt by yourself, I found nothing to criticize or correct – you sang it to me with the interpretation, with the method and the expression which I desired. So I have reason to have every confidence in your ability and knowledge. In short, you are capable – most capable – so that all that I ask you (and this I do beg you most earnestly to do) is to be so good as to re-read my letters now and then and to follow my advice – resting assured and convinced that my sole object when I say and when I used to say all these things, is, and always will be, to do as much for you as I possibly can.

Dearest friend! I hope that you are in excellent health – I beg you to take great care of it – for good health is the best thing in the world. Thank God, I am very well, as far as my health is concerned, because I watch it. But my mind is not at rest – nor will it be until I have heard (and what a comfort that will be) that your merits have received their just reward. But

---

1. K.316, a recitative and aria composed to words taken from Gluck's 'Alceste'.
2. K.272, a recitative and aria composed to words taken from Paisiello's 'Andromeda'.

my condition and my situation will be the happiest on that day when I shall have the infinite pleasure of serving you again and embracing you with all my heart. This too is all that I can long for and desire, and my only consolation and my sole comfort lie in this hope and desire. Please write to me very often. You have no idea how much pleasure your letters afford me. Please write to me whenever you have been to see Herr Marchand – and tell me something about your study of stage acting – to which I urge you most warmly to apply yourself. Basta, you know that everything that concerns you interests me very greatly . . . Addio, for the present, dearest friend! I am very anxious to get a letter from you. So please do not keep me waiting and do not make me suffer too long. In the hope of having news from you very soon, I kiss your hands, I embrace you with all my heart, and am, and ever shall be, your true and sincere friend

W. A. MOZART

Please embrace your dear mother and all your sisters for me.

TO HIS FATHER
Paris, 31 July 1778

Monsieur mon très cher Père!

I hope you have received my two letters – I think, of the 11th and 18th. Meanwhile I have received yours of the 13th and 20th. The first brought tears of sorrow to my eyes – because I was reminded of the sad death of my dear departed mother – and everything came back to me so vividly. As long as I live I shall never forget it. You know that I had never seen anyone die, although I had often wished to. How cruel that my first experience should be the death of my mother! I dreaded that moment most of all, and I prayed earnestly to God for strength. My prayer was heard and strength was given to me. Sad as your letter made me, yet I was beside myself with joy when I heard that you had taken it all as it should be taken – and that thus I need have no fears for my most beloved father and my dearest sister. As soon as I had read your letter through, I fell on my knees and thanked our gracious God with all my heart for this blessing. I am quite calm now, for I know that I have nothing to fear for the two persons who are dearest to me in this world. Had it been otherwise, it would have been the greatest misfortune for me – and would have certainly crushed me. Do take care, both of you, of your health, which is so precious to me, and grant to him who flatters himself that he is now the dearest thing in the world to you, the happiness, the joy and the bliss of folding you soon in his arms. Your last letter drew tears of joy from me, for it convinced me completely of your true fatherly love and care. I shall strive with all my might to deserve still more your fatherly affection. I kiss your hand in tender gratitude for sending me the powders, and am sure you will be glad to know that I do not need them. Once during my dear departed mother's illness a dose was almost necessary – but now, thank God, I am perfectly well and healthy. From time to time I have fits of melancholy – but I find that the best way to get rid of them is to write or receive letters, which invariably cheer me up again. But, believe me, there is always a cause for these sad feelings. Would you like to know how much I had to pay for your last letter containing the powders? Forty-five *sous*. You would like to have a short account of her illness and of all its circumstances? You shall have it, but I must ask you to let it be short – and I shall only allude to the main facts, as it is all over now and, unfortunately, cannot be undone – and I need room to write about things which have to do with our present situation. First of all, I must tell you that my dear departed mother had to die. No doctor in the world could have saved her this time – for it was clearly the will of God; her time had come – and God wanted to take her to Himself. You think she put off being bled until it was too late? That may be. She did postpone it a little. But I rather agree with the people here who tried to dissuade her from being bled – and to persuade her to take a *lavement*. She would not, however, have this – and I did not venture to say anything, as I do not understand these things and consequently should have been to blame if it had not suited her. If it had been my own case, I should have consented at once – for this treatment is very popular here – whoever has an inflammation takes a *lavement* – and the cause of my mother's illness was nothing but an internal inflammation – or at least was diagnosed as such. I cannot tell you accurately how much blood she was let, for it is measured here not by the ounce but by the plate; they took a little less than two platefuls. The surgeon said that it was very necessary – but it was so terribly hot that day that he did not dare to bleed her any more. For a few days she was all right. Then diarrhoea started – but no one paid much attention to it, as foreigners who drink a good deal of water commonly find it a laxative. And that is true. I had it myself when I first came to Paris, but since I have given up drinking plain water and always add a little wine, I have been free of this trouble, though indeed, as I cannot altogether do without drinking plain water, I purify it with ice and drink it *en glace* – and take two tumblerfuls before going to bed. Well, to continue. On the 19th she complained of headache, and for the first time she had to spend the day in

bed; she was up for the last time on the 18th. On the 20th she complained of shivers – and then fever – so that I gave her an antispasmodic powder. All this time I was very anxious to send for a doctor, but she would not consent; and when I urged her very strongly, she said she had no confidence in a French physician. So I looked about for a German – but as of course I could not go out and leave her, I waited anxiously for M. Heina, who was in the habit of coming regularly every day to see us – but, needless to say, on this occasion he had to stay away for two days! At last he came, but as the doctor was prevented from coming the following day, we could not consult him. Thus he did not come until the 24th. On the previous day, when I had wanted him so badly, I had a great fright – for all of a sudden she lost her hearing. The doctor (an old German of about seventy) gave her a rhubarb powder in wine. I cannot understand that, for people usually say that wine is heating. But when I said so, they all exclaimed: 'How on earth can you say so? Wine is not heating, but strengthening – water is heating' – and meanwhile the poor patient was longing for a drink of fresh water. How gladly would I have given it to her! Most beloved father, you cannot imagine what I endured. But there was no help for it, for by Heaven I had to leave her in the hands of the doctor. All I could do with a good conscience was to pray to God without ceasing that He would order all things for her good. I went about as if I was bereft of my reason. I had ample leisure then for composing, but I could not have written a single note. On the 25th the doctor did not come. On the 26th he visited her again. Imagine my feelings when he said to me quite unexpectedly: 'I fear she will not last out the night. If she is taken with pains and has to go to the night-stool, she may die at any moment. You had better see that she makes her confession.' So I ran out to the end of the Chaussée d'Antin, well beyond the Barrière, to find Heina, who I knew was at a concert at the house of a certain Count. He told me he would bring a German priest next day. On my way back, as I was passing, I went in for a moment to see Grimm and Mme D'Épinay. They were distressed that I had not told them sooner, for they would have sent their own doctor at once. I had not said anything to them before, because my mother would not have a French doctor – but now I was at my wits' end. They said therefore that they would send their doctor that very evening. When I got home, I told my mother that I had met Herr Heina with a German priest who had heard a great deal about me and was longing to hear me play, and that they were coming on the morrow to pay me a visit. She was quite satisfied, and as I thought that she seemed better (although I am no doctor), I said nothing more. I see now that it is impossible for me to tell a thing briefly. I like to write about everything in detail and I think that you too will prefer it. So, as I have more urgent matters to write about, I shall continue this story in my next letter. Meanwhile, you must have seen from my last letters where I am living and that all my possessions and those of my beloved mother are in good order. When I come to this point I shall explain fully how this was arranged. Heina and I did everything. Clothes, linen, jewels, indeed everything belonging to her I shall send to Salzburg on the first suitable occasion and with every precaution. I shall arrange all that with Gschwendner. Now for our own affairs. But first of all I must beg you again not to worry at all about what I told you in my letter of the 3rd, in which I asked you not to insist on my disclosing my ideas until the time should be ripe. I cannot tell you about it yet, for indeed it is not yet time – and, if I did, I should do more harm than good. But for your peace of mind let me say that it only concerns myself. It will not affect your circumstances either for better or for worse and I shall not think about it until I see you in a better position. But when we are happily reunited and can live somewhere together (which is my sole ambition) – when that happy time comes – and God grant it may be soon! – then the moment will have arrived and the rest will depend on you. So do not worry about it now – and rest assured that in all matters where I know that your peace and happiness are involved, I shall always put my trust in you, my most beloved father and my truest friend, and shall tell you everything in detail. If I have not always done so hitherto – it has not been entirely my fault. M. Grimm said to me the other day: 'What am I to write to your father? What course do you intend to pursue? Are you staying here or going to Mannheim?' I really could not help laughing. 'What could I do in Mannheim now?' I said, 'would that I had never come to Paris – but so it is. Here I am and I must use every effort to make my way.' 'Well', he said, 'I hardly think that you will make a success of things in Paris.' 'Why?' I asked. 'I see a crowd of miserable bunglers here who are able to get on, and with my talents should I not be able to do so? – I assure you that I liked being at Mannheim – and should be glad to have an appointment there – but it must be an honourable and reputable one. I must be certain how I stand before I move a step.' 'Well, I am afraid', said he, 'that you have not been active enough here – you do not go about enough.' 'Well,' I replied, 'that is just what I find most difficult to do here.' After all, during my mother's long illness I couldn't go anywhere – and two of my pupils are in the country – and the third (the daughter of the Duc de Guines) is getting married – and (what is no great loss to my reputation) will not continue her studies. Moreover I shall lose no money, for he only pays me what everyone else does. Just imagine, the Duc de Guines, to whose house I have had to go daily for two hours, let me give twenty-four lessons and (although it is the custom to pay after every twelve) went off into the country and came back after ten days without letting me know a word about it, so that had I not enquired out of mere curiosity – I should not have known that they were here! And when I did go, the house-keeper pulled out a purse and said: 'Pray forgive me if I only pay you for twelve lessons this time, but I haven't enough money.' There's noble treatment for you! She paid me three *louis d'or*, adding: 'I hope you will be satisfied – if not,

Louis d'Epinay, the mistress of Baron Grimm, by Jean-Etienne Liotard.

please let me know.' So M. le Duc hasn't a spark of honour and must have thought, 'After all, he's a young man and a stupid German into the bargain – (for all Frenchmen talk like this about the Germans) – so he'll be quite glad of it.' – But the stupid German was not at all glad of it, in fact he didn't take it. It amounted to this, that the Duke wanted to pay me for one hour instead of two – and that from *égard*. For he has already had, for the last four months, a concerto of mine for flute and harp, for which he has not yet paid me. So I am only waiting until the wedding is over and then I shall go to the house-keeper and demand my money. What annoys me most of all here is that these stupid Frenchmen seem to think I am still seven years old, because that was my age when they first saw me. This is perfectly true. Mme D'Épinay said as much to me quite seriously. They treat me here as a beginner – except, of course, the real musicians, who think differently. But it is the majority that counts. After my conversation with Grimm I went the very next day to Count Sickingen. He was entirely of my opinion – that I should have patience and wait for the arrival of Raaff, who will do everything in his power to help me. Then, if that is no use, Count Sickingen himself has offered to get me an appointment at Mainz. So that is my prospect at present. Meanwhile I shall do my utmost to get along here by teaching and to earn as much money as possible, which I am now doing in the fond hope that my circumstances may soon change; for I cannot deny, and must indeed confess, that I shall be delighted to be released from this place. For giving lessons here is no joke. Unless you wear yourself out by taking a large number of pupils, you cannot make much money. You must not think that this is laziness on my part. No, indeed! It just goes utterly against my genius and my manner of life. You know that I am, so to speak, soaked in music, that I am immersed in it all day long and that I love to plan works, study and meditate. Well, I am prevented from all this by my way of life here. I shall have a few free hours, it is true, but these few hours I shall need more for rest than for work. I told you in my last letter about the opera. I cannot help it – I must write a grand opera or none at all; if I write a small one, I shall get very little for it (for everything is taxed here). And should it have the misfortune not to please these stupid Frenchmen, all would be over – I should never get another commission to compose – I should have gained nothing by it – and my reputation would have suffered. If, on the other hand, I write a grand opera – the remuneration will be better – I shall be doing the work in which I delight – and I shall have better hopes of success, for with a big work you have a better chance of making your name. I assure you that if I am commissioned to write an opera, I shall have no fears whatever. True, the devil himself must certainly have invented the language of these people – and I fully realize the difficulties with which all composers have had to contend. But in spite of this I feel I am as well able to overcome them as anyone else. *Au contraire*, when I fancy, as I often do, that I have got the commission, my whole body seems to be on fire and I tremble from head to foot with eagerness to teach the French more thoroughly to know, appreciate and fear the Germans. For why is a grand opera never entrusted to a Frenchman? Why must it always be a foreigner? For me the most detestable part of the business would be the singers. Well, I am ready – I wish to avoid quarrels – but if I am challenged, I shall know how to defend myself. But I should prefer to avoid a duel, for I do not care to wrestle with dwarfs. God grant that a change may come soon! Meanwhile I shall certainly not fall short in industry, pains and labour. My hopes are centred on the winter, when everyone returns from the country. Meanwhile farewell – and continue to love me. My heart leaps up when I think of the happy day when I shall have the joy of seeing you again and embracing you with all my heart. *Adieu.* I kiss your hands 100,000 times, embrace my sister in brotherly fashion and remain your most obedient son

WOLFGANG AMADÉ MOZART

TO THE ABBÉ BULLINGER AT SALZBURG
Paris, 7 August 1778

Dearest Friend!

Allow me above all to thank you most warmly for the new proof of friendship you have given me by your kind interest in my dear father – first in preparing him for his loss and then in consoling him so sympathetically. You played your part most admirably – these are my father's own words. Most beloved friend, how can I thank you sufficiently? You have saved my dear father for me; I have you to thank that I still have him. Permit me to say no more on this subject and not to attempt to express my gratitude, for indeed I feel far too weak, too incompetent – too weary to do so. Most beloved friend! I am always your debtor. But patience! On my honour I am not yet in a position to repay what I owe you – but do not doubt me, for God will grant me the opportunity of showing by deeds what I am unable to express in words . . . You say that I should now think only of my father and that I should disclose all my thoughts to him with entire frankness and put my trust in him. How unhappy should I be if I needed the reminder! It was expedient that you should suggest it, but I am glad to say (and you will be glad to hear it) that I do not need this advice. In my last letter to my dear father I told him what I myself knew up to the time, assuring him that I should always report everything to him very fully and inform him candidly of my views, because I placed my entire confidence in him and trusted completely to his fatherly care, love and goodness. I feel sure that some day he will not deny me a request on which the whole happiness and peace of my life depend and which will certainly be quite fair and reasonable, for he cannot expect anything else from me. Dearest friend, do not let my father read this. You know him. He would only worry, and quite unnecessarily.

Now for our Salzburg story. You, most beloved friend, are well aware how I detest Salzburg – and not only on account of the injustices which my dear father and I have endured there, which in themselves would be enough to make us wish to forget such a place and blot it out of our memory for ever! . . . Perhaps you will misunderstand me and think that Salzburg is too small for me? If so, you are greatly mistaken. I have already given some of my reasons to my father. In the meantime, content yourself with this one, that Salzburg is no place for my talent. In the first place, professional musicians there are not held in much consideration; and, secondly, one hears nothing, there is no theatre, no opera; and even if they really wanted one, who is there to sing? For the last five or six years the Salzburg orchestra has always been rich in what is useless and superfluous, but very poor in what is necessary, and absolutely destitute of what is indispensable; and such is the case at the present moment . . .

TO HIS FATHER
Saint-Germain, 27 August 1778

. . . I should like to have written to you long ago, but just as I had started a letter (which is now lying in Paris) I was obliged to drive to St Germain, intending to return the same day. But I have now been here a week. I shall return to Paris as soon as possible, though I shall not lose much there by my absence, for I have now only one pupil, the others being in the country. I could not write to you before from here either, as we have been obliged to wait patiently for an opportunity to send a letter to Paris. Thank God, I am quite well, and I trust that both of you are the same. You must have patience – everything goes very slowly. I must make friends – France is rather like Germany in feeding people with praises. Yet there is some hope that by means of your friends you can make your fortune. The best part of the business is ⟨that food and lodging cost me nothing. When you write to the friends with whom I am staying[1], don't be too obsequious in your thanks. There are reasons for this of which I shall tell you some other time.⟩ . . .

TO HIS FATHER
Paris, 11 September 1778

Mon très cher Père!

I have received your three letters of August 13th, 27th and 31st, but I shall only reply to the last one, as it is the most important. When I read it through (M. Heina, who sends his compliments to you both, was with me), I trembled with joy, for I fancied myself already in your arms. It is true (and you will confess this yourself) that no great fortune is awaiting me in Salzburg. Yet, when I think of once more embracing you and my dear sister with all my heart, I care for no other advantage. This indeed is the only real excuse I can make to the people here who keep on shouting in my ears that I must remain in Paris: for I always reply at once: 'What do you mean? I am satisfied, and that settles it. There is one place where I can say I am at home, where I can live in peace and quiet with my most beloved father and my dearest sister, where I can do as I like, where apart from the duties of my appointment I am my own master, and where I have a permanent income and yet can go off when I like, and travel every second year. What more can I desire?' To tell you my real feelings, the only thing that disgusts me about Salzburg is the impossibility of mixing freely with the people and the low estimation in which the musicians are held there – and – that the Archbishop has no confidence in the experience of intelligent people, who have seen the world. For I assure you that people who do not travel (I mean those who cultivate the arts and learning) are indeed miserable creatures; and I protest that unless the Archbishop allows me to travel every second year, I can't possibly accept the engagement. A fellow of mediocre talent will remain a mediocrity,

1. Grimm and Mme d'Épinay.

whether he travels or not; but one of superior talent (which without impiety I cannot deny that I possess) will go to seed, if he always remains in the same place. If the Archbishop would only trust me, I should soon make his orchestra famous; of this there can be no doubt. I can assure you that this journey has not been unprofitable to me, I mean, from the point of view of composition, for, as for the clavier, I play it as well as I ever shall. But there is one thing more I must settle about Salzburg and that is that I shall not be kept to the violin, as I used to be. I will no longer be a fiddler. I want to conduct at the clavier and accompany arias. It would indeed have been a good thing if I could have obtained a written agreement regarding the post of *Kapellmeister*, for otherwise it may be that I shall have the honour of filling two posts and being paid for one – and in the end the Archbishop may again promote some stranger over my head. Dearest father! I must confess that were it not for the pleasure of seeing you both again, I really could not decide to accept . . .

. . . Well, I shall be able to . . . make it plain to you that M. Grimm may be able to help children, but not grown-up people – and – but no, I had better not write anything – and yet I must. Do not imagine that he – is the same as he was; were it not for Madame D'Épinay, I should not be in this house. And he need not be so proud of his hospitality – for there are four houses where I could have had both board and lodging. The good fellow doesn't know that, if I had remained in Paris, I should have cleared out of his house next month and gone to a less boorish and stupid household, where people can do you a kindness without constantly casting it in your teeth. Such conduct is enough to make me forget a benefit. But I will be more generous than he is – I am only sorry that I am not remaining here, for I would show him that I do not need him – and that I can do as well as his Piccinni – although I am only a German. The greatest kindness he has shown me has taken the form of fifteen *louis d'or*, which he lent me bit by bit during my mother's illness and death. – Is he afraid of losing them, I wonder? If he has any doubts about it, he really deserves to be kicked, for in that case he is distrusting my honesty (which is the only thing which is capable of driving me into a rage) and also my talents – but I know that he distrusts the latter, for he himself once said to me that he did not believe I was capable of composing a French opera. When I leave I shall return the fifteen *louis d'or* with thanks and I shall say a few very polite words . . . I am only sorry that when the Salzburg people flock to Mannheim for the next carnival and 'Rosemunde' is given, poor Mlle Weber will probably not please, or at least that they will not be able to judge her as she

deserves – for she has a miserable part – almost that of a *persona muta* – and has only to sing a few lines between the choruses. She has one aria where something good might be expected from the *ritornello*, but the voice part is *alla* Schweitzer, as if dogs were yelping. She has only one song, a sort of rondo in the second act, where she has an opportunity of sustaining her voice a little and showing what she can do. Yes, unhappy indeed is the singer, male or female, who falls into Schweitzer's hands, for as long as he lives he will never learn how to write for the voice! When I return to Salzburg, I shall certainly not fail to plead with great enthusiasm for my dear friend. Meanwhile, please do all you can for her, for you cannot give your son greater pleasure . . .

TO HIS FATHER
Strasbourg, 26 October–2 November 1778

Mon très cher Père!

As you see, I am still here and that too on the advice of Herr Frank and some other Strassburg bigwigs; but I am leaving to-morrow. In my last letter, which I hope you have received safely, I told you that on Saturday the 17th I was giving a concert of sorts, as to give a concert here is an even worse undertaking than in Salzburg. That, of course, is over now – I played quite alone and I engaged no musicians, so that at least I might lose nothing. Briefly, I took in three *louis d'or* in all. The chief receipts consisted in the shouts of *Bravo!* and *Bravissimo!* which echoed on all sides. Prince Max von Zweibrücken too honoured the concert with his presence. I need not tell you that everyone was pleased. I wanted to leave Strassburg at once, but they advised me to stay on until the following Saturday and give a grand concert in the theatre. I did so and to the surprise, indignation and disgrace of all the people of Strassburg, my receipts were exactly the same. The Director, M. Villeneuve, cursed the inhabitants of this really detestable town in a way that was delightful to listen to. I took in a little more money certainly, but the cost of the orchestra (who are very bad but demand to be paid handsomely), the lighting, the guard, the printing, the crowds of attendants at the entrances and so forth made up a considerable sum. Still I must tell you that the applause and clapping of hands made my ears ache as much as if the whole theatre had been full. All who were present loudly and publicly abused their fellow-citizens – and I told them all, that if I could have reasonably supposed that so few people would have come, I should gladly have given the concert gratis merely for the pleasure of

A print made in 1820 by François Jacques Oberthur, showing the market hall and cathedral in Strasbourg.

seeing the theatre well filled. And indeed I should have preferred it, for upon my word there is nothing more depressing than a large T-shaped table laid for eighty with only three at dinner. Besides, it was so cold – though indeed I soon warmed myself, for, in order to show these gentlemen of Strassburg how little I cared, I played a very long time for my own amusement, giving one more concerto than I had promised – and, in the end, extemporizing for quite a while. Well, that is over – and at least I have won honour and glory . . .

I trust that you received my last letter of October 15th from Strassburg. I don't want to run down M. Grimm any more; but I cannot help saying that it is entirely due to his stupidity in hurrying up my departure that my sonatas have not yet been engraved, or have not appeared – or at any rate that I have not yet received them. And when they do come, I shall probably find them full of mistakes. If I had only stayed three days longer in Paris, I could have corrected them myself and brought them with me. The engraver was in despair when I told him that I should not be able to revise them myself, but should have to commission someone else to do so. Why? Because, when I told Grimm that, as I could not spend three more days in his house, I was going to stay with Count Sickingen for the sake of the sonatas, he replied, his eyes sparkling with rage: 'Look here. If you leave my house before you leave Paris, I shall never look at you again as long as I live. In that case you must never come near me, for I shall be your worst enemy.' Well, self-control was indeed very necessary. Had it not been for you, who knew nothing about the whole affair, I should certainly have replied: 'Well, be my enemy; be so by all means. You are my enemy as it is, or you would not be preventing me from putting my affairs in order here – from doing what I have promised to do – and thereby preserving my honour and reputation – from making money and perhaps even my fortune. For if I present my sonatas to the Electress when I go to Munich, I shall be keeping my promise, I shall get a present – or even make my fortune.' But, as it was, I only bowed and went off without saying a word. Before I left Paris, however, I did say all this to him – but he answered me like an idiot – or like some wicked fellow who now and then prefers to behave like one . . . Strassburg is loth to let me go! You cannot think how much they esteem and love me here. They say that everything about me is so distinguished – that I am so composed – and polite – and have such excellent manners. Everyone knows me. As soon as they heard my name, the two Herren Silbermann and Herr Hepp, the organist, came to call on me, and also *Kapellmeister* Richter. The latter now lives very economically, for instead of forty bottles of wine a day he only swills about twenty . . .

The Place d'Armes, Strasbourg; an 18th-century engraving by Weis.

TO HIS FATHER
Mannheim, 12 November 1778

. . . God be praised that I am back again in my beloved Mannheim! I assure you, if you were here, you would say the same. I am staying with Madame Cannabich, who, with her family and all my good friends here, was almost beside herself with joy at seeing me again. We have not finished talking yet, for she is telling me of all the events and changes which have taken place during my absence. Since I came here I have not been able to lunch at home once, as there is a regular scramble to have me. In a word, Mannheim loves me as much as I love Mannheim. And I am not positive, but I believe that I may yet obtain an appointment here – here, not in Munich; for my belief is that the Elector ⟨will be glad to have his residence again in Mannheim, as he will not long be able to stand the insolence of those Bavarian gentry!⟩ You know that the Mannheim company is in Munich. Well, the Bavarians have already hissed there the two best actresses, Madame Toscani and Madame Urban, and there was such an uproar that ⟨the Elector himself⟩ leaned over his ⟨box⟩ and called out – 'Sh' – and when nobody took the slightest notice, he sent someone down to put a stop to it – and ⟨Count Seeau⟩, who had asked certain officers not to make such a noise, as ⟨the Elector⟩ did not like it, got the reply ⟨that they had paid to come in and would take orders from no one⟩. . . .

I beg you, dearest father, to make use of this affair at Salzburg and to speak so strongly and emphatically that the Archbishop may be led to think that perhaps I shall not come after all, so that he may thus be induced to give me a better salary; for I declare that I cannot think of the whole business with composure. Indeed the Archbishop cannot pay me enough for that slavery in Salzburg! As I said before, I feel the greatest pleasure at the thought of paying you a visit – but only annoyance and anxiety when I see myself back at that beggarly court! The Archbishop had better not begin to play the high and mighty with me as he used to – for it is not at all unlikely that I shall pull a long nose at him! Indeed it is quite likely; and I am sure that you too will share the pleasure which I shall have in so doing . . .

TO HIS FATHER
Mannheim, 3 December 1778

. . . Do answer the following questions. What do people in Salzburg think of the players? Is not the girl who sings called Kaiser? Does Herr Feiner play the *cor anglais* as well? Ah, if only we had clarinets too! You cannot imagine the glorious effect of a symphony with flutes, oboes and clarinets. I shall have much that is new to tell the Archbishop at my first audience and I shall make some suggestions as well. Ah, how much finer and better our orchestra might be, if only the Archbishop desired it. Probably the chief reason why it is not better is because there are far too many performances. I have no objection to the chamber music, only to the concerts on a larger scale. A propos – you do not mention it, but I assume that you have received the trunk; if not, Herr von Grimm is responsible. You will find in it the aria I wrote for Mlle Weber.[1] You have no idea what an effect it produces with instruments; you cannot judge of it by the score, for it must be rendered by a singer like Mlle Weber. Please do not give it to anyone, for that would be the greatest injustice, as it is written solely for her and fits her like a well-tailored garment. . . .

TO HIS FATHER
Kaysersheim, 18 December 1778

. . . As for the watch, you guessed rightly. I pawned it, but I only got five *louis d'or* for it, and that on account of the works, which were in good order – for the shape, as you know, was out of date and completely out of fashion. Talking of watches, I must tell you that I am bringing with me one for myself – a real Parisian one. You know the sort of thing my jewelled watch was – how inferior the little stones were, how clumsy and awkward its shape; but I would not have minded all that, had I not been obliged to spend so much money on having it repaired and regulated; yet in spite of that the watch would one day gain and the next day lose an hour or two. The watch the Elector gave me did just the same and, moreover, the works were even worse and more fragile. I exchanged these two watches and their chains for a Parisian one worth twenty *louis d'or*. So now at last I know what the time is – which I never managed to do with my five watches. At present, out of four watches I have at least one on which I can rely. . . .

1. K.294. 'Non so d'onde viene'.

TO HIS FATHER
Munich, 29 December 1778

... Thank God, I arrived here safely on the 25th, but until now it has been impossible for me to write to you. I am saving up everything until our happy and joyous meeting, for to-day I can only weep. . . .

TO HIS FATHER
Munich, 8 January 1779

... I swear to you on my honour that I cannot bear Salzburg or its inhabitants (I mean, the natives of Salzburg). Their language – their manners are quite intolerable to me. You have no idea what I suffered during Madame Robinig's visit here, for indeed it is a long time since I met such a fool; and, to annoy me still more, that idiotic and deadly dull Mosmayer was with her! Well, let's talk about something else. I went yesterday with my dear friend Cannabich to the Electress and presented my sonatas. . . . We spent over half an hour with her and she was very gracious. So that I may be paid soon, I have managed to let her know that I am leaving here in a few days. . . . Please believe that I have the most aching longing to embrace you and my dear sister once more. If only it were not in Salzburg! . . .

TO ARCHBISHOP HIERONYMUS COLLOREDO AT SALZBURG
Salzburg, January 1779

Your Grace,
  Most worthy Prince of the Holy Roman Empire!
    Most gracious Prince and Lord!
  After the decease of Cajetan Adlgasser your Grace was so good as to take me into your service. I therefore humbly beseech you to grant me a certificate of my appointment as Court Organist.
    I remain,
      Your Grace's most humble and obedient servant,
                    WOLFGANG AMADÉ MOZART

MUNICH
1780-81

Mon très cher Père!

My arrival here was happy and pleasant – happy, because no mishap occurred during the journey; and pleasant, because we could hardly wait for the moment to reach our destination, on account of our drive, which though short was most uncomfortable. Indeed, I assure you that none of us managed to sleep for a moment the whole night through. Why, that carriage jolted the very souls out of our bodies – and the seats were as hard as stone! After we left Wasserburg I really believed that I should never bring my behind to Munich intact. It became quite sore and no doubt was fiery red. For two whole stages I sat with my hands dug into the upholstery and my behind suspended in the air. But enough of this; it is all over now, though it will serve me as a warning rather to go on foot than to drive in a mail coach.

Now for Munich. We arrived here at one o'clock in the afternoon and on the very same evening I called on Count Seeau, for whom, as he was not at home, I left a note. On the following morning I went there with Becke, who sends his greetings to you all. Seeau has been moulded like wax by the Mannheim people ... I have just one request to make of the Abbate. Ilia's aria in Act II, Scene 2, should be altered slightly to suit what I require. 'Se il padre perdei, in te lo ritrovo'; this verse could not be better. But now comes what has always seemed unnatural to me – I mean, in an aria – and that is, a spoken aside. In a dialogue all these things are quite natural, for a few words can be spoken aside hurriedly; but in an aria where the words have to be repeated, it has a bad effect, and even if this were not the case, I should prefer an uninterrupted aria. The beginning may stand, if it suits him, for the poem is charming and, as it is absolutely natural and flowing and therefore as I have not got to contend with difficulties arising from the words, I can go on composing quite easily; for we have agreed to introduce here an aria *andantino* with obbligatos for four wind-instruments, that is, a flute, oboe, horn and bassoon. I beg you therefore to let me have the text as soon as possible. Now for a sorry story. I have not, it is true, the honour of being acquainted with the hero Dal Prato; but from the description I have been given of him I should say that Ceccarelli is almost the better of the two; for often in the middle of an aria his breath gives out; and, mark you, he has never been on any stage – and Raaff is like a statue. Well, just picture to yourself the scene in Act I. Now for a cheerful story. Madame Dorothea Wendling is *arcicontentissima* with her scene and insisted on hearing it played three times in succession. . . .

TO HIS FATHER
Munich, 13 November 1780

... Shall I soon have the aria for Madame Wendling?

The second duet is to be omitted altogether – and indeed with more profit than loss to the opera. For, when you read through the scene, you will see that it obviously becomes limp and cold by the addition of an aria or a duet, and very *gênant* for the other actors who must stand by doing nothing; and, besides, the noble struggle between Ilia and Idamante would be too long and thus lose its whole force. ...

The Krautermarkt in Munich; an 18th-century engraving by Georg Balthazar Probst.

The "Sonneck" house in Munich, where on the second floor Mozart spent the winter of 1780-81, and wrote Idomeneo; *an etching by Domenico Quaglio, 1811.*

TO HIS FATHER
Munich, 15 November 1780

... The aria is excellent now, but there is still one more alteration, for which Raaff is responsible. He is right, however, – and even if he were not, some courtesy ought to be shown to his grey hairs. He was with me yesterday. I ran through his first aria for him and he was very well pleased with it. Well – the man is old and can no longer show off in such an aria as that in Act II – 'Fuor del mar ho un mar nel seno'. So, as he has no aria in Act III and as his aria in Act I, owing to the expression of the words, cannot be as *cantabile* as he would like, he wishes to have a pretty one to sing (instead of the quartet) after his last speech, 'O Creta

129

Elisabeth Auguste Wendling, the soprano whom Mozart had known at Mannheim. She sang Elettra *in* Idomeneo.

fortunata! O me felice!' Thus too a useless piece will be got rid of – and Act III will be far more effective. In the last scene of Act II Idomeneo has an aria or rather a sort of cavatina between the choruses. Here it will be better to have a mere recitative, well supported by the instruments. For in this scene which will be the finest in the whole opera (on account of the action and grouping which were settled recently with Le Grand), there will be so much noise and confusion on the stage that an aria at this particular point would cut a poor figure – and moreover there is the thunderstorm, which is not likely to subside during Herr Raaff's aria, is it? The effect, therefore, of a recitative between the choruses will be infinitely better. Lisel Wendling has also sung through her two arias half a dozen times and is delighted with them. I have it from a third party that the two Wendlings praised their arias very highly; and as for Raaff, he is my best and dearest friend!

But to my *molto amato castrato* Dal Prato I shall have to teach the whole opera. He has no notion how to sing a cadenza effectively, and his voice is so uneven!
. . .

My sister must not be lazy, but practise hard, for people are already looking forward to hearing her play. My lodging is in the Burggasse at M. Fiat's. But it is not at all necessary to add the address, for at the post office they know me – and know too where I am living. *Adieu.* . . .

TO HIS FATHER
Munich, 22 November 1780

. . . The day before yesterday Dal Prato sang at the concert – most disgracefully. I bet you that fellow will never get through the rehearsals, still less the opera. Why, the rascal is rotten to the core. – Come in! Why, it's Herr Panzacchi, who has already paid me three visits and has just invited me to lunch on Sunday. I hope I shall not have the same experience as the two of us had with the coffee. He has enquired very meekly whether instead of '*se la sa*' he may not sing '*se co la*' – Well, why not '*ut re mi fa sol la*'? . . . When the *castrato* comes, I have to sing with him, for I have to teach him his whole part as if he were a child. He has not got a farthing's worth of method. . . .

131

TO HIS FATHER
Munich, 29 November 1780

. . . Tell me, don't you think that the speech of the subterranean voice is too long?
Consider it carefully. Picture to yourself the theatre, and remember that the voice
must be terrifying – must penetrate – that the audience must believe that it really
exists. Well, how can this effect be produced if the speech is too long, for in this
case the listeners will become more and more convinced that it means nothing. If
the speech of the Ghost in 'Hamlet' were not so long, it would be far more
effective. It is quite easy to shorten the speech of the subterranean voice and it
will gain thereby more than it will lose.

For the march in Act II, which is heard in the distance, I require mutes for the
trumpets and horns, which it is impossible to get here. Will you send me one of
each by the next mail coach, so that I may have them copied?

Dorothea Wendling, Elisabeth's sister-in-law. Mozart wrote the aria K.486a for her.

TO HIS FATHER
Munich, 1 December 1780

... Yesterday morning Mr Raaff came to see me again in order to hear the aria in Act II. The fellow is as infatuated with it as a young and ardent lover might be with his fair one, for he sings it at night before going to sleep and in the morning when he awakes. As I heard first from a reliable source and now from his own lips, he said to Herr von Viereck, Chief Equerry, and to Herr von Castel: 'Hitherto both in recitatives and arias I have always been accustomed to alter my parts to suit me, but here everything remains as it was written, for I cannot find a note which does not suit me, etc.' *Enfin*, he is as happy as a king. ...

TO HIS FATHER
Munich, 5 December 1780

... I am very much disappointed, because in that particular letter I asked you for something which I urgently require for my opera – and that is – to send me a trumpet mute – of the kind we had made in Vienna – and also one for the horn – which you can get from the watchmen. I need them for the march in Act II. Please send them soon. In regard to the *ultima aria* for Raaff, I mentioned that we both wished to have more pleasing and gentle words. The *era* is forced. The beginning would do quite well, but *gelida massa* – again is hard. In short, far-fetched or unusual words are always unsuitable in an aria which ought to be pleasing.

... You must accustom yourself a little to kissing. You could practise in the meantime on Madame Maresquelle. For here whenever you call at Dorothea Wendling's (where everything is rather in the French style) you will have to embrace both mother and daughter – but on the chin, of course, so that their rouge may not become blue. But more of this next time. Adieu. I kiss your hands a thousand times and embrace my sister with all my heart and am ever your most obedient son

WOLFGANG AMADÉ MOZART

P.S. – Do not forget about my black suit; I must have it, or I shall be laughed at, which is never very pleasant.

TO HIS FATHER
Munich, 19 December 1780

... The scene between father and son in Act I and the first scene in Act II between Idomeneo and Arbace are both too long. They would certainly bore the audience, particularly as in the first scene both the actors are bad, and in the second, one of them is; besides, they only contain a narrative of what the spectators have already seen with their own eyes. These scenes are being printed as they stand. But I should like the Abbate to indicate how they may be shortened – and as drastically as possible, – for otherwise I shall have to shorten them myself. These two scenes cannot remain as they are – I mean, when set to music. ...

TO HIS FATHER
Munich, 27 December 1780

... In regard to the two scenes which are to be shortened, it was not my suggestion, but one to which I have consented – my reason being that Raaff and Dal Prato spoil the recitative by singing it without any spirit or fire, and so monotonously. They are the most wretched actors that ever walked on a stage. ... The Elector was there too. This time we rehearsed with the whole orchestra. ... After the first act the Elector called out to me quite loudly: *Bravo!* ... As he was not sure whether he could remain much longer, we had to perform the aria with obbligatos for wind-instruments and the thunderstorm at the beginning of Act II, when he again expressed his approval in the kindest manner and said with a laugh: 'Who would believe that such great things could be hidden in so small a head?'

... To return, Raaff is the best and most honest fellow in the world, but so tied to old-fashioned routine that flesh and blood cannot stand it. Consequently, it is very difficult to compose for him, but very easy if you choose to compose commonplace arias, as, for instance, the first one, 'Vedrommi intorno'. When you hear it, you will say that it is good and beautiful – but if I had written it for Zonca it would have suited the words much better. Raaff is too fond of everything which is cut and dried, and he pays no attention to expression. I have just had a bad time with him over the quartet. The more I think of this quartet, as it will be performed on the stage, the more effective I consider it; and it has pleased all those who have heard it played on the clavier. Raaff alone thinks it will produce no effect whatever. He said to me when we were by ourselves: *'You can't let yourself go in it. It gives me no scope.'* As if in a quartet the words should not be spoken much more than sung. That kind of thing he does not understand at all. All I said was:

*Leopold Mozart with his daughter and son at the keyboard, with a portrait of his wife
behind, painted in Salzburg by Johann Nepomuk de la Croce, 1780-81.*

'My very dear friend, if I knew of one single note which ought to be altered in this
quartet, I would alter it at once. But so far there is nothing in my opera with
which I am so pleased as with this quartet; and when you have once heard it sung
in concert, you will talk very differently. I have taken great pains to serve you
well in your two arias, I shall do the same with your third one – and shall hope to
succeed. But as far as trios and quartets are concerned, the composer must have a
free hand.' Whereupon he said that he was satisfied. . . .

TO HIS FATHER
Munich, 30 December 1780

Mon très cher Père!

A Happy New Year! Forgive me for not writing much this time, but I am up to
the eyes in work. I have not quite finished the third act, and, as there is no extra
ballet, but only an appropriate divertissement in the opera, I have the honour of
composing the music for that as well; but I am glad of it, for now all the music

135

will be by the same composer. The third act will turn out to be at least as good as the first two – in fact, I believe, infinitely better – and I think that it may be said with truth, *finis coronat opus*. The Elector was so pleased at the rehearsal that, as I wrote to you the other day, he praised my opera most highly at his *levée* on the following morning – and again at court in the evening. I have heard too from a very good source that on the same evening after the rehearsal he spoke of my music to everyone with whom he conversed, saying: 'I was quite surprised. No music has ever made such an impression on me. It is magnificent music.' The day before yesterday we had a rehearsal of recitatives at Wendling's and we went through the quartet together. We repeated it six times and now it goes well. The stumbling-block was Dal Prato; the fellow is utterly useless. His voice would not be so bad if he did not produce it in his throat and larynx. But he has no intonation, no method, no feeling. He sings – well, like the best of the boys who come to be tested in the hope of getting a place in the chapel choir. Raaff is delighted that he was mistaken about the quartet and no longer doubts its effect. I

LEFT Johann Baptist Wendling, Dorothea's husband, a flautist with the Mannheim orchestra.
RIGHT Antaon Raaff, the tenor, an engraving by G.F. Touchemolin.

am now in a difficulty in regard to his last aria, and you must help me out of it. He cannot stomach the *'rinvigorir'* and *'ringiovenir'* – and these two words make the whole aria distasteful to him. It is true that *mostrami* and *vienmi* are also not good, but the two final words are the worst of all. To avoid the shake on the *i* in the first *rinvigorir*, I really ought to transfer it to the *o* . . . Please give my greetings to all my good friends and my New Year wishes too. I drew the fifteen *gulden* yesterday. I shall not have very much left, for there are a hundred trifles which make inroads on my money; and I certainly do not spend it unnecessarily. Why, it cost me seven *gulden*, twenty-four *kreutzer*, just to have my black coat turned, a new damask lining put in, and a sleeve of my brown costume patched. So I must ask you to send me another draft. It is just as well to have something in hand, as I really can't go about in a penniless condition. *Adieu.* I kiss your hands a thousand times and embrace my sister with all my heart and am ever your most obedient son

WOLFGANG AMADÉ MOZART

My compliments to dear Theresa. The maid who waits on me here is also a Theresa – but, Heavens! how different from our Theresa from Linz, in beauty, virtue, charms – and a thousand other merits! . . .

TO HIS FATHER
Munich, 3 January 1781

Mon très cher Père!

My head and my hands are so full of Act III that it would be no wonder if I were to turn into a third act myself. This act alone has cost me more trouble than a whole opera, for there is hardly a scene in it which is not extremely interesting. The accompaniment to the subterranean voice consists of five instruments only, that is, three trombones and two French horns, which are placed in the same quarter as that from which the voice proceeds. At this point the whole orchestra is silent. The dress rehearsal will take place for certain on January 20th, and the first performance on the 22nd. All you will both require and all that you need bring with you is one black dress – and another, for everyday wear – when you are just visiting intimate friends, where there is no standing on ceremony – so that you may save your black one a little; and, if you like, a more elegant dress to wear at the ball and the *académie masquée.* . . .

137

No doubt we shall have a good many points to raise in Act III, when it is staged. For example, in Scene 6, after Arbace's aria, I see that Varesco has Idomeneo, Arbace, etc. How can the latter reappear immediately? Fortunately he can stay away altogether. But for safety's sake I have composed a somewhat longer introduction to the High Priest's recitative. After the mourning chorus the King and all his people go away; and in the following scene the directions are, '*Idomeneo in ginocchione nel tempio*'. That is quite impossible. He must come in with his whole suite. A march must be introduced here, and I have therefore composed

IDOMENEO.
DRAMMA
PER
MUSICA
DA RAPPRESENTARSI
NEL TEATRO NUOVO DI
CORTE
PER COMANDO
DI S. A. S E.
CARLO TEODORO
Come Palatino del Rheno, Duca dell'
alta, e bafsa Baviera, e del Palatinato
Superiore, etc. etc. Archidapifero,
et Elettore, etc. etc.

NEL CARNOVALE
1 7 8 1.

La Poesia è del Signor Abate Gianbattista Varesco
Capellano di Corte di S. A. R. l'Arcivescovo, e Principe di Salisburgo.
La Musica è del Signor Maestro Wolfgango Amadeo Mozart Academico di Bologna, e di Verona, in
fin attual servizio di S. A. R. l'Arcivescovo, e Principe
di Salisburgo.
La Traduzione è del Signor Andrea Schachtner,
pure in attual servizio di S. A. R. l'Arcivescovo, e
Principe di Salisburgo.

MONACO.
Aprefso Francesco Giuseppe Thuille.

The title page of the libretto of Idomeneo, Re di Creta, *first performed in Munich on 29
January 1781.*

a very simple one for two violins, viola, cello and two oboes, to be played *a mezza voce*. While it is going on, the King appears and the priests prepare the offerings for the sacrifice. The King then kneels down and begins the prayer.

In Elettra's recitative, after the subterranean voice has spoken, there ought to be an indication – *Partono*. I forgot to look at the copy which has been made for the printer to see whether there is one, and if so, where it comes. It seems to me very silly that they should hurry away so quickly for no better reason than to allow Madame Elettra to be alone. . . .

FIRST YEARS IN VIENNA

TO HIS FATHER
Vienna, 17 March 1781

. . . Now for the Archbishop. I have a charming room in the very same house where he is staying. Brunetti and Ceccarelli are lodging in another. *Che distinzione!* . . . We lunch about twelve o'clock, unfortunately somewhat too early for me. Our party consists of the two valets, that is, the body and soul attendants of His Worship, the *contrôleur*, Herr Zetti, the confectioner, the two cooks, Ceccarelli, Brunetti and – my insignificant self. By the way, the two valets sit at the top of the table, but at least I have the honour of being placed above the cooks. Well, I almost believe myself back in Salzburg! A good deal of silly, coarse joking goes on at table, but no one cracks jokes with me, for I never say a word, or, if I have to speak, I always do so with the utmost gravity; and as soon as I have finished my lunch, I get up and go off. We do not meet for supper, but we each receive three ducats – which goes a long way! The Archbishop is so kind as to add to his lustre by his household, robs them of their chance of earning and pays them nothing. . . . Well, I must wait and see whether I shall get anything. If I get nothing, I shall go to the Archbishop and tell him with absolute frankness that if he will not allow me to earn anything, then he must pay me, for I cannot live at my own expense.

TO HIS FATHER
Vienna, 24–28 March 1781

... Oh, had I but known that I should be in Vienna during Lent, I should have written a short oratorio and produced it in the theatre for my benefit, as they all do here. I could easily have written it beforehand, for I know all the voices. How gladly would I give a public concert, as is the custom here. But I know for certain that I should never get permission to do so – for just listen to this! You know that there is a society in Vienna which gives concerts for the benefit of the widows of musicians, at which every professional musician plays gratis. . . . No virtuoso who has any love for his neighbour, refuses to give his services, if the society asks him to do so. Besides, in this way he can win the favour both of the Emperor and of the public. Starzer was commissioned to invite me and I agreed at once, adding, however, that I must first obtain the consent of my Prince, which I had not the slightest doubt that he would give – as it was a matter of charity, or at any rate a good work, for which I should get no fee. He would not permit me to take part. All the nobility in Vienna have made a grievance of it. . . .

I could not finish this letter, because Herr von Kleinmayr fetched me in his carriage to go to a concert at Baron Braun's. So I can now add that ⟨the Archbishop has given me permission to play at the concert for the widows⟩. For Starzer went to the concert at ⟨Galitsin's⟩ and he and ⟨all the nobility worried the Archbishop until he gave his consent⟩. I am so glad.

TO HIS FATHER
Vienna, 4 April 1781

You want to know how we are getting on in Vienna – or rather, I hope, how I am getting on; for the other two I do not count as having anything to do with me. I told you in a recent letter that ⟨the Archbishop⟩ is a great hindrance to me here, for he has done me out of at least a hundred ducats, which I could certainly have made by giving ⟨a concert in the theatre⟩. Why, the ladies themselves offered of their own accord to distribute the tickets. I can say with truth that I was very well pleased with the Viennese public yesterday, when I played at the concert for the widows in the Kärntnerthor theatre. I had to begin all over again, because there was no end to the applause. Well, how much do you suppose I should make if I were to give a concert of my own, now that the public has got to know me? But this ⟨arch-booby⟩ of ours will not allow it. He does not want his people to have

The Kärntnerthortheater in Vienna, one of two official court theatres in the 1780s.

any profit – only loss. Still, he will not be able to achieve this in my case, for if I have two pupils I am better off in Vienna than in Salzburg. Nor do I need his board and lodging. Now listen to this. Brunetti said to-day at table that Arco had told him on behalf of the Archbishop that he ⟨Brunetti⟩ was to inform us that we were to receive the money for our mail coach fares and to leave before Sunday. On the other hand, whoever wanted to stay on ⟨oh, how judicious!⟩ could do so, but would have to live at his own expense, as he would no longer get board and lodging from the Archbishop.

... ⟨I shall certainly fool the Archbishop to the top of his bent and how I shall enjoy doing it!⟩ I shall do it with the greatest politesse – ⟨and he will not be able to dodge me⟩. Enough of this. In my next letter I shall be able to tell you more. Rest assured that unless I am in a good position and can see clearly that it is to my advantage to do so. I shall certainly not remain in Vienna. But if it is to my advantage, why should I not profit by it? Meanwhile, ⟨you are drawing two salaries and have not got to feed me⟩. If I stay here, I can promise you that I shall soon ⟨be able to send home some money.⟩ ...

TO HIS FATHER
Vienna, 11 April 1781

. . . Sunday week, April 22nd, Ceccarelli and I are to go home. When I think that I must leave Vienna without bringing home at least a thousand *gulden*, my heart is sore indeed. So, for the sake of a ⟨malevolent Prince⟩ who ⟨plagues me⟩ every day and only pays me a ⟨lousy salary of four hundred *gulden*⟩, I am to ⟨kick away a thousand⟩? For I should ⟨certainly⟩ make that sum if I ⟨were to give a concert⟩.

Maria Wilhelmine, Countess Thun-Hohenstein, to whose house in Vienna Mozart was frequently invited after March 1781; a silhouette by G.F. Meischner, 1784.

When we had our first grand concert in this house, ⟨the Archbishop sent each of us four ducats⟩. At the last concert for which I composed ⟨a new rondo for Brunetti⟩, a ⟨new sonata⟩ for myself, and ⟨also a new rondo for Ceccarelli⟩, I received ⟨nothing⟩. But what made me almost ⟨desperate⟩ was that the very same ⟨evening⟩ we had this ⟨foul⟩ concert I was invited to Countess Thun's, but of course could not go; and who should be there but ⟨the Emperor⟩! Adamberger and Madame Weigl were there and received fifty ducats each! Besides, what an opportunity! I cannot, of course, arrange for ⟨the Emperor to be told that if he wishes to hear me he must hurry up⟩, as ⟨I am leaving⟩ Vienna in a few days. One has to ⟨wait for⟩ things like that. Besides, I ⟨neither can nor will remain here unless I give a concert⟩. Still, even if I have only two ⟨pupils⟩, I am better off here than in Salzburg. But if I had 1,000 or 1,200 *gulden* ⟨in my pocket, I should be a little more solicited⟩ and therefore ⟨exact better terms⟩. That is what he ⟨will not

allow, the inhuman villain⟩. I must ⟨call him that, for he is a villain and all the nobility call him so⟩. But enough of this. Oh, how I hope to hear by the next post whether I am to go on ⟨burying my youth and my talents in Salzburg, or whether I may make my fortune as best I can, and not wait until it is too late⟩. It is true ⟨that I cannot make my fortune⟩ in a fortnight or three weeks, any more than I ⟨can make it in a thousand years in Salzburg⟩. Still, it is more pleasant to wait ⟨with a thousand *gulden* a year⟩ than with ⟨four hundred⟩. . . .

TO HIS FATHER
Vienna, 28 April 1781

Mon très cher Père!

You are looking forward to my return with great joy, my dearest father! That is the only thing that can make me decide to leave Vienna. I am writing all this in our plain language, because the whole world knows and should know that the Archbishop of Salzburg has only you to thank, my most beloved father, that he did not lose me yesterday for ever (I mean, as far as he himself is concerned). We had a grand concert here yesterday, probably the last of them. It was a great success, and in spite of all the obstacles put in my way by His Archiepiscopal Grace, I still had a better orchestra than Brunetti. Ceccarelli will tell you about it. I had a great deal of worry over arranging this. Oh, it is far easier to talk than to write about it. If, however, anything similar should happen again, which I hope may not be the case, I can assure you that I shall lose all patience; and certainly you will forgive me for doing so. And I beg you, dearest father, to allow me to return to Vienna during Lent towards the end of the next carnival. This depends on you alone and not on the Archbishop. For if he does not grant me permission, I shall go all the same; and this visit will certainly not do me any harm. . . .

TO HIS FATHER
Vienna, 9 May 1781

Mon très cher Père!

I am still seething with rage! And you, my dearest and most beloved father, are doubtless in the same condition. My patience has been so long tried that at last it

143

has given out. I am no longer so unfortunate as to be in Salzburg service. To-day is a happy day for me. Just listen.

Twice already that – I don't know what to call him – has said to my face the greatest *sottises* and *impertinences*, which I have not repeated to you, as I wished to spare your feelings, and for which I only refrained from taking my revenge on the spot because you, my most beloved father, were ever before my eyes. He called me a ⟨rascal⟩ and a ⟨dissolute fellow⟩ and told me to be off. And I – endured it all, although I felt that not only my honour but yours also was being attacked. But, as you would have it so, I was silent. Now listen to this. A week ago the footman came up unexpectedly and told me to clear out that very instant. All the others had been informed of the day of their departure, but not I. Well, I shoved everything into my trunk in haste, and old Madame Weber has been good enough to take me into her house, where I have a pretty room. Moreover, I am living with people who are obliging and who supply me with all the things which one often requires in a hurry and which one cannot have when one is living alone. I decided to travel home by the *ordinaire* on Wednesday, that is, to-day, May 9th. But as I could not collect the money still due to me within that time, I postponed my departure until Saturday. When I presented myself to-day, the valets informed me that the Archbishop wanted to give me a parcel to take charge of. I asked whether it was urgent. They told me, 'Yes, it is of the greatest importance.' 'Well,' said I, 'I am sorry that I cannot have the privilege of serving His Grace, for ⟨on account of the reason mentioned above⟩ I cannot leave before Saturday. I have left this house, and must live at my own expense. So it is evident that I cannot leave Vienna until I am in a position to do so. For surely no one will ask me to ruin myself.' Kleinmayr, Moll, Bönike and the two valets all said that I was perfectly right. When I went in to the Archbishop – that reminds me, I must tell you first of all that ⟨Schlauka⟩ advised me to ⟨make the excuse⟩ that the ⟨*ordinaire* was already full⟩, a reason which would carry more weight with him than if I gave him the true one, – well, when I entered the room, his first words were:– Archbishop: 'Well, young fellow, when are you going off?' I: 'I intended to go to-night, but all the seats were already engaged.' Then he rushed full steam ahead, without pausing for breath – I was the ⟨most dissolute fellow he knew – no one⟩ served him so badly as I did – I had better leave to-day or else he would write home and have my ⟨salary⟩ stopped. I couldn't get a word in edgeways, for he blazed away like a fire. I listened to it all very calmly. He lied to my face that my salary was five hundred *gulden*, called me ⟨a scoundrel, a rascal, a vagabond⟩. Oh,

I really cannot tell you all he said. At last my blood began to boil, I could no longer contain myself, and I said, 'So Your Grace is not satisfied with me?' 'What, you dare to threaten me – you ⟨scoundrel⟩? There is the ⟨door⟩! Look out, for I will have nothing more to do with such ⟨a miserable wretch⟩.' At last I said: 'Nor I with you!' 'Well, be off!'[1] When leaving the room, I said, 'This is final. You shall have it to-morrow in writing.' Tell me now, most beloved father, did I not say the word too late rather than too soon? Just listen for a moment. My honour is more precious to me than anything else and I know that it is so to you also. Do not be the least bit anxious about me. I am so sure of my success in Vienna that I would have resigned even without the slightest reason; and now that I have a very good reason – and that too thrice over – I cannot make a virtue of it. *Au contraire*, I had twice played the coward and I could not do so a third time.

As long as ⟨the Archbishop⟩ remains here, I shall not ⟨give a concert⟩. You are altogether mistaken if you think that I shall ⟨get a bad name with the Emperor and the nobility⟩, for ⟨the Archbishop⟩ is detested here and ⟨most of all by the Emperor⟩. In fact, he is furious because the Emperor did not invite him to Laxenburg. By the next post I shall send you a little ⟨money⟩ to show you that I am not starving. Now please be cheerful, for my good luck is just beginning, and I trust that my good luck will be yours also. Write to me ⟨in cipher⟩ that you are pleased – and indeed you may well be so – ⟨but in public rail at me as much as you like, so that none of the blame may fall on you. But if, in spite of this, the Archbishop should be the slightest bit impertinent to you⟩, come at once with my ⟨sister to Vienna, for I give you my word of honour that there is enough for all three of us to live on⟩. Still, I should prefer it if you could ⟨hold out⟩ for another year. . . .

1. Throughout this conversation, as reported by Mozart, the Archbishop used the contemptuous form of address 'Er'.

A view of Vienna from the Upper Belvedere by Canaletto, c. 1760.

TO HIS FATHER
Vienna, 12 May 1781

Mon très cher Père!

You will know from my last letter that I have asked the Prince for my discharge, because he himself has told me to go. For already in the two previous audiences he said to me: 'Clear out of this, if you will not serve me properly.' He will deny it, of course, but all the same it is as true as that God is in His Heaven. Is it any wonder then if, after being roused to fury by 'knave, scoundrel, rascal, dissolute fellow', and other similar dignified expressions uttered by a Prince, I at last took 'Clear out of this' in its literal sense? On the following day I gave Count Arco a petition to present to His Grace, and I returned my travelling expenses, which consisted of fifteen *gulden*, forty *kreutzer* for the diligence, and two ducats for my keep. He refused to take either and assured me that I could not resign without your consent, my father. 'That is your duty', said he. I retorted that I knew my duty to my father as well as he did and possibly better, and that I should be very sorry if I had to learn it first from him. 'Very well', he replied, 'if he is satisfied, you can ask for your discharge; if not, you can ask for it all the same.' A pretty distinction! All the edifying things which the Archbishop said to me during my three audiences, particularly during the last one, all the subsequent remarks which this fine servant of God made to me, had such an excellent effect on my health that in the evening I was obliged to leave the opera in the middle of the first act and go home and lie down. For I was very feverish. I was trembling in every limb, and I was staggering along the street like a drunkard. I also stayed at home the following day, yesterday, and spent the morning in bed, as I had taken tamarind water.

The Count has also been so kind as to write very flattering things about me to his father, all of which you will probably have had to swallow by now. They will certainly contain some astounding passages. But whoever writes a comedy and wants to win applause, must exaggerate a little and not stick too closely to the truth. Besides, you must remember how very anxious these gentlemen are to serve the Archbishop.

Well, without losing my temper (for my health and my life are very precious to me and I am only sorry when circumstances force me to get angry) I just want to set down the chief accusation which was brought against me in respect of my service. I did not know that I was a valet – and that was the last straw. I ought to have idled away a couple of hours every morning in the antechamber. True, I was often told that I ought to present myself, but I could never remember that this was part of my duty, and I only turned up punctually whenever the Archbishop sent for me.

I will now confide to you very briefly my inflexible determination, but so that the whole world may hear it. If I were offered a salary of 2,000 *gulden* by the Archbishop of Salzburg and only 1,000 *gulden* somewhere else, I should still take the second offer. For instead of the extra 1,000 *gulden* I should enjoy good health and peace of mind. I trust, therefore, by all the fatherly love which you have lavished on me so richly from my childhood and for which I can never thank you enough (though indeed I can show it least of all in Salzburg), that, if you wish to see your son well and happy, you will say nothing to me about this affair and that you will bury it in the deepest oblivion. For one word about it would suffice to embitter me again and – if you will only admit it – to fill you too with bitterness.

Now farewell, and be glad that your son is no coward. I kiss your hands a thousand times, embrace my sister with all my heart and am ever your most obedient son

WOLFGANG AMADÉ MOZART

TO HIS FATHER

Vienna, 16 May 1781

Mon très cher Père!

I could hardly have supposed otherwise than that in the heat of the moment you would have written just such a letter as I have been obliged to read, for the event must have taken you by surprise (especially as you were actually expecting my arrival). But by this time you must have considered the matter more carefully and, as a man of honour, you must feel the insult more strongly, and must know and realize that ⟨what you have thought likely to happen, has happened already. It is always more difficult to get away in Salzburg, for there he is lord and master, but here he is – a nobody, an underling, just as I am in his eyes⟩. Besides, pray believe me when I say that I know you and know ⟨the strength of my affection⟩ for you. Even if ⟨the Archbishop had given me another two hundred *gulden*⟩ – and I – I had agreed – we should have had the ⟨same old story⟩ over again. Believe me, most beloved father, I need all my manliness to write to you what common sense dictates. God knows how hard it is for me to leave you; but, even if I had to beg, I could never serve such a master again; for, as long as I live, I shall never forget what has happened. I implore you, I adjure you, by all you hold dear in this

Aloysia Lange (née Weber), the young singer with whom Mozart fell in love in 1778.

world, to strengthen me in this resolution instead of trying to dissuade me from it, for if you do you will only make me unproductive. ⟨My desire and my hope is to gain honour, fame and money⟩, and I have every confidence that I shall be ⟨more useful to you in Vienna than if I were to return to Salzburg. The road to Prague⟩ is now less closed to me than ⟨if I were in Salzburg⟩. What you ⟨say about the Webers⟩, I do assure you is not true. I was a fool, I admit, about Aloysia Lange, but what does not a man do ⟨when he is in love⟩? Indeed I loved her truly, and even now I feel that she is not a matter of indifference to me. It is, therefore, a good thing for me that her husband is a jealous fool and lets her go nowhere, so that I seldom have an opportunity of seeing her. Believe me when I say that ⟨old Madame Weber is a very obliging woman⟩ and that I cannot do enough for her in return for her kindness, as unfortunately I have no time to do so. Well, I am longing for a letter from you, my dearest and most beloved father. Cheer up your son, for it is only the thought of displeasing you that can make him unhappy in his very promising circumstances. *Adieu.* A thousand farewells. I am ever, and I kiss your hands a thousand times as, your most obedient son

W. A. M

TO HIS FATHER
Vienna, 19 May 1781

Mon très cher Père!

I too do not know how to begin this letter[1], my dearest father, for I have not yet recovered from my astonishment and shall never be able to do so, if you continue to think and to write as you do. I must confess that there is not a single touch in your letter by which I recognize my father! I see a father, indeed, but not that most beloved and most loving father, who cares for his own honour and for that of his children – in short, not my father. But it must have been a dream. You are awake now and need no reply from me to your points in order to be fully convinced that – now more than ever – I can never abandon my resolve. Yet, because in certain passages my honour and my character are most cruelly assailed, I must reply to these points. You say that you can never approve of my having tendered my resignation while I was in Vienna. I should have thought that if I wished to do so (although at the time I did not, or I should have done so on the first occasion) the most sensible thing was to do it in a place where I had a good standing and the finest prospects in the world. It is possible that you will not approve this in the presence of the Archbishop, but to me you cannot but applaud my action. You say that the only way to save my honour is to abandon my resolve. How can you perpetrate such a contradiction! When you wrote this you surely did not bear in mind that such a recantation would prove me to be the basest fellow in the world. All Vienna knows that I have left the Archbishop, and all Vienna knows the reason! Everyone knows that it was because my honour was insulted – and, what is more, insulted three times. And am I publicly to prove the contrary? Am I to make myself out to be a cowardly sneak and the Archbishop a worthy prince? No one would like to do the former, and I least of all; and the latter God alone can accomplish, if it be His will to enlighten him. You say that I have never shown you any affection and therefore ought now to show it for the first time. Can you really say this? You add that I will never sacrifice any of my pleasures for your sake. But what pleasures have I here? The pleasure of taking trouble and pains to fill my purse? You seem to think that I am revelling in pleasures and amusements. Oh, how you deceive yourself indeed! . . . If you call it pleasure to be rid of a prince, who does not pay a fellow and bullies him to death, then it is true that my pleasure is great. If I were to do nothing but think and work from early morning till late at night, I would gladly do so, rather than depend upon the favour of such a – I dare not call him by his right name. I

1. Mozart is obviously quoting the opening sentence of his father's last letter

151

have been forced to take this step, so I cannot deviate from my course by a hair's breadth – it is quite impossible! All that I can say to you is this, that on your account – but solely on your account, my father – I am very sorry that I was driven to take this step, and that I wish that the Archbishop had acted more judiciously, if only in order that I might have been able to devote my whole life to you. To please you, my most beloved father, I would sacrifice my happiness, my health and my life. But my honour – that I prize, and you too must prize it, above everything. You may show this to Count Arco and to all Salzburg too. After that insult, that threefold insult, were the Archbishop to offer me 1,200 *gulden* in person, I would not accept them. I am no skunk, no rascal; and, had it not been for you, I should not have waited for him to say to me for the third time, 'Clear out of this', without taking him at his word! What am I saying? Waited! Why, I should have said it, and not he! I am only surprised that the Archbishop should have behaved with so little discretion, particularly in a place like Vienna! Well, he will see that he has made a mistake. Prince Breuner and Count Arco need the Archbishop, but I do not; and if the worst comes to the worst and he forgets all the duties of a prince – of a spiritual prince – then come and join me in Vienna. You can get four hundred *gulden* anywhere. Just imagine how he would disgrace himself in the eyes of the Emperor, who already hates him, if he were to do that! My sister too would get on much better in Vienna than in Salzburg. There are many distinguished families here who hesitate to engage a male teacher, but would give handsome terms to a woman. Well, all these things may happen some day. . . .

TO HIS FATHER
Vienna, between 26 May and 2 June 1781

. . . The Archbishop runs me down to everyone here and has not the sense to see that such a proceeding does him no credit; for I am more highly respected in Vienna than he is. He is only known as a presumptuous, conceited ecclesiastic, who despises everyone here, whereas I am considered a very amiable person . . .

TO HIS FATHER
Vienna, 2 June 1781

Mon très cher Père!

You will have gathered from my last letter that I have spoken to Count Arco himself. Praise and thanks be to God that everything has passed off so well! Do not be anxious; you have nothing whatever ⟨to fear⟩ from ⟨the Archbishop⟩, for Count Arco did not say a single word to suggest that I ought to take care or the affair ⟨might injure you⟩. When he told me that you had written to him and had complained bitterly about me, I immediately interrupted him and said: 'And have I not heard from him too? He has written to me in such a strain that I have often thought I should go crazy. But, however much I reflect, I simply cannot, etc.' Upon which he said: 'Believe me, you allow yourself to be far too easily dazzled in Vienna. A man's reputation here lasts a very short time. At first, it is true, you are overwhelmed with praises and make a great deal of money into the bargain – but how long does that last? After a few months the Viennese want something new.' 'You are right, Count', I replied. 'But do you suppose that I mean to settle in Vienna? Not at all. I know where I shall go. That this affair should have occurred in Vienna is the Archbishop's fault and not mine. If he knew how to treat people of talent, it would never have happened. I am the best tempered fellow in the world, Count Arco, provided that people are the same with me.' 'Well', he said, 'the Archbishop considers you a dreadfully conceited person.' 'I daresay he does', I rejoined, 'and indeed I am so towards him. I treat people as they treat me. When I see that someone despises me and treats me with contempt, I can be as proud as a peacock.' Among other things he asked me whether I did not think that he too often had to swallow very disagreeable words. I shrugged my shoulders and said: 'You no doubt have your reasons for putting up with it, and I – have my reasons for refusing to do so.' . . .

TO HIS FATHER
Vienna, 9 June 1781

Mon très cher Père!

Well, Count Arco has made a nice mess of things! So that is the way to persuade people and to attract them! To refuse petitions from innate stupidity, not to say a word to your master from lack of courage and love of toadyism, to keep a fellow dangling about for four weeks, and finally, when he is obliged to present the petition in person, instead of at least granting him admittance, to

*The Burgtheater in Vienna, where four of Mozart's operas had their first Vienna
performances; an aquatint by C. Postle after Karl Schütz, 1783.*

throw him out of the room and give him a kick on his behind – that is the Count,
who, according to your last letter, has my interest so much at heart – and that is
the court where I ought to go on serving – the place where whoever wants to
make a written application, instead of having its delivery facilitated, is treated in
this fashion! . . . Your comparison of me to Madame Lange positively amazed me
and made me feel distressed for the rest of the day. That girl lived on her parents
as long as she could earn nothing for herself. But as soon as the time came when
she could show them her gratitude (remember that her father died before she had
earned anything in Vienna), she deserted her poor mother, attached herself to an
actor and married him – and her mother has never had a farthing from her. Good
God! He knows that my sole aim is to help you and to help us all. Must I repeat it
a hundred times that I can be of more use to you here than in Salzburg? I implore
you, dearest, most beloved father, for the future to spare me such letters. I entreat
you to do so, for they only irritate my mind and disturb my heart and spirit; and I,
who must now keep on composing, need a cheerful mind and a calm
disposition . . .

TO HIS FATHER
Vienna, 13 June 1781

... Instead of taking my petition or procuring me an audience or advising me to send in the document later or persuading me to let the matter lie and to consider things more carefully, – *enfin*, whatever he wanted – Count Arco hurls me out of the room and gives me a kick on my behind. Well, that means in our language that Salzburg is no longer the place for me, except to give me a favourable opportunity of returning the Count's kick, even if it should have to be in the public street ...

TO HIS FATHER
Vienna, 16 June 1781

... The present season is, as you know, the worst for anyone who wants to make money. The most distinguished families are in the country. So all I can do is to work hard in preparation for the winter, when I shall have less time to compose ... At present I have only one pupil, Countess Rumeck, Cobenzl's cousin. I could have many more, it is true, if I chose to lower my terms, but by doing so, I should lose credit ... I would rather have three pupils who pay me well than six who pay badly. With this one pupil I can just make both ends meet, and that is enough for the present. I simply mention this in order that you may not think me guilty of selfishness in sending you only thirty ducats. Believe me, I would gladly deprive myself of everything, if only I had it! But things are bound to improve. We must never let people know how we really stand financially ...

I went to Stephanie, *en forme de visite*. For we thought it possible that his partiality for Umlauf might make him play me false. This suspicion proved, however, quite unfounded. For I heard afterwards that he had commissioned someone to ask me to go and see him, as there was something he wished to discuss with me. And the moment I entered his room, he said: 'Ah, you are just the very person I wanted to see' ...

Well, I must now explain why we were suspicious of Stephanie. I regret to say that the fellow has the worst reputation in Vienna, for he is said to be rude, false and slanderous and to treat people most unjustly. But I pay no attention to these reports. There may be some truth in them, for everyone abuses him. On the other hand, he is in great favour with the Emperor. He was most friendly to me the very first time we met, and said: 'We are old friends already and I shall be delighted if it be in my power to render you any service.' I believe and hope too

that he himself may write an opera libretto for me. Whether he has written his plays alone or with the help of others, whether he has plagiarized or created, he still understands the stage, and his plays are invariably popular . . . I have not the slightest doubt about the success of the opera, provided the text is a good one. For do you really suppose that I should write an *opéra comique* in the same style as an *opera seria*? There should be as little frivolity in an *opera seria* and as much seriousness and solidity as there should be little seriousness in an *opera buffa*, and the more frivolity and gaiety. That people like to have a little comic music in an *opera seria*, I cannot help. But in Vienna they make the proper distinction on this point. I do certainly find that in music the Merry Andrew has not yet been banished, and in this respect the French are right. I hope to receive my clothes safely by the next mail coach. I do not know when it goes, but as I think this letter will reach you first, I beg you to keep the stick for me. People carry sticks here, but for what purpose? To walk with, and for that purpose any little stick will do. So please use the stick instead of me, and always carry it if you can. Who knows whether in your hand it may not avenge its former master on Arco? I mean, of course, *accidentaliter*, or by chance. That arrogant jackass will certainly get a very palpable reply from me, even if he has to wait twenty years for it. For to see him and to return his kick will be one and the same thing, unless I am so unlucky as to meet him first in some sacred place . . .

TO HIS FATHER
Vienna, 20 June 1781

. . . As for Arco, I have but to consult my own feelings and judgement and therefore do not need the advice of a lady or a person of rank to help me to do what is right and fitting, and neither too much nor too little. It is the heart that ennobles a man; and though I am no count, yet I have probably more honour in me than many a count. Whether a man be count or valet, the moment he insults me, he is a scoundrel. I intend at first to tell him quite reasonably how badly and clumsily he has played his part. But in conclusion I shall feel bound to assure him in writing that he may confidently expect from me a kick on his behind and a few boxes on the ear in addition. For when I am insulted, I must have my revenge; and if I do no more than was done to me, I shall only be getting even with him and not punishing him. Besides, I should be placing myself on a level with him, and really I am too proud to measure myself with such a stupid booby. . . .

*Karl Schütz's engraving of St Peter's Church, Vienna, 1799. From May to September 1781,
Mozart lodged with the widowed Frau Weber and her three daughters on the second floor of
the second house on the left.*

TO HIS FATHER
Vienna, 25 July 1781

Mon très cher Père!

I repeat that I have long been thinking of moving to another lodging, and that
too solely because people are gossiping. I am very sorry that I am obliged to do
this on account of silly talk, in which there is not a word of truth. I should very
much like to know what pleasure certain people can find in spreading entirely
groundless reports. Because I am living with them, therefore I am going to marry
the daughter. There has been no talk of our being in love. They have skipped that
stage. No, I just take rooms in the house and marry. If ever there was a time when
I thought less of getting married, it is most certainly now! For (although the last
thing I want is a rich wife) even if I could now make my fortune by a marriage, I
could not possibly pay court to anyone, for my mind is running on very different
matters. God has not given me my talent that I might attach it to a wife and waste

my youth in idleness. I am just beginning to live, and am I to embitter my own life? To be sure, I have nothing against matrimony, but at the moment it would be a misfortune for me ... I will not say that, living in the same house with the Mademoiselle to whom people have already married me, I am ill-bred and do not speak to her; but I am not in love with her. I fool about and have fun with her when time permits (which is only in the evenings when I take supper at home, for in the morning I write in my room and in the afternoon I am rarely in the house) and – that is all. If I had to marry all those with whom I have jested, I should have two hundred wives at least ...

TO HIS FATHER
Vienna, 1 August 1781

... Well, the day before yesterday Stephanie junior gave me a libretto to compose. I must confess that, however badly he may treat other people, about which I know nothing, he is an excellent friend to me. The libretto is quite good. The subject is Turkish and the title is: 'Belmonte und Konstanze', or 'Die Verführung aus dem Serail'. I intend to write the overture, the chorus in Act I and the final chorus in the style of Turkish music ...

TO HIS FATHER
Vienna, 22 August 1781

Mon très cher Père!

I cannot let you know the address of my new lodging, as I have not yet got one. But I am bargaining about the prices of two, one of which I shall certainly take, as I cannot stay here next month and so must move out. It appears that Herr von Aurnhammer wrote and told you that I had actually found a lodging! I had one, it is true, but what a habitation! fit for rats and mice, but not for human beings. At noon I had to look for the stairs with a lantern. The room was a little closet and to get to it I had to pass through the kitchen. In the door there was a tiny window and although they promised me to put up a curtain inside, they asked me at the same time to draw it back as soon as I was dressed, for otherwise they would not be able to see anything either in the kitchen or in the adjoining rooms. The owner's wife herself called the house the rats' nest – in short, it was a dreadful place to look at. Ah, what a splendid dwelling for me indeed, who have to receive visits from various distinguished people . . . You know Frau Adlgasser? Well, this *meuble* is even more aggravating, for she is *médisante* into the bargain – I mean, she is both stupid and malicious. Now for the daughter. If a painter wanted to portray the devil to the life, he would have to choose her face. She is as fat as a farm-wench, perspires so that you feel inclined to vomit, and goes about so scantily clad that really you can read as plain as print: 'Pray, do look here'. True, there is enough to see, in fact, quite enough to strike one blind; but – one is thoroughly well punished for the rest of the day if one is unlucky enough to let one's eyes wander in that direction – tartar is the only remedy! So loathsome, dirty and horrible! Faugh, the devil! Well, I have told you how she plays, and also why she begged me to assist her. I am delighted to do people favours, provided they do not plague me incessantly. But she is not content if I spend a couple of hours with her every day. She wants me to sit there the whole day long – and, what is more, she tries to be attractive. But, what is worse still, she is *sérieusement* in love with me! I thought at first it was a joke, but now I know it to be a fact. When I perceived it – for she took liberties with me – for example, she made me tender reproaches if I came somewhat later than usual or could not stay so long, and more nonsense of the same kind – I was obliged, not to make a fool of the girl, to tell her the truth very politely. But that was no use: she became more loving than ever. In the end I was always very polite to her except when she started her nonsense – and then I was very rude. Whereupon she took my hand and said: 'Dear Mozart, please don't be so cross. You may say what you like, I am really very fond of you.' Throughout the town people are saying that we are to be married, and they are very much surprised at me, I mean, that I have chosen such a face. She told me that when anything of the kind was said to her, she always laughed at it; but I know from a certain person that she confirmed the rumour, adding that we would then travel together. That enraged me. So the other day I gave her my mind pretty plainly and warned her not to abuse my kindness. Now I no longer go there every day, but only every other day, and I shall gradually drop it altogether. She is nothing but an amorous fool . . .

TO HIS FATHER
Vienna, 5 September 1781

... From the way in which you have taken my last letter – as if I were an arch-scoundrel or a blockhead or both! – I am sorry to see that you rely more on the gossip and scribblings of other people than you do on me – and that in fact you have no trust in me whatever. But I assure you that all this does not disturb me; people may write themselves blind – and you may believe them as much as you please – but I shall not alter by a hair's breadth; I shall remain the same honest fellow as ever. And I swear to you that if you had not wanted me to move into another lodging, I should not have left the Webers; for I feel just like a person who has left his own comfortable travelling carriage for a post-chaise. But not another word on the subject. It is really no use talking about it. For the nonsense which God knows who puts into your head always outweighs any reasons of mine. But one thing I do beg of you. When you write to me about something I have done, of which you disapprove or which you think might have been done better, and in reply I send you my ideas on the subject, please regard the whole matter as one between father and son alone, a secret, I mean, and something which is not to be told to others, as I myself always regard it. I therefore entreat you to leave it at that and not to apply to other people, for, by God, I will not give the smallest account to others of what I do or leave undone, no, not even to the Emperor himself. Do trust me always, for indeed I deserve it. I have trouble and worry enough here to support myself, and it therefore does not help me in the very least to read unpleasant letters ...

TO HIS FATHER
Vienna, 26 September 1781

Mon très cher Père!

Forgive me for having made you pay an extra heavy postage fee the other day. But I happened to have nothing important to tell you and thought that it would afford you pleasure if I gave you some idea of my opera. As the original text began with a monologue, I asked Herr Stephanie to make a little arietta out of it – and then to put in a duet instead of making the two chatter together after Osmin's short song. As we have given the part of Osmin to Herr Fischer, who certainly has an excellent bass voice (in spite of the fact that the Archbishop told me that he sang too low for a bass and that I assured him that he would sing higher next time), we must take advantage of it, particularly as he has the whole Viennese

Announcement of the first performance of Die Entführung aus dem Serail *on 16 July 1782, at the Burgtheater in Vienna.*

public on his side. But in the original libretto Osmin has only this short song and nothing else to sing, except in the trio and the finale; so he has been given an aria in Act I, and he is to have another in Act II. I have explained to Stephanie the words I require for this aria – indeed I had finished composing most of the music for it before Stephanie knew anything whatever about it. I am enclosing only the beginning and the end, which is bound to have a good effect. Osmin's rage is rendered comical by the accompaniment of the Turkish music. In working out the aria I have given full scope now and then to Fischer's beautiful deep notes (in spite of our Salzburg Midas). The passage 'Drum beim Barte des Propheten' is indeed in the same tempo, but with quick notes; but as Osmin's rage gradually increases, there comes (just when the aria seems to be at an end) the *allegro assai*, which is in a totally different measure and in a different key; this is bound to be very effective. For just as a man in such a towering rage oversteps all the bounds of order, moderation and propriety, and completely forgets himself, so must the music too forget itself. But as passions, whether violent or not, must never be

expressed in such a way as to excite disgust, and as music, even in the most terrible situations, must never offend the ear, but must please the hearer, or in other words must never cease to be music, I have gone from F (the key in which the aria is written), not into a remote key, but into a related one, not, however, into its nearest relative D minor, but into the more remote A minor. Let me now turn to Belmonte's aria in A major, 'O wie ängstlich, o wie feurig'. Would you like to know how I have expressed it – and even indicated his throbbing heart? By the two violins playing octaves. This is the favourite aria of all those who have heard it, and it is mine also. I wrote it expressly to suit Adamberger's voice. You feel the trembling – the faltering – you see how his throbbing breast begins to swell; this I have expressed by a *crescendo*. You hear the whispering and the sighing – which I have indicated by the first violins with mutes and a flute playing in unison.

The Janissary chorus is, as such, all that can be desired, that is, short, lively, and written to please the Viennese. I have sacrificed Constanze's aria a little to the flexible throat of Mlle Cavalieri, 'Trennung war mein banges Los und nun schwimmt mein Aug' in Tränen'. I have tried to express her feelings, as far as an Italian *bravura* aria will allow it. I have changed the 'Hui' to 'schnell', so it now runs thus – 'Doch wie schnell schwand meine Freude'. I really don't know what our German poets are thinking of. Even if they do not understand the theatre, or at all events operas, yet they should not make their characters talk as if they were addressing a herd of swine. Hui, sow!

Now for the trio at the close of Act I. Pedrillo has passed off his master as an architect – to give him an opportunity of meeting his Constanze in the garden. Bassa Selim has taken him into his service. Osmin, the steward, knows nothing of this, and being a rude churl and a sworn foe to all strangers, is impertinent and refuses to let them into the garden. It opens quite abruptly – and because the words lend themselves to it, I have made it a fairly respectable piece of real three-part writing. Then the major key begins at once *pianissimo* – it must go very quickly – and wind up with a great deal of noise, which is always appropriate at the end of an act. The more noise the better, and the shorter the better, so that the audience may not have time to cool down with their applause.

I have sent you only fourteen bars of the overture, which is very short with alternate fortes and pianos, the Turkish music always coming in at the fortes. The overture modulates through different keys; and I doubt whether anyone, even if his previous night has been a sleepless one, could go to sleep over it. Now comes the rub! The first act was finished more than three weeks ago, as was also one aria in Act II and the drunken duet (*per i signori viennesi*) which consists entirely of my Turkish tattoo. But I cannot compose any more, because the whole story is being altered – and, to tell the truth, at my own request. At the beginning of Act III there is a charming quintet or rather finale, but I should prefer to have it at the end of Act II. In order to make this practicable, great changes must be made, in fact an entirely new plot must be introduced – and Stephanie is up to the eyes in other work. So we must have a little patience. Everyone abuses Stephanie. It may be that in my case he is only very friendly to my face. But after all he is arranging the libretto for me – and, what is more, as I want it – exactly – and, by Heaven, I do not ask anything more of him. Well, how I have been chattering to you about my opera! But I cannot help it . . .

TO HIS FATHER
Vienna, 13 October 1781

. . . Why, an opera is sure of success when the plot is well worked out, the words written solely for the music and not shoved in here and there to suit some miserable rhyme (which, God knows, never enhances the value of any theatrical performance, be it what it may, but rather detracts from it) – I mean, words or even entire verses which ruin the composer's whole idea. Verses are indeed the most indispensable element for music – but rhymes – solely for the sake of rhyming – the most detrimental. Those high and mighty people who set to work in this pedantic fashion will always come to grief, both they and their music. The best thing of all is when a good composer, who understands the stage and is talented enough to make sound suggestions, meets an able poet, that true phoenix; in that case no fears need be entertained as to the applause even of the ignorant. Poets almost remind me of trumpeters with their professional tricks! If we composers were always to stick so faithfully to our rules (which were very good at a time when no one knew better), we should be concocting music as unpalatable as their libretti . . .

TO HIS FATHER
Vienna, 15 December 1781

... Dearest father! You demand an explanation of the words in the closing sentence of my last letter! Oh, how gladly would I have opened my heart to you long ago, but I was deterred by the reproaches you might have made to me for thinking of such a thing at an unseasonable time – although indeed thinking can never be unseasonable. Meanwhile I am very anxious to secure here a small but certain income, which, together with what chance may provide, will enable me to live here quite comfortably – and then – to marry! You are horrified at the idea? But I entreat you, dearest, most beloved father, to listen to me. I have been obliged to reveal my intentions to you. You must, therefore, allow me to disclose to you my reasons, which, moreover, are very well founded. The voice of nature speaks as loud in me as in others, louder, perhaps, than in many a big strong lout of a fellow. I simply cannot live as most young men do in these days. In the first place, I have too much religion; in the second place, I have too great a love of my neighbour and too high a feeling of honour to seduce an innocent girl; and, in the third place, I have too much horror and disgust, too much dread and fear of diseases and too much care for my health to fool about with whores. So I can swear that I have never had relations of that sort with any woman. Besides, if such a thing had occurred, I should not have concealed it from you; for, after all, to err is natural enough in a man, and to err once would be mere weakness – although indeed I should not undertake to promise that if I had erred once in this way, I should stop short at one slip. However, I stake my life on the truth of what I have told you. I am well aware that this reason (powerful as it is) is not urgent enough. But owing to my disposition, which is more inclined to a peaceful and domesticated existence than to revelry, I who from my youth up have never been accustomed to look after my own belongings, linen, clothes and so forth, cannot think of anything more necessary to me than a wife. I assure you that I am often obliged to spend unnecessarily, simply because I do not pay attention to things. I am absolutely convinced that I should manage better with a wife (on the same income which I have now) than I do by myself. And how many useless expenses would be avoided! True, other expenses would have to be met, but – one knows what they are and can be prepared for them – in short, one leads a well-ordered existence. A bachelor, in my opinion, is only half alive. Such are my views and I cannot help it. I have thought the matter over and reflected sufficiently, and I shall not change my mind. But who is the object of my love? Do not be horrified again, I entreat you. Surely not one of the Webers? Yes, one of the Webers – but not Josefa, nor Sophie, but Constanze, the middle one. In no other family have I ever come across such differences of character. The eldest is a lazy, gross, perfidious woman, and as cunning as a fox. Mme Lange is a false, malicious person and a coquette. The youngest is still too young to be anything in particular – she is just a good-natured, but feather-headed creature! May God protect her from seduction! But the middle one, my good, dear Constanze, is the martyr of the family, and, probably for that very reason, is the kindest-hearted, the cleverest and in short, the best of them all. She makes herself responsible for the whole household and yet in their opinion she does nothing right. Oh, my most beloved father, I could fill whole sheets with descriptions of all the scenes that I have witnessed in that house. If you want to read them, I shall do so in my next letter. But before I cease to plague you with my chatter, I must make you better acquainted with the character of my dear Constanze. She is not ugly, but at the same time far from beautiful. Her whole beauty consists in two little black eyes and a pretty figure. She has no wit, but she has enough common sense to enable her to fulfil her duties as a wife and mother. It is a downright lie that she is inclined to be extravagant. On the contrary, she is accustomed to be shabbily dressed, for the little that her mother has been able to do for her children, she has done for the two others, but never for Constanze. True, she would like to be neatly and cleanly dressed, but not smartly, and most things that a woman needs she is able to make for herself; and she dresses her own hair every day. Moreover she understands housekeeping and has the kindest heart in the world. I love her and she loves me with all her heart. Tell me whether I could wish myself a better wife? . . .

TO HIS FATHER
Vienna, 22 December 1781

. . . As for the marriage contract, I want to make the most frank confession, fully convinced as I am that you will forgive me for taking this step; for had you been in my place, you would most certainly have done the same thing. But for one thing alone I ask your pardon – that is, that I did not tell you all about this long ago. In my last letter I apologised to you for my delay and gave you the reason which deterred me. So I hope that you will forgive me, particularly as no one has suffered more by it than I have – and even if you had not provided the occasion for doing so in your last letter, I should have written to you and disclosed everything. For, by Heaven, I could not have stood it – much – much longer.

Well, let's come to the marriage contract, or rather to the written assurance of my honourable intentions towards the girl. You know, of course, that as the father is no longer alive (unhappily for the whole family as well as for my Constanze and myself) a guardian has taken his place. Certain busybodies and impudent gentlemen like Herr Winter must have shouted in the ears of this person (who doesn't know me at all) all sorts of stories about me – as, for example, that he should beware of me – that I have no settled income – that I was far too intimate with her – that I should probably jilt her – and that the girl would then be ruined, and so forth. All this made him smell a rat – for the mother who knows me and knows that I am honourable, let things take their course and said nothing to him about the matter. For my whole association with her consisted in my lodging with the family and later in my going to their house every day. No one ever saw me with her outside the house. But the guardian kept on pestering the mother with his representations until she told me about them and asked me to speak to him myself, adding that he would come some day to her house. He came – and we had a talk – with the result (as I did not explain myself as clearly as he desired) that he told the mother to forbid me to associate with her daughter until I had come to a written agreement with him. The mother replied: 'Why, his whole association with her consists in his coming to my house, and – I cannot forbid him my house. He is too good a friend – and one to whom I owe a great deal. I am quite satisfied. I trust him. You must settle it with him yourself.' So he forbade me to have anything more to do with Constanze, unless I would give him a written undertaking. What other course was open to me? I had either to give him a written contract or – to desert the girl. What man who loves sincerely and honestly can forsake his beloved? Would not the mother, would not my loved one herself place the worst interpretation upon such conduct? That was my predicament. So I drew up a document to the effect that I bound myself to marry Mlle Constanze Weber within the space of three years and that if it should prove impossible for me to do so owing to my changing my mind, she should be entitled to claim from me three hundred *gulden* a year. Nothing in the world could have been easier for me to write. For I knew that I should never have to pay these three hundred *gulden*, because I should never forsake her, and that even should I be so unfortunate as to change my mind, I should only be too glad to get rid of her for three hundred *gulden*, while Constanze, if I know her, would be too proud to let herself be sold. But what did the angelic girl do when the guardian was

Constanze Mozart, née Weber, by Joseph Lange, 1782.

167

gone? She asked her mother for the document, and said to me: 'Dear Mozart! I need no written assurance from you. I believe what you say,' and tore up the paper. This action made my dear Constanze yet more precious to me, and the document having been destroyed and the guardian having given his *parole d'honneur* to keep the matter to himself, I was to a certain extent easy in my mind on your account, my most beloved father. For I had no fear but that ultimately you would give your consent to our marriage (as the girl has everything but money), because I know your sensible ideas on this subject. Will you forgive me? Indeed I hope so! Nor do I doubt it for a moment ...

TO HIS FATHER
Vienna, 16 January 1782

Mon très cher Père!

I thank you for your kind and affectionate letter. If I were to give you detailed replies to every point, I should have to fill a quire of paper. As this is impossible, I shall deal only with the most important of them. The guardian's name is Herr von Thorwart; he is Inspector of theatrical properties ... I quite agree with you in thinking that Madame Weber and Herr von Thorwart have been to blame in showing too much regard for their own interests, though the Madame is no longer her own mistress and has to leave everything, particularly all matters of this kind, to the guardian, who (as he has never made my acquaintance) is by no means bound to trust me. But that he was too hasty in demanding from me a written undertaking is undeniable, especially as I told him that as yet you knew nothing about the affair and that at the moment I could not possibly disclose it to you. I asked him to have patience for a short time until my circumstances should take another turn, when I should give you a full account of everything and then the whole matter would be settled. However, it is all over now; and love must be my excuse. Herr von Thorwart did not behave well, but not so badly that he and Madame Weber 'should be put in chains, made to sweep streets and have boards hung round their necks with the words "seducers of youth"'. That too is an

*The composer Muzio Clementi, about whom Mozart made some ungenerous remarks in a
letter of 16 January 1782; an engraving by Johann Neidl after Thomas Hardy.*

exaggeration. And even if what you say were true, that in order to catch me she opened her house, let me have the run of it, gave me every opportunity, etc., even so the punishment would be rather drastic. But I need hardly tell you that it is not true. And it hurts me very much to think that you could believe that your son could frequent a house where such things went on. Let me only say that you should believe precisely the opposite of all you have been told. But enough of this. Now a word about Clementi. He is an excellent cembalo-player, but that is all. He has great facility with his right hand. His star passages are thirds. Apart from this, he has not a farthing's worth of taste or feeling; he is a mere *mechanicus*.

After we had stood on ceremony long enough, the Emperor declared that Clementi ought to begin. '*La Santa Chiesa Cattolica*,' he said, Clementi being a Roman. He improvised and then played a sonata. The Emperor then turned to me: '*Allons*, fire away.' I improvised and played variations. The Grand Duchess produced some sonatas by Paisiello (wretchedly written out in his own hand), of which I had to play the Allegros and Clementi the Andantes and Rondos. We then selected a theme from them and developed it on two pianofortes. The funny thing was that although I had borrowed Countess Thun's pianoforte, I only played on it when I played alone; such was the Emperor's desire – and, by the way, the other instrument was out of tune and three of the keys were stuck. 'That doesn't matter,' said the Emperor. Well, I put the best construction on it I could, that is that the Emperor, already knowing my skill and my knowledge of music, was only desirous of showing especial courtesy to a foreigner. Besides, I have it from a very good source that he was extremely pleased with me . . .

TO HIS FATHER
Vienna, 30 January 1782

. . . Just one thing more (for if I did not say it I could not sleep in peace). Please do not suspect my dear Constanze of harbouring such evil thoughts. Believe me, if she had such a disposition, I could not possibly love her. Both she and I long ago observed her mother's designs. But the latter is very much mistaken, for she wishes us (when we marry) to live with her, as she has apartments to let. This is out of the question, for on no account would I consent to it, and my Constanze still less. *Au contraire*, she intends to see very little of her mother and I shall do my best to stop it altogether, for we know her too well. Dearest, most beloved father, my only wish is that we may soon meet, so that you may see her and – love her, for you love those who have kind hearts – that I know . . .

TO HIS SISTER
Vienna, 13 February 1782

. . . I can never work before five or six o'clock in the evening, and even then I am often prevented by a concert. If I am not prevented, I compose until nine. I then go to my dear Constanze, though the joy of seeing one another is nearly always spoilt by her mother's bitter remarks. I shall explain this in my next letter to my father. For that is the reason why I am longing to be able to set her free, and to rescue her as soon as possible. At half-past ten or eleven I come home – it depends on her mother's darts and on my capacity to endure them! . . .

TO HIS SISTER
Vienna, 20 April 1782

Dearest Sister!

My dear Constanze has at last summoned up courage to follow the impulse of her kind heart – that is, to write to you, my dear sister! Should you be willing to favour her with a reply (and indeed I hope you will, so that I may see the sweet creature's delight reflected on her face), may I beg you to enclose your letter to me? I only mention this as a precaution and so that you may know that her mother and sisters are not aware that she has written to you. . . . The reason why I did not reply to your letter at once was that on account of the wearisome labour of writing these small notes, I could not finish the composition any sooner. And,

even so, it is awkwardly done, for the prelude ought to come first and the fugue to follow. But I composed the fugue first and wrote it down while I was thinking out the prelude. I only hope that you will be able to read it, for it is written so very small; and I hope further that you will like it. Another time I shall send you something better for the clavier. My dear Constanze is really the cause of this fugue's coming into the world. Baron van Swieten, to whom I go every Sunday, gave me all the works of Handel and Sebastian Bach to take home with me (after I had played them to him). When Constanze heard the fugues, she absolutely fell in love with them. Now she will listen to nothing but fugues, and particularly (in this kind of composition) the works of Handel and Bach. Well, as she had often heard me play fugues out of my head, she asked me if I had ever written any down, and when I said I had not, she scolded me roundly for not recording some of my compositions in this most artistic and beautiful of all musical forms and never ceased to entreat me until I wrote down a fugue for her. So this is its origin. I have purposely written above it *Andante maestoso*, as it must not be played too fast. For if a fugue is not played slowly, the ear cannot clearly distinguish the theme when it comes in and consequently the effect is entirely missed. . . .

Baron Gottfried van Swieten (1733–1803), an important patron and supporter of Mozart in his last years; an engraving by J.E. Mansfield after J.C. de Lakner.

TO CONSTANZE WEBER
Vienna, 29 April 1782

Dearest, most beloved Friend!

Surely you will still allow me to address you by this name? Surely you do not hate me so much that I may be your friend no longer, and you – no longer mine? And even if you will not be my friend any longer, yet you cannot forbid me to wish you well, my friend, since it has become very natural for me to do so. Do think over what you said to me to-day. In spite of all my entreaties you have thrown me over three times and told me to my face that you intend to have nothing more to do with me. I (to whom it means more than it does to you to lose the object of my love) am not so hot-tempered, so rash and so senseless as to accept my dismissal. I love you far too well to do so. I entreat you, therefore, to ponder and reflect upon the cause of all this unpleasantness, which arose from my being annoyed that you were so impudently inconsiderate as to say to your sisters – and, be it noted, in my presence – that you had let a _chapeau_ measure the calves of your legs. No woman who cares for her honour can do such a thing. It is quite a good maxim to do as one's company does. At the same time there are many other factors to be considered – as, for example, whether only intimate friends and acquaintances are present – whether I am a child or a marriageable girl – more particularly, whether I am already betrothed – but, above all, whether only people of my own social standing or my social inferiors – or, what is even more important, my social superiors are in the company? If it be true that the Baroness herself allowed it to be done to her, the case is still quite different, for she is already past her prime and cannot possibly attract any longer – and besides, she is inclined to be promiscuous with her favours. I hope, dearest friend, that, even if you do not wish to become my wife, you will never lead a life like hers. If it was quite impossible for you to resist the desire to take part in the game (although it is not always wise for a man to do so, and still less for a woman), then why in the name of Heaven did you not take the ribbon and measure your own calves yourself (as all self-respecting women have done on similar occasions in my presence) and not allow a _chapeau_ to do so? – Why, I myself in the presence of others would never have done such a thing to you. I should have handed you the ribbon myself. Still less, then, should you have allowed it to be done to you by a stranger – a man about whom I know nothing. But it is all over now; and the least acknowledgement of your somewhat thoughtless behaviour on that occasion would have made everything all right again; and if you will not make a grievance of it, dearest friend, everything will still be all right. You realize now how much I love you. I do not fly into a passion as you do. I think, I reflect and I feel. If you will but surrender to your feelings, then I know that this very day I shall be able to say with absolute confidence that Constanze is the virtuous, honourable, prudent and loyal sweetheart of her honest and devoted

MOZART

Martha Elisabeth, Baroness von Waldstätten, in whose house Constanze had taken refuge before her marriage; a silhouette by François Gonord, 1781.

TO HIS FATHER
Vienna, 8 May 1782

Mon très cher Père!

I have received your last letter of April 30th and yesterday too my sister's letter with the enclosure for my dear Constanze, to whom I gave it at once. It caused her sincere pleasure and she will take the liberty of writing to her again very soon. Meanwhile (as I cannot possibly find time to write to my sister to-day) I must put a question to you on behalf of Constanze, which is, whether fringes are being worn in Salzburg? Whether my sister is wearing them already? Whether she can make them herself? Constanze has just trimmed two *piqué* dresses with them, for they are all the fashion in Vienna. As she can make them herself now, she would like to send some to my sister, if the latter will tell her which shade she prefers. For they are worn in all colours, white, black, green, blue, puce, etc . . .

173

TO HIS FATHER
Vienna, 20 July 1782

Mon très cher Père!

I hope that you received safely my last letter informing you of the good reception of my opera. It was given yesterday for the second time. Can you really believe it, but yesterday there was an even stronger cabal against it than on the first evening! The whole first act was accompanied by hissing. But indeed they could not prevent the loud shouts of *bravo* during the arias. I was relying on the closing trio, but, as ill-luck would have it, Fischer went wrong, which made Dauer (Pedrillo) go wrong too; and Adamberger alone could not sustain the trio,

Johann Ernest Dauer, the first Pedrillo in Die Entführung; *a silhouette by Hieronymus Löschenkohl, 1785.*

with the result that the whole effect was lost and that this time it was not repeated. I was in such a rage (and so was Adamberger) that I was simply beside myself and said at once that I would not let the opera be given again without having a short rehearsal for the singers. In the second act both duets were repeated as on the first night, and in addition Belmonte's rondo 'Wenn der Freude Tränen fliessen'. The theatre was almost more crowded than on the first night and on the preceding day no reserved seats were to be had, either in the stalls or in the third circle, and not a single box. My opera has brought in 1,200 *gulden* in the two days . . .

TO HIS FATHER
Vienna, 27 July 1782

... Dearest, most beloved father, I implore you by all you hold dear in the world to give your consent to my marriage with my dear Constanze. Do not suppose that it is just for the sake of getting married. If that were the only reason, I would gladly wait. But I realize that it is absolutely necessary for my own honour and for that of my girl, and for the sake of my health and spirits. My heart is restless and my head confused; in such a condition how can one think and work to any good purpose? And why am I in this state? Well, because most people think that we are already married. Her mother gets very much annoyed when she hears these rumours, and as for the poor girl and myself, we are tormented to death. This state of affairs can be remedied so easily. Believe me, it is just as easy to live in expensive Vienna as anywhere else. It all depends on economy and good management, which cannot be expected from a young fellow, particularly if he is in love. Whoever gets a wife like my Constanze will certainly be a happy man. We intend to live very modestly and quietly and yet we shall be happy ...

TO THE BARONESS VON WALDSTÄDTEN
Vienna, [?2] August 1782

Most highly esteemed Baroness!

Madame Weber's maid-servant has brought me my music, for which I have had to give her a written receipt. She has also told me something in confidence which, although I do not believe it could happen, as it would be a disgrace to the whole family, yet seems possible when one remembers Madame Weber's stupidity, and which consequently causes me anxiety. It appears that Sophie went to the maid-servant in tears and when the latter asked her what was the matter, she said: 'Do tell Mozart in secret to arrange for Constanze to go home, for my mother is absolutely determined to have her fetched by the police.' Are the police in Vienna allowed to go into any house? Perhaps the whole thing is only a trap to make her return home. But if it could be done, then the best plan I can think of is to marry Constanze to-morrow morning – or even to-day, if that is possible. For I should not like to expose my beloved one to this scandal – and there could not be one, if she were my wife ...

175

St Stephen's Cathedral, Vienna, engraved by Karl Schütz, 1792.

TO HIS FATHER
Vienna, 7 August 1782

Mon très cher Père!

You are very much mistaken in your son if you can suppose him capable of acting dishonestly. My dear Constanze – now, thank God, at last my wife – knew my circumstances and heard from me long ago all that I had to expect from you. But her affection and her love for me were so great that she willingly and joyfully sacrificed her whole future to share my fate. I kiss your hands and thank you with all the tenderness which a son has ever felt for a father, for your kind consent and fatherly blessing. But indeed I could safely rely on it. For you know that I myself could not but see only too clearly all the objections that could be raised against such a step. At the same time you also know that I could not act otherwise without injury to my conscience and my honour. Consequently I could certainly rely on having your consent. So it was that having waited two post-days in vain

176

for a reply and the ceremony having been fixed for a day by which I was certain to have received it, I was married by the blessing of God to my beloved Constanze. I was quite assured of your consent and was therefore comforted. The following day I received your two letters at once – Well, it is over! I only ask your forgiveness for my too hasty trust in your fatherly love . . .

TO HIS FATHER
Vienna, 17 August 1782

. . . In regard to Gluck, my ideas are precisely the same as yours, my dearest father. But I should like to add something. The Viennese gentry, and in particular the ⟨Emperor⟩, must not imagine that I am on this earth solely for the sake of Vienna. There is no monarch in the world whom I should be more glad to serve than the Emperor, but I refuse to beg for any post. I believe that I am capable of doing credit to any court. If Germany, my beloved fatherland, of which, as you know, I am proud, will not accept me, then in God's name let France or England become the richer by another talented German, to the disgrace of the German nation. . . . Latterly I have been practising my French daily and have already

Christoph Willibald von Gluck (1714-87) (Simon Charles Miger after Joseph Duplessis).

taken three lessons in English. In three months I hope to be able to read and understand English books fairly easily. Now farewell. My wife and I kiss your hands a thousand times and I am ever your most obedient son

W. A. MOZART

TO HIS FATHER
Vienna, 24 August 1782

... You are perfectly right about France and England! It is a step which I can always take, and it is better for me to remain in Vienna a little longer. Besides, times may change too in those countries. Last Tuesday (after, thank Heaven! an interval of a fortnight) my opera was again performed with great success.
... My wife sheds tears of joy when she thinks of our journey to Salzburg. Farewell. We kiss your hands a thousand times and embrace our dear sister with all our hearts and are ever your most obedient children

W. A. MOZART
MAN AND WIFE
ARE ONE LIFE.

TO HIS FATHER
Vienna, 31 August 1782

... You say that I have never told you on what floor we are living? That in truth must have stuck in my pen! Well, I am telling you now – that we are living on the second floor. But I cannot understand how you got the idea that my highly honoured mother-in-law is living here too. For indeed I did not marry my sweetheart in such a hurry in order to live a life of vexations and quarrels, but to enjoy peace and happiness; and the only way to ensure this was to cut ourselves off from that house. Since our marriage we have paid her two visits, but on the second occasion quarrelling and wrangling began again, so that my poor wife started to cry. I put a stop to the bickering at once by saying to Constanze that it was time for us to go. We have not been there since and do not intend to go until we have to celebrate the birthday or name-day of the mother or of one of the two sisters ...

TO HIS FATHER
Vienna, 19 October 1782

. . . Indeed I have heard about England's victories[1] and am greatly delighted too, for you know that I am an out-and-out Englishman.

The Russian Royalties left Vienna to-day. My opera was performed for them the other day, and on this occasion I thought it advisable to resume my place at the clavier and conduct it. I did so partly in order to rouse the orchestra who had gone to sleep a little, partly (since I happen to be in Vienna) in order to appear before the royal guests as the father of my child.

My dearest father, I must confess that I have the most impatient longing to see you again and to kiss your hands; and for this reason I wanted to be in Salzburg on November 15th, which is your name-day. But the most profitable season in Vienna is now beginning. The nobility are returning from the country and are taking lessons. Moreover, concerts are starting again. I should have to be back in Vienna by the beginning of December. How hard it would be for my wife and myself to be obliged to leave you so soon! For we would much rather enjoy for a longer period the company of our dear father and our dear sister. So it depends on you – whether you prefer to have me for a longer or shorter time. We are thinking of going to you in the spring. If I only mention Salzburg to my dear wife, she is already beside herself with joy. The barber of Salzburg (not of Seville) called on me and delivered kind messages from you, from my sister and from Katherl. Now farewell. We both kiss your hands a thousand times and embrace my dear sister with all our hearts and are ever your most obedient children

M: C: ET W: A: MOZART

TO HIS FATHER
Vienna, 13 November 1782

Mon très cher Père!

We are in considerable perplexity. I did not write to you last Saturday, because I thought we were certain to leave Vienna on Monday. But on Sunday the weather became so dreadful that carriages could scarcely make their way through the town. I still wished to set off on Monday afternoon, but I was told at the post

---

1. The relief of Gibraltar by Lord Howe and Sir Edward Hughes's crushing defeat of the French navy off Trincomalee.

that not only would each stage take four or five hours, but we should not be able to get much beyond the first and should have to turn back. The mail coach with eight horses did not even reach the first stage and has returned to Vienna. I then intended to leave tomorrow, but my wife has such a severe headache to-day that, although she insists on setting out, I dare not allow her to run such a risk in this odious weather. So I am waiting for another letter from you (I trust that in the meantime road conditions will have improved) and then we shall be off. For the pleasure of embracing you again, my dearest father, outweighs all other considerations. My pupils can quite well wait for me for three or four weeks. For although the Countesses Zichy and Rumbeck have returned from the country and have already sent for me, it is not at all likely that they will engage another master in the meantime. Well, as I have not been so fortunate as to be able to congratulate you in person, I now do so in writing and send you the wishes of my wife and your future grandson or granddaughter. We wish you a long and happy life, health and contentment and whatever you wish for yourself. We kiss your hands a thousand times and embrace our dear sister with all our hearts and are ever your most obedient children

W: ET C: MOZART

TO HIS FATHER
Vienna, 20 November 1782

Mon très cher Père!

I see alas! that the pleasure of embracing you must be postponed until the spring, for my pupils positively refuse to let me go, and indeed the weather is at present far too cold for my wife. Everyone implores me not to take the risk. In spring then (for I call March, or the beginning of April at latest spring, as I reckon it according to my circumstances), we can certainly travel to Salzburg, for my wife is not expecting her confinement before the month of June. So I am unpacking our trunks to-day, as I left everything packed until I heard from you

. . .

W: ET C: MOZART

TO HIS FATHER
Vienna, 21 December 1782

Mon très cher Père!

Passionate as was my longing to get a letter from you again after a silence of three weeks, I was none the less amazed at its contents. In short, we have both been in the same state of anxiety. You must know that I replied to your last letter on December 4th and expected an answer from you in eight days. Nothing came. Well, I thought that perhaps you had not had time to write; and from a rather pleasant hint in your previous letter, we almost thought that you would arrive yourself. The next post again brought us nothing. All the same I intended to write, but was unexpectedly summoned to the Countess Thun and consequently was prevented from doing so. Then our anxiety began. We consoled ourselves, however, with the thought that if anything had been wrong, one of you would have written. At last your letter came to-day, by which I perceive that you never received my last letter. I can scarcely think that it was lost in the post, so no doubt the maid must have pocketed the money. But, by Heavens! I would far rather have made a present of six *kreutzer* to such a brute than have lost my letter so *mal à propos*; and yet it is not always possible to post the letter oneself . . . Confound the creature! For how can I know whether that letter did not contain something which I should be very sorry to see falling into other hands? But I do not think that it did and I trust that it didn't; and I am only pleased and happy to hear that you are both in good health. My wife and I, thank God, are very well . . .

A new opera, or rather a comedy with ariettas by Umlauf, entitled 'Welche ist die beste Nation?' was performed the other day – a wretched piece which I could have set to music, but which I refused to undertake, adding that whoever should compose music for it without altering it completely would run the risk of being hooted off the stage; had it not been Umlauf's, it would certainly have been hooted; but, being his, it was only hissed. Indeed it was no wonder, for even with the finest music no one could have tolerated such a piece. But, what is more, the music is so bad that I do not know whether the poet or the composer will carry off the prize for inanity. To its disgrace it was performed a second time; but I think we may now say, *Punctum satis* . . .

TO HIS FATHER

Vienna, 28 December 1782

... There are still two concertos wanting to make up the series of subscription concertos. These concertos are a happy medium between what is too easy and too difficult; they are very brilliant, pleasing to the ear, and natural, without being vapid. There are passages here and there from which connoisseurs alone can derive satisfaction; but these passages are written in such a way that the less learned cannot fail to be pleased, though without knowing why. I am distributing the tickets at six ducats apiece. I am now finishing too the piano arrangement of my opera, which is about to be published; and at the same time I am engaged in a very difficult task, the music for a bard's song by Denis about Gibraltar. But this is a secret, for it is a Hungarian lady who wishes to pay this compliment to Denis. The ode is sublime, beautiful, anything you like, but too exaggerated and pompous for my fastidious ears. But what is to be done? The golden mean of truth in all things is no longer either known or appreciated. In order to win applause one must write stuff which is so inane that a *fiacre* could sing it, or so unintelligible that it pleases precisely because no sensible man can understand it. This is not what I have been wanting to discuss with you; but I should like to write a book, a short introduction to music, illustrated by examples, but, I need hardly add, not under my own name. ...

TO HIS FATHER

Vienna, 5 February 1783

... On Friday, the day after to-morrow, a new opera is to be given, the music of which, a *galimatias*, is by a young Viennese, a pupil of Wagenseil, who is called *gallus cantans, in arbore sedens, gigirigi faciens*. It will probably not be a success. Still, it is better stuff than its predecessor, an old opera by Gassmann, 'La notte critica', in German 'Die unruhige Nacht', which with difficulty survived three performances. This in its turn had been preceded by that execrable opera of Umlauf, about which I wrote to you and which never got so far as a third performance. It really seems as if they wished to kill off before its time the German opera, which in any case is to come to an end after Easter; and Germans themselves are doing this – shame upon them! ... Let me now tell you of my plan. I do not believe that the Italian opera will keep going for long, and besides, I hold with the Germans. I prefer German opera, even though it means more trouble for me. Every nation has its own opera and why not Germany? Is not

An engraving by Johann Adam Delsenbach of Neumarkt, Vienna with the Schwartzenberg Palace in the background, 1750.

German as singable as French and English? Is it not more so than Russian? Very well then! I am now writing a German opera for myself. I have chosen Goldoni's comedy 'Il servitore di due padroni', and the whole of the first act has now been translated. Baron Binder is the translator. But we are keeping it a secret until it is quite finished . . .

TO THE BARONESS VON WALDSTÄDTEN
Vienna, 15 February 1783

Most highly esteemed Baroness!

Here I am in a fine dilemma! Herr von Tranner and I discussed the matter the other day and agreed to ask for an extension of a fortnight. As every merchant does this, unless he is the most disobliging man in the world, my mind was quite at ease and I hoped that by that time, if I were not in the position to pay the sum myself, I should be able to borrow it. Well, Herr von Tranner now informs me that the person in question absolutely refuses to wait and that if I do not pay the sum before to-morrow, he will bring an action against me. Only think, your Ladyship, what an unpleasant business this would be for me! At the moment I cannot pay – not even half the sum! If I could have foreseen that the subscriptions

for my concertos would come in so slowly, I should have raised the money on a longer time-limit. I entreat your Ladyship for Heaven's sake to help me to keep my honour and my good name!

My poor little wife is slightly indisposed, so I cannot leave her; otherwise I should have come to you myself to ask in person for your Ladyship's assistance. We kiss your Ladyship's hands a thousand times and are both your Ladyship's most obedient children

W. A. AND C. MOZART

TO HIS FATHER
Vienna, 29 March 1783

Mon très cher Père!

I need not tell you very much about the success of my concert, for no doubt you have already heard of it. Suffice it to say that the theatre could not have been more crowded and that every box was full. But what pleased me most of all was that His Majesty the Emperor was present and, goodness! – how delighted he was and how he applauded me! It is his custom to send the money to the box-office before going to the theatre; otherwise I should have been fully justified in counting on a larger sum, for really his delight was beyond all bounds. He sent twenty-five ducats . . .

TO HIS FATHER
Vienna, 7 May 1783

. . . Well, the Italian *opera buffa* has started again here and is very popular. The *buffo* is particularly good – his name is Benucci. I have looked through at least a hundred libretti and more, but I have hardly found a single one with which I am satisfied; that is to say, so many alterations would have to be made here and there, that even if a poet would undertake to make them, it would be easier for him to write a completely new text – which indeed it is always best to do. Our poet here is now a certain Abbate Da Ponte. He has an enormous amount to do in revising pieces for the theatre and he has to write *per obbligo* an entirely new libretto for Salieri, which will take him two months. He has promised after that to write a new libretto for me. But who knows whether he will be able to keep his word – or will want to? For, as you are aware, these Italian gentlemen are very civil to your face. Enough, we know them! If he is in league with Salieri, I shall never get anything out of him. But indeed I should dearly love to show what I can do in an Italian opera! So I have been thinking that unless Varesco is still very much annoyed with us about the Munich opera, he might write me a new libretto for seven characters. *Basta!* You will know best if this can be arranged. In the meantime he could jot down a few ideas, and when I come to Salzburg we could then work them out together. The most essential thing is that on the whole the story should be really comic; and, if possible, he ought to introduce two equally good female parts, one of these to be *seria*, the other *mezzo carattere*, but both parts equal in importance and excellence. The third female character, however, may be entirely *buffa*, and so may all the male ones, if necessary. If you think that something can be got out of Varesco, please discuss it with him soon. But you must not tell him that I am coming to Salzburg in July, or he will do no work; for I should very much like to have some of it while I am still in Vienna. Tell him too that his share will certainly amount to 400 or 500 *gulden*, for the custom here is that the poet gets the takings of the third performance . . .

Antonio Salieri (1750-1825), maestro di capella *at the court of Joseph II, and composer of numerous operas; engraving by Johanne Gottfried Scheffner.*

TO HIS FATHER
Vienna, 21 May 1783

. . . Now our sole desire is to have the happiness of embracing you both soon. But do you think that this will be in ⟨Salzburg⟩? I ⟨hardly⟩ think so, unfortunately! An idea has been worrying me for a long time, but as it never seemed to occur to you, my dearest father, I banished it from my mind. Herr von Edelbach and Baron Wetzlar, however, have confirmed ⟨my suspicion, which is that when I come to Salzburg, the Archbishop may have me arrested⟩ or at least – *Basta!* – What chiefly makes me ⟨dread⟩ this, is the fact that I have not yet received my formal ⟨dismissal⟩. Perhaps he has ⟨purposely held it back, in order to catch me later⟩. Well, you are the best judge; and, if your opinion is to the contrary, then ⟨we shall certainly come⟩; but if you agree with me, then we must choose a third ⟨place⟩ for our meeting – perhaps ⟨Munich. For a priest⟩ is capable of anything. . . .

TO HIS FATHER
Vienna, 7 June 1783

Mon très cher Père!

Praise and thanks be to God, I am quite well again! But my illness has left me a cold as a remembrance, which was very charming of it! I have received my dear sister's letter. My wife's name-day is neither in March nor in May, but on February 16th; and is not to be found in any calendar. She thanks you both, however, most cordially for your kind good wishes, which are always acceptable, even though it is not her name-day. She wanted to write to my sister herself, but in her present condition she must be excused if she is a little bit *commode* – or, as we say, indolent. According to the midwife's examination she ought to have had her confinement on the 4th, but I do not think that the event will take place before the 15th or 16th. She is longing for it to happen as soon as possible, particularly that she may have the happiness of embracing you and my dear sister in Salzburg. As I did not think that this would happen so soon, I kept on postponing going down on my knees, folding my hands and entreating you most submissively, my dearest father, to be godfather! As there is still time, I am doing so now. Meanwhile (in the confident hope that you will not refuse) I have already arranged (I mean, since the midwife took stock of the *visum repertum*) that someone shall present the child in your name, whether it is *generis masculini* or *feminini*! So we are going to call it Leopold or Leopoldine.

Well, I have a few words to say to my sister about Clementi's sonatas.

Everyone who either hears them or plays them must feel that as compositions they are worthless. They contain no remarkable or striking passages except those in sixths and octaves. And I implore my sister not to practise these passages too much, so that she may not spoil her quiet, even touch and that her hand may not lose its natural lightness, flexibility and smooth rapidity. For after all what is to be gained by it? Supposing that you do play sixths and octaves with the utmost velocity (which no one can accomplish, not even Clementi) you only produce an atrocious chopping effect and nothing else whatever. Clementi is a *ciarlatano*, like all Italians. He writes *Presto* over a sonata or even *Prestissimo* and *Alla breve*, and plays it himself *Allegro* in ¼ time. I know this is the case, for I have heard him do so. What he really does well are his passages in thirds; but he sweated over them day and night in London. Apart from this, he can do nothing, absolutely nothing, for he has not the slightest expression or taste, still less, feeling . . .

Constanze Mozart in 1783, a drawing by Joseph Lange.

TO HIS FATHER
Vienna, 18 June 1783

Mon très cher Père!

Congratulations, you are a grandpapa! Yesterday, the 17th, at half-past six in the morning my dear wife was safely delivered of a fine sturdy boy, as round as a ball . . . My mother-in-law by her great kindness to her daughter has made full

amends for all the harm she did her before her marriage. She spends the whole day with her ... I wanted the child to be brought up on water, like my sister and myself. However, the midwife, my mother-in-law and most people here have begged and implored me not to allow it, if only for the reason that most children here who are brought up on water do not survive, as the people here don't know how to do it properly. That induced me to give in, for I should not like to have anything to reproach myself with ...

Now for the godfather question. Let me tell you what has happened. After my wife's delivery I immediately sent a message to Baron Wetzlar, who is a good and true friend of mine. He came to see us at once and offered to stand godfather. I could not refuse and thought to myself: 'After all, my boy can still be called Leopold.' But while I was turning this round in my mind, the Baron said very cheerfully: 'Ah, now you have a little Raimund' – and kissed the child. What was I to do? Well, I have had the child christened Raimund Leopold ...

TO HIS FATHER

Vienna, 2 July 1783

... And now for a trick of Salieri's, which has injured poor Adamberger more than me. I think I told you that I had composed a rondo for Adamberger. During a short rehearsal, before the rondo had been copied, Salieri took Adamberger aside and told him that Count Rosenberg would not be pleased if he put in an aria and that he advised him as his good friend not to do so. Adamberger, provoked by Rosenberg's objection and not knowing how to retaliate, was stupid enough to say, with ill-timed pride, 'All right. But to prove that Adamberger has already made his reputation in Vienna and does not need to make a name for himself by singing music expressly written for him, he will only sing what is in the opera and will never again, as long as he lives, introduce any aria.' What was the result? Why, that was a complete failure, as was only to be expected! Now he is sorry, but it is too late. For if he were to ask me this very day to give him the rondo, I should refuse. I can easily find a place for it in one of my own operas. But the most annoying part of the whole affair is that his wife's prophecy and mine have come true, that is, that Count Rosenberg and the management knew nothing whatever about it, so that it was only a ruse on the part of Salieri. Thank God, my

wife is quite well again, save for a slight cold. We and our little Raimund, aged a fortnight, kiss your hands and embrace our dear sister with all our hearts and are ever your most obedient children

W: A: C: MOZART

TO HIS FATHER
Vienna, 5 July 1783

. . . I feel sure that we shall be able to set out in September; and indeed you can well imagine that our most ardent longing is to embrace you both. Yet I cannot conceal from you, but must confess quite frankly that many people here are alarming me to such an extent that I cannot describe it. You already know what it is all about. However much I protest I am told: 'Well, you will see, you will ⟨never get away again⟩. You have no idea of what ⟨that wicked malevolent Prince is capable of⟩! And you ⟨cannot⟩ conceive what ⟨low tricks⟩ are resorted to in affairs of this kind. Take my advice and ⟨meet your father⟩ in some third place.' This, you see, is what has been worrying my wife and me up to the present and what is still perturbing us. I often say to myself: 'Nonsense, it's quite impossible!' But the next moment it occurs to me that after all it might be possible and that it would not be the ⟨first injustice⟩ which he has ⟨committed⟩. *Basta!* In this matter no one can comfort me but you, my most beloved father! And so far as I am concerned, whatever happened would not worry me very much, for I can now adapt myself to any circumstances. But when I think of my wife and my little Raimund, then my indifference ceases. Think it over . . .

TO HIS FATHER
Linz, 31 October 1783

We arrived here safely yesterday morning at nine o'clock.
. . . Young Count Thun (brother of the Thun in Vienna) called on me immediately and said that his father had been expecting me for a fortnight and would I please drive to his house at once for I was to stay with him. I told him that I could easily put up at an inn. But when we reached the gates of Linz on the following day, we found a servant waiting there to drive us to old Count Thun's,

A posthumous portrait of Nannerl Mozart, dated 1875.

at whose house we are now staying. I really cannot tell you what kindnesses the family are showering on us. On Tuesday, November 4th, I am giving a concert in the theatre here and, as I have not a single symphony with me, I am writing a new one at break-neck speed, which must be finished by that time . . .

TO HIS FATHER

Vienna, 24 April 1784

We now have here the famous Strinasacchi from Mantua, a very good violinist. She has a great deal of taste and feeling in her playing. I am this moment composing a sonata which we are going to play together on Thursday at her concert in the theatre. I must tell you that some quartets have just appeared, composed by a certain Pleyel, a pupil of Joseph Haydn. If you do not know them, do try and get hold of them; you will find them worth the trouble. They are very well written and most pleasing to listen to. You will also see at once who was his master. Well, it will be a lucky day for music if later on Pleyel should be able to replace Haydn.

TO HIS FATHER

Vienna, 15 May 1784

Mon très cher Père!

I gave to-day to the mail coach the symphony which I composed in Linz for old Count Thun and also four concertos. I am not particular about the symphony, but I do ask you to have the four concertos copied at home, for the Salzburg copyists are as little to be trusted as the Viennese. I know for a positive fact that Hofstetter made two copies of Haydn's music. For example, I really possess the last three symphonies he wrote. And as no one but myself possesses these new concertos in B♭ and D, and no one but myself and Fräulein von Ployer (for whom I composed them) those in E♭ and G, the only way in which they could fall into other hands is by that kind of cheating. I myself have everything copied in my room and in my presence. . . .

TO HIS FATHER
Vienna, 26 May 1784

. . . The concerto Herr Richter praised to her so warmly is the one in B♭, the first one I composed and which he praised so highly to me at the time. I really cannot choose between the two of them, but I regard them both as concertos which are bound to make the performer perspire. From the point of view of difficulty the B♭ concerto beats the one in D. Well, I am very curious to hear which of the three in B♭, D and G you and my sister prefer. The one in E♭ does not belong at all to the same category. It is one of a quite peculiar kind, composed rather for a small orchestra than for a large one. So it is really only a question of the three grand concertos. I am longing to hear whether your judgement will coincide with the general opinion in Vienna and with my own view. Of course it is necessary to hear all three well performed and with all the parts. I am quite willing to wait patiently until I get them back, so long as no one else is allowed to get hold of them. Only to-day I could have got twenty-four ducats for one of them, but I think that it will be more profitable to me to keep them by me for a few years more and then have them engraved and published. . . .

TO HIS SISTER
Vienna, 18 August 1784

. . . My wife and I wish you all joy and happiness in your change of state and are only heartily sorry that we cannot have the pleasure of being present at your wedding. But we hope to embrace you as Frau von Sonnenburg and your husband also next spring both at Salzburg and at St Gilgen. Our only regrets are for our dear father, who will now be left so utterly alone! . . .

TO JOSEPH HAYDN AT EISENSTADT
Vienna, 1 September 1785

To my dear friend Haydn

A father who had decided to send out his sons into the great world, thought it his duty to entrust them to the protection and guidance of a man who was very celebrated at the time and who, moreover, happened to be his best friend.

In like manner I send my six sons to you, most celebrated and very dear friend. They are, indeed, the fruit of a long and laborious study; but the hope which many friends have given me that this toil will be in some degree rewarded, encourages me and flatters me with the thought that these children may one day prove a source of consolation to me.

ABOVE *Mozart and Joseph Haydn, with Mozart's wife listening. Contemporary silhouette by an unknown artist.*

ABOVE *A silhouette of Mozart by Hiernonymus Löschenkohl, published in 1786.*

LEFT *The title page of the six string quartets which Mozart dedicated to Joseph Haydn in 1785.*

Joseph Haydn, a portrait by Thomas Hardy, 1791.

Anna Selina (Nancy) Storace, who first played Susanna in Le nozze di Figaro; *an engraving by Pietro Bertelini, 1788.*

During your last stay in this capital you yourself, my very dear friend, expressed to me your approval of these compositions. Your good opinion encourages me to offer them to you and leads me to hope that you will not consider them wholly unworthy of your favour. Please then receive them kindly and be to them a father, guide and friend! From this moment I surrender to you all my rights over them. I entreat you, however, to be indulgent to those faults which may have escaped a father's partial eye, and, in spite of them, to continue your generous friendship towards one who so highly appreciates it. Meanwhile, I remain with all my heart, dearest friend, your most sincere friend

W. A. MOZART

THE GREAT OPERAS
1785-91

TO FRANZ ANTON HOFFMEISTER
Vienna, 20 November 1785

My dear Hoffmeister!

I turn to you in my distress and beg you to help me out with some money, which I need very badly at the moment. Further, I entreat you to endeavour to procure for me as soon as possible the thing you know about. Forgive me for constantly worrying you, but as you know me and are aware how anxious I am that your business should succeed, I am convinced that you will not misconstrue my importunity and that you will help me as readily as I shall help you.

MZT

TO BARON GOTTFRIED VON JACQUIN
Prague, 14 January 1787

... At six o'clock I drove with Count Canal to the so-called Bretfeld ball, where the cream of the beauties of Prague are wont to gather. Why – you ought to have been there, my friend! I fancy I see you running, or rather, limping after all those pretty women, married and unmarried! I neither danced nor flirted with any of them, the former, because I was too tired, and the latter owing to my natural bashfulness. I looked on, however, with the greatest pleasure while all these people flew about in sheer delight to the music of my 'Figaro', arranged for quadrilles and waltzes. For here they talk about nothing but 'Figaro'. Nothing is played, sung, or whistled but 'Figaro'. No opera is drawing like 'Figaro'. Nothing, nothing but 'Figaro'. Certainly a great honour for me! ... When I remember that after my return I shall enjoy only for a short while the pleasure of your valued society and shall then have to forgo this happiness for such a long

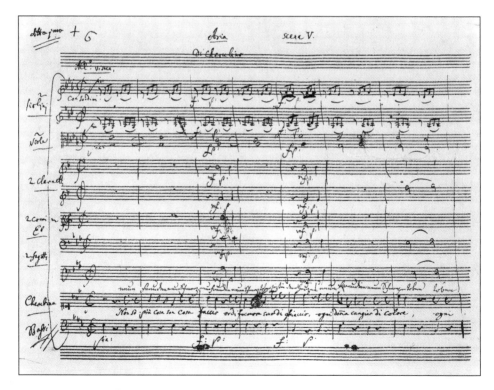

The autograph of Cherubino's aria from Le Nozze di Figaro.

196

Announcement of the first performance of Le nozze di Figaro *on 1 May 1785 at the Burgtheater.*

time, perhaps for ever, then indeed I realize the extent of the friendship and regard which I cherish for your whole family. Now farewell, dearest friend, dearest Hinkity Honky! That is your name, as you must know. We all invented names for ourselves on the journey. Here they are. I am Punkitititi – My wife is Schabla Pumfa. Hofer is Rozka-Pumpa. Stadler is Nàtschibinitschibi. My servant Joseph is Sàgadaratà. My dog Gaukerl is Schamanuzky – Madame Quallenberg is Runzifunzi – Mlle Crux Ps—Ramlo is Schurimuri. Freistädtler is Gaulimauli. Be so kind as to tell him his name. Well, adieu. My concert is to take place in the theatre on Friday, the 19th, and I shall probably have to give a second one, which unfortunately will prolong my stay here. Please give my kind regards to your worthy parents and embrace your brother (who by the way could be christened Blatterrizi) a thousand times for me; and I kiss your sister's hands (her name is Signora Dinimininimi) a hundred thousand times and urge her to practise hard on her new pianoforte. But this admonition is really unnecessary, for I must confess that I have never yet had a pupil who was so diligent and who showed so much zeal – and indeed I am looking forward to giving her lessons again according to my small ability. . . .

TO HIS FATHER
Vienna, 4 April 1787

Mon très cher Père!

I am very much annoyed that owing to the stupidity of Madame Storace my letter never reached you. Amongst other things it contained, I expressed the hope that you had received my last letter; but as you do not mention this particular one, I mean, my second letter from Prague, I do not know what to think. It is quite likely that some servant of Count Thun's had the brilliant idea of pocketing the postage money. Indeed I would rather pay double postage than suspect that my letters have fallen into the wrong hands. Ramm and the two Fischers, the bass singer and the oboist from London, came here this Lent. If the latter when we knew him in Holland played no better than he does now, he certainly does not deserve the reputation he enjoys. But this is between ourselves. In those days I was not competent to form an opinion. All that I remember is that I liked his playing immensely, as indeed everyone did. This is quite understandable, of course, on the assumption that taste can undergo remarkable changes. Possibly he plays in some old-fashioned style? Not at all! The long and short of it is that he plays like a bad beginner. Young André, who took some lessons from Fiala, plays a thousand times better. And then his concertos! His own compositions! Why, each ritornello lasts a quarter of an hour; and then our hero comes in, lifts up one leaden foot after the other and stamps on the floor with each in turn. His tone is entirely nasal, and his held notes like the tremulant on the organ. Would you ever have thought that his playing is like this? Yet it is nothing but the truth, though a truth which I should only tell to you.

This very moment I have received a piece of news which greatly distresses me, the more so as I gathered from your last letter that, thank God, you were very well indeed. But now I hear that you are really ill. I need hardly tell you how greatly I am longing to receive some reassuring news from yourself. And I still expect it; although I have now made a habit of being prepared in all affairs of life for the worst. As death, when we come to consider it closely, is the true goal of our existence, I have formed during the last few years such close relations with this best and truest friend of mankind, that his image is not only no longer terrifying to me, but is indeed very soothing and consoling! ... I hope and trust that while I am writing this, you are feeling better. But if, contrary to all expectation, you are not recovering, I implore you by ... not to hide it from me, but to tell me the whole truth or get someone to write it to me, so that as quickly as is humanly possible I may come to your arms. I entreat you by all that is sacred – to both of us. Nevertheless I trust that I shall soon have a reassuring letter from

you; and cherishing this pleasant hope, I and my wife and our little Karl kiss your hands a thousand times and I am ever your most obedient son

W. A. MOZART

TO BARON GOTTFRIED VON JACQUIN
Vienna, 29 May 1787

. . . I inform you that on returning home to-day I received the sad news of my most beloved father's death. You can imagine the state I am in.

Joseph Quaglio's watercolour set for the graveyard scene in Don Giovanni, *1789.*

TO HIS SISTER
Vienna, 2 June 1787

Dearest Sister!

You can easily imagine, as our loss is equally great, how pained I was by the sad news of the sudden death of our dearest father – Since at the moment it is impossible for me to leave Vienna (which I would gladly do if only to have the pleasure of embracing you) and since it would be hardly worth my while to do so for the sake of our late father's estate, I must confess that I too am entirely of your opinion about having a public auction. But before it takes place I should like to see the inventory, so as to be able to choose some personal effects – But if, as Herr F. D'Yppold has written to tell me, there is a *dispositio paterna inter liberos,* then, of course, I must be informed of this *dispositio* beforehand, so as to be able to make further arrangements – Hence I am now expecting an accurate copy of it and after a rapid perusal of its contents I shall let you have my opinion at once – Please see that the enclosed letter is handed to our kind and sincere friend Herr F. D'Yppold – As he has already proved his friendship to our family on so many occasions, I trust that he will again be a friend to me also and act for me in any necessary events – Farewell, dearest sister! I am

ever your faithful brother

W. A. MOZART

P.S. – My wife wishes to be remembered to you and your husband, and so do I –

TO HIS SISTER
Vienna, 16 June 1787

Dearest, most beloved Sister!

I was not at all surprised, as I could easily guess the reason, that you yourself did not inform me of the sad death of our most dear father, which to me was quite unexpected. May God take him to Himself! Rest assured, my dear, that if you desire a kind brother to love and protect you, you will find one in me on every occasion. My dearest, most beloved sister! If you were still unprovided for, all this would be quite unnecessary, for, as I have already said and thought a thousand times, I should leave everything to you with the greatest delight. But as the property would really be of no use to you, while, on the contrary, it would be a considerable help to me, I think it my duty to consider my wife and child.

TO HIS SISTER

Vienna, 1 August 1787

Dearest, most beloved Sister!

At the moment I am simply replying to your letters, so I am writing very little and in great haste, as I really have far too much to do. As both your husband, my dear brother-in-law, whom I ask you to kiss a thousand times for me, and I are particularly anxious to wind up the whole business as soon as possible, I am accepting his offer, on the understanding, however, that the thousand *gulden* shall be paid to me not in Imperial but in Viennese currency and, moreover, as a bill of exchange. Next post-day I shall send your husband the draft of an agreement or rather of a contract between us. Then the two original documents will follow, one signed by me, the other to be signed by him. I shall send you as soon as possible some new compositions of mine for the clavier. Please do not forget about my scores. A thousand farewells to you. I must close. My wife and our Karl send a thousand greetings to you and your husband, and I am ever your brother who loves you sincerely,

W. A. MOZART

TO HIS BROTHER-IN-LAW BARON VON BERCHTOLD ZU SONNENBURG AT ST GILGEN

Vienna, 29 September 1787

Dearest Brother!

In great haste. If you are sending me the bill of exchange, please address it to Herr Michael Puchberg. For he has instructions to take charge of the money, as I am leaving very early on Monday morning for Prague – Farewell. Kiss our dear sister a thousand times on our behalf. . . .

TO BARON GOTTFRIED VON JACQUIN

Prague, 15–25 October 1787

Dearest Friend!

You probably think that my opera is over by now. If so, you are a little mistaken. In the first place, the stage personnel here are not as smart as those in Vienna, when it comes to mastering an opera of this kind in a very short time. Secondly, I found on my arrival that so few preparations and arrangements had

201

Prague, in an anonymous 18th-century view.

been made that it would have been absolutely impossible to produce it on the 14th, that is, yesterday. So yesterday my 'Figaro' was performed in a fully lighted theatre and I myself conducted.

In this connexion I have a good joke to tell you. A few of the leading ladies here, and in particular one very high and mighty one, were kind enough to find it very ridiculous, unsuitable, and Heaven knows what else that the Princess[1] should be entertained with a performance of Figaro, the 'Crazy Day'[2], as the management were pleased to call it. It never occurred to them that no opera in the world, unless it is written specially for it, can be exactly suitable for such an occasion and that therefore it was of absolutely no consequence whether this or that opera were given, provided that it was a good opera and one which the Princess did not know; and 'Figaro' at least fulfilled this last condition. In short by her persuasive tongue the ringleader brought things to such a pitch that the government forbade the impresario to produce this opera on that night. So she was triumphant! *'Ho vinto'* she called out one evening from her box. No doubt she never suspected that the *ho* might be changed to a *sono*. But the following day Le

1. Prince Anton of Saxony and his bride, the Archduchess Maria Theresa, a sister of the Emperor Joseph II, spent a few days in Prague during their honeymoon.
2. The sub-title of Beaumarchais's comedy 'Le mariage de Figaro' is 'La folle journée'.

Noble appeared, bearing a command from His Majesty to the effect that if the new opera could not be given, 'Figaro' was to be performed! My friend, if only you had seen the handsome, magnificent nose of this lady! Oh, it would have amused you as much as it did me! 'Don Giovanni' has now been fixed for the 24th.

October 21st. It was fixed for the 24th, but a further postponement has been caused by the illness of one of the singers. As the company is so small, the impresario is in a perpetual state of anxiety and has to spare his people as much as possible, lest some unexpected indisposition should plunge him into the most awkward of all situations, that of not being able to produce any show whatsoever!

So everything dawdles along here because the singers, who are lazy, refuse to rehearse on opera days and the manager, who is anxious and timid, will not force them. But what is this? – Is it possible? What vision meets my ears, what sound

The Karlsbrücke, Prague; engraving by J. Balzar after Scotti di Casano.

bombards my eyes? A letter from – I am almost rubbing my eyes sore – Why, it is – The devil take me † God protect us † It actually is from you – indeed! If winter were not upon us, I would smash the stove in good earnest. But as I frequently use it now and intend to use it more often in future, you will allow me to express my surprise in a somewhat more moderate fashion and merely tell you in a few words that I am extraordinarily pleased to have news from you and your most precious family.

October 25th. To-day is the eleventh day that I have been scrawling this letter. You will see from this that my intentions are good. Whenever I can snatch a moment, I daub in another little piece. But indeed I cannot spend much time over it, because I am far too much at the disposal of other people and far too little at my own. I need hardly tell you, as we are such old friends, that this is not the kind of life I prefer.

My opera is to be performed for the first time next Monday, October 29th. You shall have an account of it from me a day or two later. . . .

Announcement of the first performance of Don Giovanni *in the National Theatre, Prague, on 29 October 1787.*

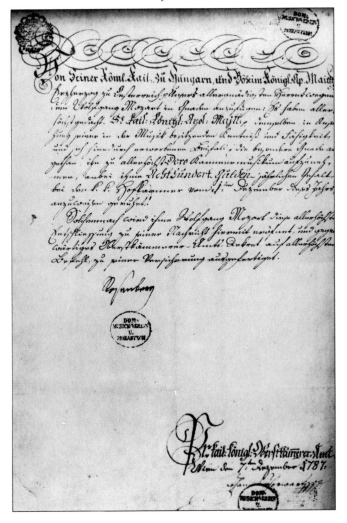

On 7 December 1787 Mozart was appointed Chamber Composer to Joseph II, a post in which he succeeded Gluck.

TO HIS SISTER
Vienna, 19 December 1787

Dearest Sister,

I most humbly beg your pardon for having left you so long without an answer. Of my writing 'Don Giovanni' for Prague and of the opera's triumphant success you may have heard already, but that His Majesty the Emperor has now taken me into his service will probably be news to you. I am sure you will be pleased to hear it. . . .

205

TO MICHAEL PUCHBERG
Vienna, early June 1788

Dearest Brother![1]

Your true friendship and brotherly love embolden me to ask a great favour of you. I still owe you eight ducats. Apart from the fact that at the moment I am not in a position to pay you back this sum, my confidence in you is so boundless that I dare to implore you to help me out with a hundred *gulden* until next week, when my concerts in the Casino are to begin. By that time I shall certainly have received my subscription money and shall then be able quite easily to pay you back 136 *gulden* with my warmest thanks.[2]

1. Brother Freemason.
2. Puchberg noted on this letter: 'Sent 100 *gulden*.'

An anonymous painting showing a meeting of a masonic lodge in Vienna, in about 1790, with Prince Nicolaus Esterházy officiating. Mozart is seated in the foreground on the right.

TO MICHAEL PUCHBERG
Vienna, 17 June 1788

Most honourable Brother of the Order,
 dearest, most beloved Friend!

The conviction that you are indeed my friend and that you know me to be a man of honour encourages me to open my heart to you completely and to make you the following request. In accordance with my natural frankness I shall go straight to the point without affectation.

If you have sufficient regard and friendship for me to assist me for a year or two with one or two thousand *gulden*, at a suitable rate of interest, you will help me enormously! You yourself will surely admit the sense and truth of my statement when I say that it is difficult, nay impossible, to live when one has to wait for various odd sums. If one has not at least a minimum of capital behind one, it is impossible to keep one's affairs in order. Nothing can be done with nothing. If you will do me this kindness then, *primo*, as I shall have some money to go on with, I can meet necessary expenses whenever they occur, and therefore more easily, whereas now I have to postpone payments and then often at the most awkward time I have to spend all I receive at one go; *secondo*, I can work with a mind more free from care and with a lighter heart, and thus earn more. As to security I do not suppose that you will have any doubts. You know more or less how I stand and you know my principles. You need not be anxious about the subscription: I am now extending the time by a few months. I have hopes of finding more patrons abroad than here.

I have now opened my whole heart to you in a matter which is of the utmost importance to me; that is, I have acted as a true brother. But it is only with a true brother that one can be perfectly frank. And now I look forward eagerly to your reply, which I do hope will be favourable. I do not know, but I take you to be a man who, provided he can do so, will like myself certainly assist a friend, if he be a true friend, or his brother, if he be indeed a brother. If you should find it inconvenient to part with so large a sum at once, then I beg you to lend me until to-morrow at least a couple of hundred *gulden*, as my landlord in the Landstrasse has been so importunate that in order to avoid an unpleasant incident I have had to pay him on the spot, and this has made things very awkward for me! We are sleeping to-night, for the first time, in our new quarters, where we shall remain both summer and winter. On the whole the change is all the same to me, in fact I prefer it. As it is, I have very little to do in town, and as I am not exposed to so many visitors, I shall have more time for work. If I have to go to town on business, which will certainly not be very often, any *fiacre* will take me there for ten *kreutzer*. Moreover our rooms are cheaper and during the spring, summer and autumn more pleasant, as I have a garden too. The address is Währingergasse, bei den Drei Sternen, No. 135. Pray regard this letter as a real proof of my complete confidence in you and remain ever my friend and brother as I shall be until the grave, your true, most devoted friend and brother.

W. A. MOZART

P.S. – When are we to have a little musical party at your house again? ...

TO MICHAEL PUCHBERG
Vienna, 27 June 1788

Most honourable B.O.,

    dearest, most beloved Friend!

    I have been expecting to go to town myself one of these days and to be able to thank you in person for the kindness you have shown me. But now I should not even have the courage to appear before you, as I am obliged to tell you frankly that it is impossible for me to pay back so soon the money you have lent me and that I must beg you to be patient with me! I am very much distressed that your circumstances at the moment prevent you from assisting me as much as I could wish, for my position is so serious that I am unavoidably obliged to raise money somehow. But, good God, in whom can I confide? In no one but you, my best friend! If you would only be so kind as to get the money for me through some other channel! I shall willingly pay the interest and whoever lends it to me will, I believe, have sufficient security in my character and my income. I am only too grieved to be in an extremity; but that is the very reason why I should like a fairly substantial sum for a somewhat longer period, I mean, in order to be able to prevent a recurrence of this state of affairs. If you, my most worthy brother, do not help me in this predicament, I shall lose my honour and my credit, which of all things I wish to preserve. I rely entirely on your genuine friendship and brotherly love and confidently expect that you will stand by me in word and deed. If my wish is fulfilled, I can breathe freely again, because I shall then be able to put my affairs in order and keep them so. Do come and see me. I am always at home. During the ten days since I came to live here I have done more work than in two months in my former quarters, and if such black thoughts did not come to me so often, thoughts which I banish by a tremendous effort, things would be even better, for my rooms are pleasant – comfortable – and – cheap. I shall not detain you longer with my drivel but shall stop talking – and hope.

Ever your grateful servant, true friend and B.O.

W. A. MOZART

TO MICHAEL PUCHBERG
Vienna, early July 1788

Dearest Friend and B.O.

Owing to great difficulties and complications my affairs have become so involved that it is of the utmost importance to raise some money on these two pawnbroker's tickets. In the name of our friendship I implore you to do me this favour; but you must do it immediately. Forgive my importunity, but you know my situation. Ah! If only you had done what I asked you! Do it even now – then everything will be as I desire.

Ever your

MOZART

TO FRANZ HOFDEMEL
Vienna, end of March 1789

Dearest Friend!

I am taking the liberty of asking you without any hesitation for a favour. I should be very much obliged to you if you could and would lend me a hundred *gulden* until the 20th of next month. On that day I receive the quarterly instalment of my salary and shall then repay the loan with thanks. I have relied too much on a sum of a hundred ducats due to me from abroad. Up to the present I have not yet received it, although I am expecting it daily. Meanwhile I have left myself too short of cash, so that at the moment I greatly need some ready money and have therefore appealed to your goodness, as I am absolutely convinced of your friendship.

Well, we shall soon be able to call one another by a more delightful name! For your novitiate is very nearly at an end!

MOZART

Dearest little Wife!

While the Prince is busy bargaining about horses, I am delighted to seize this opportunity to write a few lines to you, dearest little wife of my heart. How are you? I wonder whether you think of me as often as I think of you? Every other moment I look at your portrait – and weep partly for joy, partly for sorrow. Look after your health which is so precious to me and fare well, my darling! Do not worry about me, for I am not suffering any discomforts or any annoyance on this journey – apart from your absence – which, as it can't be helped, can't be remedied. I write this note with eyes full of tears. *Adieu.* I shall write a longer and more legible letter to you from Prague, for then I shan't have to hurry so much. *Adieu.* I kiss you millions of times most tenderly and am ever yours, true till death

stu – stu

MOZART

Kiss Karl for me and give all sorts of messages to Herr and Frau von Puchberg. More very soon.

Dearest, most beloved little Wife!

We expected to reach Dresden after dinner on Saturday, but we did not arrive until yesterday, at two o'clock in the afternoon, as the roads were so bad. All the same I went yesterday to the Neumanns, where Madame Duschek is staying, in order to deliver her husband's letter. Her room is on the third floor beside the corridor and from it you can see anyone who is coming to the house. When I arrived at the door, Herr Neumann was already there and asked me to whom he had the honour to speak. 'That I shall tell you in a moment', I replied, 'but please be so kind as to call Madame Duschek, so that my joke may not be spoilt.' But at the same moment Madame Duschek stood before me, for she had recognized me from the window and had said at once: 'Why, here comes someone who is very like Mozart.' Well, we were all delighted. There was a large party, consisting entirely of ugly women, who by their charm, however, made up for their lack of beauty. ....

Dearest little wife, if only I had a letter from you! If I were to tell you all the things I do with your dear portrait, I think that you would often laugh. For instance, when I take it out of its case, I say, 'Good-day, Stanzerl! – Good-day, little rascal, pussy-pussy, little turned-up nose, little bagatelle, *Schluck und Druck*', and when I put it away again, I let it slip very slowly, saying all the time, 'Nu – Nu – Nu – Nu!' with the peculiar emphasis which this word so full of meaning demands, and then just at the last, quickly, 'Good night, little mouse, sleep well.' Well, I suppose I have been writing something very foolish (to the world at all events); but to us who love each other so dearly, it is not foolish at all. To-day is the sixth day since I left you and by Heaven! it seems a year. I expect you will have some difficulty here and there in reading my letter, because I am writing in a hurry and therefore rather badly. *Adieu*, my only love! The carriage is waiting. This time I do not say: 'Hurrah – the carriage has come at last', but '*male*'. Farewell, and love me for ever as I love you. I kiss you a million times most lovingly and am ever your husband who loves you tenderly

W. A. MOZART

P.S. – How is our Karl behaving? Well, I hope. Kiss him for me. . . .

TO HIS WIFE
Dresden, 16 April 1789
Half-past eleven at night

Dearest, most beloved little Wife!

What? Still in Dresden? Yes, my love. Well, I shall tell you everything as minutely as possible. On Monday, April 13th, after breakfasting with the Neumanns we all went to the Court chapel. The mass was by Naumann, who conducted it himself, and very poor stuff it was. We were in an oratory opposite the orchestra. All of a sudden Neumann nudged me and introduced me to Herr von König, who is the *Directeur des Plaisirs* (of the melancholy *plaisirs* of the Elector). He was extremely nice and when he asked me whether I should like His Highness to hear me, I replied that it would indeed be a great privilege, but that, as I was not travelling alone, I could not prolong my stay. So we left it at that. My princely travelling companion invited the Neumanns and Madame Duschek to lunch. While we were at table a message came that I was to play at court on the following day, Tuesday, April 14th, at half-past five in the evening. That is something quite out of the ordinary for Dresden, for it is usually very difficult to get a hearing, and you know that I never thought of performing at court here. We had arranged a quartet among ourselves at the Hôtel de Pologne. So we performed it in the Chapel with Anton Teiber (who, as you know, is organist here) and with Herr Kraft, Prince Esterházy's violoncellist, who is here with his son. At this little concert I introduced the trio which I wrote for Herr von Puchberg and it was played quite decently. Madame Duschek sang a number of arias from 'Figaro' and 'Don Giovanni'. The next day I played at court my new concerto in D, and on the following morning, Wednesday, April 15th, I received a very handsome snuff-box. Then we lunched with the Russian Ambassador, to whom I played a great deal. After lunch we agreed to have some organ playing and drove to the church at four o'clock – Naumann was there too. At this point you must know that a certain Hässler, who is organist at Erfurt, is in Dresden. Well, he too was there. He was a pupil of a pupil of Bach's. His *forte* is the organ and the clavier (clavichord). Now people here think that because I come from Vienna, I am quite unacquainted with this style and mode of playing. Well, I sat down at the organ and played. Prince Lichnowsky, who knows Hässler very well, after some difficulty persuaded him to play also. This Hässler's chief excellence on the organ consists in his foot-work, which, since the pedals are graded here, is not so very wonderful. Moreover, he has done no more than commit to memory the harmony and modulations of old Sebastian Bach and is not capable of executing a fugue properly; and his playing is not thorough. Thus he is far from being an Albrechtsberger. After that we decided to go back to the Russian Ambassador's, so that Hässler might hear me on the *fortepiano*. He played too. I consider Mlle Aurnhammer as good a player on the *fortepiano* as he is, so you can imagine that he has begun to sink very considerably in my estimation. After that we went to the opera, which is truly wretched. Do you know who is one of the singers? Why – Rosa Manservisi. You can picture her delight at seeing me. But the leading woman singer, Madame Allegranti, is far better than Madame Ferraresi, which, I admit, is not saying very much. When the opera was over we went home. Then came the happiest of all moments for me. I found a letter from you, that letter which I had longed for so ardently, my darling, my beloved! Madame Duschek and the Neumanns were with me as usual. But I immediately went off in triumph to my room, kissed the letter countless times before breaking the seal, and then devoured it rather than read it. I stayed in my room a long time; for I could not read it or kiss it often enough. When I rejoined the company, the

Neumanns asked me whether I had had a letter from you, and when I said that I had, they all congratulated me most heartily – as every day I had been lamenting that I had not yet heard from you. They are delightful people. Now for your dear letter. You shall receive by the next post an account of what will have taken place here up to the time of our departure.

Dear little wife, I have a number of requests to make. I beg you

(1) not to be melancholy,

(2) to take care of your health and to beware of the spring breezes,

(3) not to go out walking alone – and preferably not to go out walking at all,

(4) to feel absolutely assured of my love. Up to the present I have not written a single letter to you without placing your dear portrait before me.

(6) and lastly I beg you to send me more details in your letters. I should very much like to know whether our brother-in-law Hofer came to see us the day after my departure? Whether he comes very often, as he promised me he would? Whether the Langes come sometimes? Whether progress is being made with the portrait? What sort of life are you leading? All these things are naturally of great interest to me.

(5) I beg you in your conduct not only to be careful of your honour and mine, but also to consider appearances. Do not be angry with me for asking this. You ought to love me even more for thus valuing our honour.[1]

Now farewell, dearest, most beloved! Please remember that every night before going to bed I talk to your portrait for a good half hour and do the same when I awake. We are leaving on the 18th, the day after to-morrow. So continue to write to Berlin, *Poste Restante*.

O Stru! Stri! I kiss and squeeze you 1,095,060,437,082 times (now you can practise your pronunciation) and am ever your most faithful husband and friend

W. A. MOZART

---

1. The last two paragraphs are thus reversed in the copy of this letter in the Berlin Library. The original is lost. – E.B.

A view of the Neustadter Markt in Dresden, by Canaletto, c. 1750.

TO HIS WIFE
Leipzig, 16 May 1789

Dearest, most beloved little Wife of my Heart!

What? Still in Leipzig? My last letter, dated May 8th or 9th, told you, it is true, that I was leaving at two o'clock that night; but the insistent requests of my friends persuaded me not to make the whole of Leipzig suffer for the shortcomings of one or two persons, but to give a concert on Tuesday, the 12th. From the point of view of applause and glory this concert was absolutely magnificent, but the profits were wretchedly meagre. Madame Duschek, who happens to be in Leipzig, sang at it. The Neumanns of Dresden are all here too. The pleasure of being as long as possible in the company of these dear good people, who all send their best greetings to you, has up to the present delayed my journey. I wanted to get away yesterday, but could find no horses. I am having the same difficulty to-day. For at the present moment everyone is trying to get off and the number of travellers is simply enormous. But we shall be on the road to-morrow at five o'clock. My love! I am very sorry and yet perhaps a little glad that you are in the same state as I have been. No, no! I would rather that you had never been in the same sad situation and I hope and trust that at the time I am writing this letter, you will have received at least one of mine. God knows what the cause may be! I received in Leipzig on April 21st your letter of April 13th. Then I spent seventeen days in Potsdam without any letters. Not until May 8th did I receive your letter of April 24th, while apart from this I have not received any, with the exception of one dated May 5th, which came yesterday. For my part I wrote to you from Leipzig on April 22nd, from Potsdam on the 28th, again from Potsdam on May 5th, from Leipzig on the 9th, and now I am writing on the 16th. The strangest thing of all is that we both found ourselves at the same time in the same sad situation. I was very anxious from April 24th until May 8th, and to judge from your letter this was also the time when you were worried. But I trust that by now you will have got over this. And my consolation is that soon letters will no longer be necessary, for we shall be able to talk to each other and kiss and press each other to our hearts. In my last letter I told you not to write to me any more; and that is the safest course. But I am now asking you to send a reply to this letter, and to address it to Duschek at Prague. You must put it in a proper *couvert* and ask him to keep it until my arrival. I shall probably have to spend at least a week in Berlin. So I shall not be able to reach Vienna before June 5th or 6th – that is, ten or twelve days after you receive this letter. . . . A thousand thanks for the account of Seydelmann's opera. Indeed a more suitable name for him would be Maasmann. But if you knew him personally, as I do, you would probably call him Bluzermann, or at any rate, Zimmentmann.[1] Farewell, dear little wife. Please do all the things I have asked you to do in my letters, for what prompted me was love – real, true love; and love me as much as I do you. I am ever

your only true friend and faithful husband

W. A. MOZART

TO HIS WIFE

Berlin, 19 May 1789

Dearest, most beloved little Wife of my Heart!

Well, I trust that you will by now have received some letters from me, for they can't all have been lost. This time I can't write very much to you, as I have to pay some calls and I am only sending you this to announce my arrival. I shall probably be able to leave by the 25th; at least I shall do my best to do so. But I shall let you know definitely before then. I shall certainly get away by the 27th. Oh, how glad I shall be to be with you again, my darling! But the first thing I shall do is to take you by your front curls; for how on earth could you think, or even imagine, that I had forgotten you? How could I possibly do so? For even supposing such a thing you will get on the very first night a thorough spanking . . . and this you may count upon.

Adieu

Ever your only friend and your husband

who loves you with all his heart

W. A. MOZART

TO MICHAEL PUCHBERG

Vienna, 12–14 July 1789

Dearest, most beloved Friend and most honourable B.O.

Great God! I would not wish my worst enemy to be in my present position. And if you, most beloved friend and brother, forsake me, we are altogether lost,

---

1. The words 'Seidel, Maas, Bluzer and Zimment' are expressions in the Viennese dialect for drinking-measures. Mozart alludes, of course, to Seydelmann's tendency to drink.

both my unfortunate and blameless self and my poor sick wife and child. Only the other day when I was with you I was longing to open my heart to you, but I had not the courage to do so – and indeed I should still not have the courage – for, as it is, I only dare to write and tremble as I do so – and I should not even dare to write, were I not certain that you know me, that you are aware of my circumstances, and that you are wholly convinced of my innocence so far as my unfortunate and most distressing situation is concerned. Good God! I am coming to you not with thanks but with fresh entreaties! Instead of paying my debts I am asking for more money! If you really know me, you must sympathize with my anguish in having to do so. I need not tell you once more that owing to my unfortunate illness I have been prevented from earning anything. But I must mention that in spite of my wretched condition I decided to give subscription concerts at home in order to be able to meet at least my present great and frequent expenses, for I was absolutely convinced of your friendly assistance. But even this has failed. Unfortunately Fate is so much against me, though only in Vienna, that even when I want to, I cannot make any money. A fortnight ago I sent round a list for subscribers and so far the only name on it is that of Baron van Swieten! Now that (the 13th) my dear little wife seems to be improving every day, I should be able to set to work again, if this blow, this heavy blow, had not come. At any rate, people are consoling me by telling me that she is better – although the night before last she was suffering so much – and I on her account – that I was stunned and despairing. But last night (the 14th), she slept so well and has felt so much easier all the morning that I am very hopeful; and at last I am beginning to feel inclined for work. I am now faced, however, with misfortunes of another kind, though, it is true, only for the moment. Dearest, most beloved friend and brother – you know my present circumstances, but you also know my prospects. So let things remain as we arranged; that is, thus or thus, you understand what I mean. Meanwhile I am composing six easy clavier sonatas for Princess Friederike[1] and six quartets for the King[2], all of which Kozeluch is engraving at my expense. At the same time the two dedications will bring me in

---

1. Princess Friederike, the eldest daughter of King Frederick William II of Prussia. Mozart appears to have finished only one of these sonatas, K.576, in D major, his last clavier sonata.
2. Mozart finished three quartets, K.575, composed in 1789, and K.589 and 590, composed in 1790. K.590 was Mozart's last string quartet. Kozeluch did not engrave these works, which were published by Artaria immediately after Mozart's death.

something. In a month or two my fate must be decided in every detail. Therefore most beloved friend, you will not be risking anything so far as I am concerned. So it all depends, my only friend, upon whether you will or can lend me another 500 *gulden*. Until my affairs are settled, I undertake to pay back ten *gulden* a month; and then, as this is bound to happen in a few months, I shall pay back the whole sum with whatever interest you may demand, and at the same time acknowledge myself to be your debtor for life. That, alas, I shall have to remain, for I shall never be able to thank you sufficiently for your friendship and affection. Thank God, that is over. Now you know all. Do not be offended by my confiding in you and remember that unless you help me, the honour, the peace of mind, and perhaps the very life of your friend and brother Mason will be ruined.

   Ever your most grateful servant, true
      friend and brother

W. A. MOZART

At home, 14 July 1789.

O God! – I can hardly bring myself to despatch this letter! – and yet I must! If this illness had not befallen me, I should not have been obliged to beg so shamelessly from my only friend. Yet I hope for your forgiveness, for you know both the good and the bad prospects of my situation. The bad is temporary; the good will certainly persist, once the momentary evil has been alleviated. Adieu. For God's sake forgive me, only forgive me! – and – Adieu.

TO MICHAEL PUCHBERG
Vienna, 17 July 1789

Dearest, most beloved Friend
   and most honourable B.O.

   I fear you are angry with me, for you are not sending me a reply! When I compare the proofs of your friendship with my present demands upon it, I cannot but admit that you are perfectly right. But when I compare my misfortunes (for which I am not to blame) with your kindly disposition towards me, then I do find that there is some excuse for me. As in my last letter to you, my dear friend, I told

219

you quite frankly everything that was burdening my heart, I can only repeat to-day what I said then. But I must still add that (1) I should not require such a considerable sum if I did not anticipate very heavy expenses in connexion with the cure my wife may have to take, particularly if she has to go to Baden. (2) As I am positive that in a short time I shall be in better circumstances, the amount of the sum I shall have to repay is a matter of indifference to me. Nevertheless at the present moment I should prefer it to be a large sum, which would make me feel safer. (3) I entreat you, if it is quite impossible for you to assist me this time with such a large sum, to show your friendship and brotherly affection by helping me at once with as much as you can spare, for I am really in very great need. You certainly cannot doubt my integrity, for you know me too well for that. Nor can you distrust my assurances, my behaviour or my mode of life, as you are well acquainted with my manner of living and my conduct. Consequently, forgive me for thus confiding in you, for I am absolutely convinced that only the impossibility of doing so will prevent you from helping your friend. If you can and if you will entirely relieve me, I shall return thanks to you as my saviour, even beyond the grave, for you will be enabling me to enjoy further happiness on earth. But if you cannot do this, then I beg and implore you, in God's name, for whatever temporary assistance you can give me, and also for your advice and comforting sympathy.

Ever your most grateful servant

MOZART

P.S. – My wife was wretchedly ill again yesterday. To-day leeches were applied and she is, thank God, somewhat better. I am indeed most unhappy, and am forever hovering between hope and fear! Dr Closset came to see her again yesterday.

TO HIS WIFE AT BADEN
Vienna, middle of August 1789

Dearest little Wife!

I was delighted to get your dear letter – and I trust that you received yesterday my second one together with the infusion, the electuaries and the ants' eggs. I shall sail off to you at five o'clock to-morrow morning. Were it not for the joy of seeing you again and embracing you, I should not drive out to Baden just yet, for

'Figaro' is going to be performed very soon, and as I have some alterations to make, my presence will be required at the rehearsals. I shall probably have to be back here by the 19th. But to stay here until the 19th without you would be quite impossible. Dear little wife! I want to talk to you quite frankly. You have no reason whatever to be unhappy. You have a husband who loves you and does all he possibly can for you. As for your foot, you must just be patient and it will surely get well again. I am glad indeed when you have some fun – of course I am – but I do wish that you would not sometimes make yourself so cheap. In my opinion you are too free and easy with N.N.[1] . . . and it was the same with N.N., when he was still at Baden. Now please remember that N.N. are not half so familiar with other women, whom they perhaps know more intimately, as they are with you. Why, N.N. who is usually a well-conducted fellow and particularly respectful to women, must have been misled by your behaviour into writing the most disgusting and most impertinent *sottises* which he put into his letter. A woman must always make herself respected, or else people will begin to talk about her. My love! Forgive me for being so frank, but my peace of mind demands it as well as our mutual happiness. Remember that you yourself once admitted to me that you were inclined to comply too easily. You know the consequences of that. Remember too the promise you gave to me. Oh, God, do try, my love! Be merry and happy and charming to me. Do not torment yourself and me with unnecessary jealousy. Believe in my love, for surely you have proofs of it, and you will see how happy we shall be. Rest assured that it is only by her prudent behaviour that a wife can enchain her husband. Adieu. To-morrow I shall kiss you most tenderly.

MOZART

TO MICHAEL PUCHBERG
Vienna, 29 December 1789

Most honourable Friend and B.O.

Do not be alarmed at the contents of this letter. Only to you, most beloved friend, who know everything about me and my circumstances, have I the courage to open my heart completely. According to the present arrangement I am to

---

1. In this and the following letters to his wife certain names have been crossed out by a later hand.

Announcement of the first performance of Cosi fan tutte, *on 26 January 1790 in the Burgtheater, Vienna.*

receive from the management next month 200 ducats for my opera. If you can and will lend me 400 *gulden* until then, you will be rescuing your friend from the greatest embarrassment; and I give you my word of honour that by that time you will have the money back in full and with many thanks. In spite of the great expenses I have to incur daily, I should try to hold out until then, were it not the New Year, when I really must pay off the chemists and doctors, whom I am no longer employing, unless I wish to lose my good name. We have in particular alienated Hundschowsky[1] (for certain reasons) in a rather unfriendly fashion, so that I am doubly anxious to settle accounts with him. Beloved friend and brother! – I know only too well how much I owe you! I beg you to be patient a little longer in regard to my old debts. I shall certainly repay you, that I promise on my honour. Once more I beg you, rescue me just this time from my horrible situation. As soon as I get the money for my opera, you will have the 400 *gulden* back for certain. And this summer, thanks to my work for the King of Prussia, I

---

1. Johann Nepomuk Hunczovsky (1752–98), a physician and professor at the Military Hospital at Gumpendorf, then a suburb of Vienna. He was a Freemason.

hope to be able to convince you completely of my honesty. Contrary to our arrangements we cannot have any music at our house to-morrow – I have too much work. By the way, if you see Zistler, you might tell him this. But I invite you, you alone, to come along on Thursday at 10 o'clock in the morning to hear a short rehearsal of my opera. I am only inviting Haydn and yourself. I shall tell you when we meet about Salieri's plots, which, however, have completely failed already. *Adieu.*

Ever your grateful friend and brother,

W. A. MOZART

TO MICHAEL PUCHBERG
Vienna, end of March or beginning of April 1790

Herewith, dearest friend, I am sending you Handel's life. When I got home from my visit to you the other day, I found the enclosed note from Baron van Swieten. You will gather from it, as I did, that my prospects are now better than ever. I now stand on the threshold of my fortune; but the opportunity will be lost for ever if this time I cannot make use of it. My present circumstances, however, are such that in spite of my excellent prospects I must abandon all hope of furthering my fortunes unless I can count on the help of a staunch friend. For some time you must have noticed my constant sadness – and only the very many kindnesses which you have already rendered me, have prevented me from speaking out. Now, however – once more, but for the last time – I call upon you to stand by me to the utmost of your power in this most urgent matter which is going to determine my whole happiness. You know how my present circumstances, were they to become known, would damage the chances of my application to the court, and how necessary it is that they should remain a secret; for unfortunately at court they do not judge by circumstances, but solely by appearances. You know, and I am sure you are convinced that if, as I may now confidently hope, my application is successful, you will certainly lose nothing. How delighted I shall be to discharge my debts to you! How glad I shall be to thank you and, in addition, to confess myself eternally your debtor! What a pleasant sensation it is to reach one's goal at last – and what a blessed feeling it is when one has helped another to do so! Tears prevent me from completing the picture! In short! – my whole future happiness is in your hands. Act according to the dictates of your noble heart! Do what you can and remember that you are dealing with a right-minded and eternally grateful man, whose situation pains him even more on your account than on his own.

MOZART

TO MICHAEL PUCHBERG
Vienna, 8 April 1780

You are right, dearest friend, not to honour me with a reply! My importunity is too great. I only beg you to consider my position from every point of view, to remember my cordial friendship and my confidence in you and to forgive me! But if you can and will extricate me from a temporary embarrassment, then, for the love of God, do so! Whatever you can easily spare will be welcome. If possible, forget my importunity and forgive me.

... I would have gone to see you myself in order to have a chat with you, but my head is covered with bandages due to rheumatic pains, which make me feel my situation still more keenly. Again, I beg you to help me as much as you can just for this once; and forgive me.

Ever your

MOZART

TO MICHAEL PUCHBERG
Vienna, 23 April 1790

Dearest Friend and Brother,

If you can send me something, even though it be only the small sum you sent me last time, you will greatly oblige your ever faithful friend and brother.

MOZART

TO THE ARCHDUKE FRANCIS
Vienna, first half of May 1790

Your Royal Highness,

I make so bold as to beg your Royal Highness very respectfully to use your most gracious influence with His Majesty the King with regard to my most humble petition to His Majesty. Prompted by a desire for fame, by a love of work and by a conviction of my wide knowledge, I venture to apply for the post of second *Kapellmeister*, particularly as Salieri, that very gifted *Kapellmeister*, has never devoted himself to church music, whereas from my youth up I have made myself completely familiar with this style. The slight reputation which I have acquired in the world by my pianoforte playing, has encouraged me to ask His Majesty for the favour of being entrusted with the musical education of the Royal Family. In the sure conviction that I have applied to the most worthy mediators who, moreover, are particularly gracious to me, I remain with the utmost confidence and shall[1] . . .

TO MICHAEL PUCHBERG
Vienna, 14 August 1790

Dearest Friend and Brother,

Whereas I felt tolerably well yesterday, I am absolutely wretched to-day. I could not sleep all night for pain. I must have got over-heated yesterday from walking so much and then without knowing it have caught a chill. Picture to yourself my condition – ill and consumed with worries and anxieties. Such a state quite definitely prevents me from recovering. In a week or a fortnight I shall be better off – certainly – but at present I am in want! Can you not help me out with a trifle? The smallest sum would be very welcome just now. You would, for the moment at least, bring peace of mind to your true friend, servant and brother

W. A. MOZART

1. The autograph breaks off with these words.

The banks of the Main at Frankfurt, by Wilhelm Friedrich Hirt, 1757.

TO HIS WIFE
Frankfurt, 28 September 1790

Dearest, most beloved little Wife of my Heart!

We have this moment arrived, that is, at one o'clock in the afternoon; so the journey has only taken us six days. We could have done it still more quickly, if on three occasions we had not rested a little at night. Well, we have just alighted at an inn in the suburb of Sachsenhausen, and are in the seventh heaven of delight at having secured a room. ... The journey was very pleasant, and we had fine weather except on one day; and even this one day caused us no discomfort, as my carriage (I should like to give it a kiss!) is splendid. At Regensburg we lunched magnificently to the accompaniment of divine music, we had angelic cooking and some glorious Moselle wine. We breakfasted at Nuremberg, a hideous town. At Würzburg, a fine, magnificent town, we fortified our precious stomachs with coffee. The food was tolerable everywhere, but at Aschaffenburg, two and a half stages from here, mine host was kind enough to fleece us disgracefully.

I am longing for news of you, of your health, our affairs and so forth. I am firmly resolved to make as much money as I can here and then return to you with great joy. What a glorious life we shall have then! I will work – work so hard – that no unforeseen accidents shall ever reduce us to such desperate straits again. ...

226

TO HIS WIFE
Frankfurt, 8 October 1790

. . . I trust that you have dealt with the business about which I wrote to you, and are still dealing with it. I shall certainly not make enough money here to be able to pay back 800 or 1,000 *gulden* immediately on my return. But if the business with Hoffmeister is at least so far advanced that only my presence is required, then, after deducting interest at the rate of 20%, I shall have 1,600 out of 2,000 *gulden*. I can then pay out 1,000 *gulden* and shall have 600 left. Well, I shall begin to give little quartet subscription concerts in Advent and I shall also take pupils. I need never repay the sum, as I am composing for Hoffmeister – so everything will be quite in order. But please settle the affair with Hoffmeister, that is, if you

Joseph Lange's unfinished portrait of Mozart, painted c. 1789-90.

227

really want me to return. If you could only look into my heart. There a struggle is going on between my yearning and longing to see and embrace you once more and my desire to bring home a large sum of money. I have often thought of travelling farther afield, but whenever I tried to bring myself to take the decision, the thought always came to me, how bitterly I should regret it, if I were to separate myself from my beloved wife for such an uncertain prospect, perhaps even to no purpose whatever. I feel as if I had left you years ago. Believe me, my love, if you were with me I might perhaps decide more easily, but I am too much accustomed to you and I love you too dearly to endure being separated from you for long. Besides, all this talk about the Imperial towns is mere misleading chatter. True, I am famous, admired and popular here; on the other hand, the Frankfurt people are even more stingy than the Viennese. . . .

The Coronation is to-morrow.

Take care of your health – and be careful when you go out walking. *Adieu.*

TO HIS WIFE
Frankfurt, 15 October 1790

Dearest little Wife of my Heart!

I have not yet received a reply to any of my letters from Frankfurt, which makes me rather anxious. My concert took place at eleven o'clock this morning. It was a splendid success from the point of view of honour and glory, but a failure as far as money was concerned.

TO HIS WIFE
Munich, 2 November 1790

Dearest, most beloved little Wife of my Heart!

You have no idea how much it pains me that I have to wait until I get to Linz before I can have news from you. Patience; for if one does not know how long one is going to stay in a place, it is impossible to make better arrangements. Though I would have gladly prolonged my stay with my old Mannheim friends, I

only wanted to spend a day here; but now I am obliged to remain until the 5th or 6th, as the Elector has asked me to perform at a concert which he is giving for the King of Naples. It is greatly to the credit of the Viennese court that the King has to hear me in a foreign country . . .

TO MICHAEL PUCHBERG

Vienna, 13 April 1791

Most valued Friend and Brother!

    I shall be drawing my quarterly pay on April 20th, that is, in a week. If you can and will lend me until then about twenty *gulden*, you will oblige me very much, most beloved friend, and you will have it back with very many thanks on the 20th, as soon as I draw my money. I am anxiously awaiting the sum. Ever your most grateful friend

MOZART

TO THE MUNICIPAL COUNCIL OF VIENNA

Vienna, early May 1791

Most honourable and most learned Municipal Councillors of Vienna!

    Most worthy Gentlemen!

    When *Kapellmeister* Hofmann was ill, I thought of venturing to apply for his post, seeing that my musical talents, my works and my skill in composition are well known in foreign countries, my name is treated everywhere with some respect, and I myself was appointed several years ago composer to the distinguished court of Vienna. I trusted therefore that I was not unworthy of this post and that I deserved the favourable consideration of our enlightened municipal council.

    Kapellmeister Hofmann, however, has recovered his health and in the circumstances – for I wish him from my heart a long life – it has occurred to me that it might perhaps be of service to the Cathedral and, most worthy gentlemen, to your advantage, if I were to be attached for the time being as unpaid assistant to this ageing *Kapellmeister* and were to have the opportunity of helping this worthy man in his office, thus gaining the approbation of our learned municipal

229

council by the actual performance of services which I may justly consider myself peculiarly fitted to render on account of my thorough knowledge of both the secular and ecclesiastical styles of music.

Your most humble servant,

WOLFGANG AMADÉ MOZART
Royal and Imperial Court Composer

TO HIS WIFE AT BADEN
Vienna, 6 June 1791

I have this moment received your dear letter and am delighted to hear that you are well and in good spirits. Madame Leutgeb has laundered my nightcap and necktie, but I should like you to see them! Good God! I kept on telling her, 'Do let me show you how she (my wife) does them!' – But it was no use.

TO HIS WIFE AT BADEN
Vienna, 7 June 1791

. . . I simply cannot describe my delight at receiving your last letter of the 6th, which told me that you are well and in good health, and that, very sensibly, you are not taking baths every day. Heavens! How delighted I should have been if you had come to me with the Wildburgs! Indeed I was wild with myself for not telling you to drive into town – but I was afraid of the expense. Yet it would have been *charmant* if you had done so. At five o'clock to-morrow morning, we are all driving out, three carriagefuls of us, and so between nine and ten I expect to find in your arms all the joy which only a man can feel who loves his wife as I do! It is only a pity that I can't take with me either the clavier or the bird! That is why I would rather have gone out alone; but, as it is, I can't get out of the arrangement without offending the company. . . . If it is at all possible, I shall certainly bring your hat with me. *Adieu*, my little sweetheart. I simply cannot tell you how I am looking forward to to-morrow. Ever your

MOZART

TO HIS WIFE AT BADEN
Vienna, 11 June 1791

... I must hurry, as it is already a quarter to seven – and the coach leaves at seven. When you are bathing, do take care not to slip and never stay in alone. If I were you I should occasionally omit a day in order not to do the cure too violently. I trust that someone slept with you last night. I cannot tell you what I would not give to be with you at Baden instead of being stuck here. From sheer boredom I composed to-day an aria for my opera. I got up as early as half-past four. Wonderful to relate, I have got back my watch – but – as I have no key, I have unfortunately not been able to wind it. What a nuisance! Schlumbla! That is a word to ponder on. Well, I wound our big clock instead. *Adieu* – my love! I am lunching to-day with Puchberg. I kiss you a thousand times and say with you in thought: 'Death and despair were his reward!'[1]

Ever your loving husband

W. A. MOZART

See that Karl behaves himself. Give him kisses from me.
Take an electuary if you are constipated – not otherwise.

TO HIS WIFE AT BADEN
Vienna, 25 June 1791

Ma très chère Épouse!

I have this moment received your letter, which has given me extraordinary pleasure. I am now longing for a second one to tell me how the baths are affecting you. I too am sorry not to have been present yesterday at your fine concert, not on account of the music, but because I should have been so happy to be with you. I gave N.N.[2] a surprise to-day. First of all I went to the Rehbergs. Well, Frau Rehberg sent one of her daughters upstairs to tell him that a dear old friend had come from Rome and had searched all the houses in the town without being able to find him. He sent down a message to say, would I please wait a few minutes. Meanwhile, the poor fellow put on his Sunday best, his finest clothes, and turned up with his hair most elaborately dressed. You can imagine how we made fun of him. I can never resist making a fool of someone – if it is not N.N., then it must be

1. A quotation from the 'Zauberflöte'.
2. Probably Leutgeb.

N.N. or Snai.[1] And where did I sleep? At home, of course. And I slept very well, save that the mice kept me most excellent company. Why, I had a first-rate argument with them. I was up before five o'clock. A propos, I advise you not to go to mass to-morrow. Those peasant louts are too cheeky for my taste. . . .

P.S. – Perhaps after all it would be well to give Karl a little rhubarb. Why did you not send me that long letter? Here is a letter for him – I should like to have an answer. Catch – Catch – bis – bis – bs – bs – kisses are flying about for you – bs – why, another one is staggering after the rest!

I have this moment received your second letter. Beware of the baths! And do sleep more – and not so irregularly, or I shall worry – I am a little anxious as it is. *Adieu.*

TO MICHAEL PUCHBERG
Vienna, 25 June 1791

Dearest, most beloved Friend!

Most honourable Brother!

Business has prevented me from having the pleasure of calling on you to-day. I have a request to make. My wife writes to say that she can see that, although they are not expecting it, the people with whom she is living would be glad to receive some payment for her board and lodging and she begs me to send her some money. I had intended to settle everything when it was time for her to leave and I now find myself in very great embarrassment. I should not like to expose her to any unpleasantness; yet at the moment I cannot leave myself short of money. If you, most beloved friend, can assist me with a small sum, which I can send to her at once, you will oblige me exceedingly. I require the loan only for a few days, when you will receive 2,000 *gulden* in my name, from which you can then refund yourself.

Ever your

MOZART

---

1. A nickname for his pupil Süssmayr, who was then at Baden.

TO HIS WIFE AT BADEN
Vienna, 2 July 1791

Ma très chère Épouse!

I trust that you are very well. I have just remembered that you have very seldom been upset during pregnancy. Perhaps the baths are having a too laxative effect? I should not wait for certain proofs which would be too unpleasant. My advice is that you should stop them now! Then I should feel quite easy in my mind. To-day is the day when you are not supposed to take one and yet I wager that that little wife of mine has been to the baths? Seriously – I had much rather you would prolong your cure well into the autumn. I hope that you got my first little note.

Please tell that idiotic fellow Süssmayr to send me my score of the first act, from the introduction to the finale so that I may orchestrate it. It would be a good thing if he could put it together to-day and dispatch it by the first coach to-morrow, for I should then have it at noon. I have just had a visit from a couple of Englishmen who refused to leave Vienna without making my acquaintance. But of course the real truth is that they wanted to meet that great fellow Süssmayr and only came to see me in order to find out where he lived, as they had heard that I was fortunate enough to enjoy his favour. I told them to go to the 'Ungarische Krone' and to wait there until he should return from Baden! Snai! They want to engage him to clean the lamps. I am longing most ardently for news of you. It is half-past twelve already and I have heard nothing. I shall wait a little longer before sealing my letter. . . . Nothing has come, so I must close it! Farewell, dearest, most beloved little wife! Take care of your health, for as long as you are well and are kind to me, I don't care a fig if everything else goes wrong. Follow the advice I gave you at the beginning of this letter and farewell. *Adieu* – a thousand kisses for you and a thousand boxes on the ear for Lacci Bacci. Ever your

MOZART

TO HIS WIFE AT BADEN
Vienna, 3 July 1791

Dearest, most beloved little Wife of my Heart!

I received your letter together with Montecucoli's and am delighted to hear that you are well and in good spirits. I thought as much. If you take the baths twice in succession, you will be thoroughly spanked when I come out to you again! Thanks for the finale you sent and my clothes, but I cannot understand why you

233

did not put in a letter. I searched all the pockets in the coat and trousers. Well, perhaps the post-woman is still carrying it about in her pocket! I am only delighted that you are in good health, my dear little wife. I rely on your following my advice. If you do, I can feel a little calmer! As for my health, I feel pretty well. I trust that my affairs will improve as rapidly as possible. Until they are settled I cannot be quite easy in my mind. But I hope to be so soon.

I trust that N.N. will not forget to copy out at once what I left for him; and I am counting on receiving to-day those portions of my score for which I asked. I see from N.N.'s Latin letter that neither of you is drinking any wine. I don't like that. Have a word with your supervisor, who no doubt will only be too delighted to give you some on my account. It is a wholesome wine and not expensive, whereas the water is horrid. I lunched yesterday at Schikaneder's with the Lieutenant-Colonel, who is also taking the Antony baths. To-day I am lunching with Puchberg. *Adieu*, little sweetheart. Dear Stanzi Marini, I must close in haste, for I have just heard one o'clock strike; and you know that Puchberg likes to lunch early. *Adieu*. Ever your

MOZART

Lots of kisses for Karl and whippings for – that table-fool

TO HIS WIFE AT BADEN
Vienna, 6 July 1791

. . . the greatest pleasure of all you can give me is to be happy and jolly. And if I know for certain that you have everything you want, then all my trouble is a joy and a delight. Indeed the most difficult and complicated situation, in which I can possibly find myself, becomes a trifle, if only I know that you are well and in good spirits. And now, farewell. Make good use of your table-fool. Think of me and talk about me often, both of you. Love me for ever as I do you and be always by Stanzi Marini, as I shall always be your

Stu! Knaller Praller
Schnip-Schnapp-Schnur
Schnepeperl –
Snai! –

Give N.N. a box on the ear and tell him that you simply must kill a fly which I have spied on his face! *Adieu* – Look there! Catch them – bi – bi – bi – three kisses, as sweet as sugar, are flying over to you!

ABOVE LEFT An announcement of the first performance of the Magic Flute.
ABOVE RIGHT The title page of the libretto of La clemenza di Tito.
BELOW LEFT A silhouette of Josefa Mayer, née Weber, the first Queen of the Night.
BELOW RIGHT Emanuel Schikaneder (1751-1812), the actor-manager.

Emanuel Schikaneder as Papageno; engraving by Ignaz Alberti.

Tamino with the three ladies, from Act 1, Scene 3 of the Magic Flute; *engravings from a Brno monthly journal, 1795.*

TO HIS WIFE AT BADEN
Vienna, 7–8 October 1791

Dearest, most beloved little Wife!

I have this moment returned from the opera, which was as full as ever. As usual the duet 'Mann und Weib' and Papageno's *glockenspiel* in Act I had to be repeated and also the trio of the boys in Act II. But what always gives me most pleasure is the silent approval. You can see how this opera is becoming more and more popular. . . .

Friedrich Schinkel's designs for the 1816 Berlin production of the Magic Flute, *Act 1, Scene 4.*

Constanze Mozart, a portrait by Hans Hansen, 1802.

Dearest, most beloved little Wife,

I was exceedingly delighted and overjoyed to find your letter on my return from the opera. Although Saturday, as it is post-day, is always a bad night, the opera was performed to a full house and with the usual applause and repetition of numbers. It will be given again to-morrow, but there will be no performance on Monday. So Süssmayr must bring Stoll in on Tuesday when it will be given again for the first time. I say for the first time, because it will probably be performed several times in succession. I have just swallowed a delicious slice of sturgeon which Don Primus (who is my faithful valet) has brought me; and as I have a rather voracious appetite to-day, I have sent him off again to fetch some more if he can. So during this interval I shall go on writing to you. This morning I worked so hard at my composition that I went on until half-past one. So I dashed

A view of the parish church in Baden, near Vienna, engraved by A. Benedetti after Ferdinand von Wetzelberg. Here the Missa Brevis *(K. 275) was performed in 1791.*

off in great haste to Hofer, simply in order not to lunch alone, where I found Mamma too. After lunch I went home at once and composed again until it was time to go to the opera. Leutgeb begged me to take him a second time and I did so. I am taking Mamma to-morrow. Hofer has already given her the libretto to read. In her case what will probably happen will be that she will see the opera, but not hear it. The N.N.s had a box this evening and applauded everything most heartily. But he, the know-all, showed himself to be such a thorough Bavarian that I could not remain or I should have had to call him an ass. Unfortunately I was there just when the second act began, that is, at the solemn scene. He made fun of everything. At first I was patient enough to draw his attention to a few passages. But he laughed at everything. Well, I could stand it no longer. I called him a Papageno and cleared out. But I don't think that the idiot understood my remark. So I went into another box where Flamm and his wife happened to be. There everything was very pleasant and I stayed to the end. But during Papageno's aria with the *glockenspiel* I went behind the scenes, as I felt a sort of impulse to-day to play it myself. Well, just for fun, at the point where Schikaneder has a pause, I played an arpeggio. He was startled, looked behind the wings and saw me. When he had his next pause, I played no arpeggio. This time he stopped and refused to go on. I guessed what he was thinking and again played a chord. He then struck the *glockenspiel* and said 'Shut up.' Whereupon everyone laughed. I am inclined to think that this joke taught many of the audience for the first time that Papageno does not play the instrument himself. By the way, you have no idea how charming the music sounds when you hear it from a box close to the orchestra – it sounds much better than from the gallery. As soon as you return – you must try this for yourself. . . .

TO HIS WIFE AT BADEN

Vienna, 14 October 1791

Dearest, most beloved little Wife,

Hofer drove out with me yesterday, Thursday the 13th, to see our Karl. We lunched there and then we all drove back to Vienna. At six o'clock I called in the carriage for Salieri and Madame Cavalieri – and drove them to my box. Then I drove back quickly to fetch Mamma and Karl, whom I had left at Hofer's. You can hardly imagine how charming they were and how much they liked not only

Karl Thomas (right) and Franz Xaver Mozart, Wolfgang and Constanze's sons, at the age of 14 and 7 respectively; portrait by Hans Hansen, 1798.

my music, but the libretto and everything. They both said that it was an *operone*,
worthy to be performed for the grandest festival and before the greatest monarch,
and that they would often go to see it, as they had never seen a more beautiful or
delightful show. Salieri listened and watched most attentively and from the
overture to the last chorus there was not a single number that did not call forth
from him a *bravo*! or *bello*! It seemed as if they could not thank me enough for my
kindness. They had intended in any case to go to the opera yesterday. But they
would have had to be in their places by four o'clock. As it was, they saw and
heard everything in comfort in my box. When it was over I drove them home and
then had supper at Hofer's with Karl. Then I drove him home and we both slept
soundly. Karl was absolutely delighted at being taken to the opera. He is looking
splendid. As far as health is concerned, he could not be in a better place, but
everything else there is wretched, alas! All they can do is to turn out a good

Autograph of the Requiem K.626), where the chorus enters in 'Requiem aeternam'.

peasant into the world. But enough of this. As his serious studies (God help them!) do not begin until Monday, I have arranged to keep him until after lunch on Sunday. I told them that you would like to see him. So to-morrow, Saturday, I shall drive out with Karl to see you. You can then keep him, or I shall take him back to Heeger's after lunch. Think it over. A month can hardly do him much harm. In the meantime the arrangement with the Piarists, which is now under discussion, may come to something. On the whole, Karl is no worse; but at the same time he is not one whit better than he was. He still has his old bad manners; he never stops chattering just as he used to do in the past; and he is, if anything, less inclined to learn than before, as out at Perchtoldsdorf all he does is to run about in the garden for five hours in the morning and five hours in the afternoon, as he has himself confessed. In short, the children do nothing but eat, drink, sleep and run wild. Leutgeb and Hofer are with me at the moment. The former is

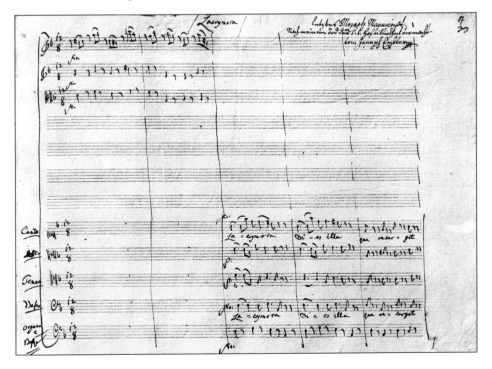

Autograph of the Requiem: the 'Lacrymosa'. Only the first eight bars are in Mozart's hand. The work was completed by his pupil Franz Xaver Süssmayer.

A posthumous portrait of Mozart by Barbara Krafft, 1819.

staying to supper with me. I have sent out my faithful comrade Primus to fetch some food from the Bürgerspital. I am quite satisfied with the fellow. He has only let me down once, when I was obliged to sleep at Hofer's, which annoyed me intensely, as they sleep far too long there. I am happiest at home, for I am accustomed to my own hours. This one occasion put me in a very bad humour. Yesterday the whole day was taken up with that trip to Perchtoldsdorf, so I could not write to you. But that you have not written to me for two days, is really unforgivable. I hope that I shall certainly have a letter from you to-day, and that to-morrow I shall talk to you and embrace you with all my heart.

Farewell. Ever your

MOZART

October 14th, 1791

I kiss Sophie a thousand times. Do what you like with N.N. *Adieu.*

INDEX TO PERSONS

Mozart's father, mother, sister and wife, who recur constantly, as a rule merely as the recipients of letters, are not incorporated in this Index; neither are his children.

---

[1] His wife, Mozart's sister, is not indexed

[1] Not indexed after her marraige to Mozart.

INDEX TO WORKS

Not all the works mentioned in the letters are identifiable.

ACKNOWLEDGEMENTS

Archiv für Kunst und Geschichte, Berlin (AKG)
8, 12, 16, 20, 28, 47, 63, 122, 123, 128, 138, 154, 183, 193T, 196, 203, 204
AKG/Bibliothèque Nationale, Paris 106
AKG/Historisches Museum, Frankfurt-am-Main 226
AKG/Musée Carnavalet, Paris, 94-5
Bridgeman Art Library/Roy Miles Fine Paintings, London 18/19
Civico Museo Bibliografico Musicale, Bologna 21R, 50
Sterling and Francine Clark Institute, Williamstown, Mass 23
Deutsches Theater Museum, Munich 33, 130, 132, 199, 235BR, 238-9
Gesellschaft der Musikfreunde, Musikverein, Vienna 246 (and Back Cover)
Giraudon/Mozart Museum, Prague 202
Giraudon/Musée Carnavalet, Paris 87, 98, 99, 103
Giraudon/Musée Conde, Chantilly 85
Historisches Museum der Stadt Wien 141, 157, 269, 174, 193BR, 206, 237
Hunterian Art Gallery, University of Glasgow 167
Internationale Stiftung Mozarteum, Salzburg Front Cover, 6, 11, 14 R, L, 64, 83, 135, 136L, 190, 193BL, 205, 227, 235 TL, BL, 240, 243
Kunsthistorisches Museum, Vienna 146
Musée d'Art et d'Histoire, Geneva 115
Österreichische Nationalbibliothek/Bildarchiv und Porträt Sammlung 21L, 142
Österreichische Nationalbibliothek/Musiksammlung 244
Österreichische Nationalbibliothek/Theatersammlung 161, 197, 222
Reichsmuseum, Mannheim 59
Residenz Museum, Munich 39
Royal College of Music, London 194
Salzburger Museum Carolino Augusteum 31, 35, 37
Scala Istituto Fotografico, Florence/Internationale Stiftung Mozarteum, Salzburg 2
Scala/Museo di Milano 26
Scala/Palazzl Barberini, Rome 214/5
Stadtsarchiv Augsburg, Mozart Gedankstätte 42, 72, 89, 92, 129, 171, 176, 177, 185, 236
University Library, Prague 235TR